TOURING CULTURES

While people tour cultures, it is also true that cultures and objects themselves travel. *Touring Cultures* analyses the complex connections between tourism and cultural change, particularly bringing out the ways that cultures themselves 'tour'.

This book examines topics on the cutting edge of conceptual and theoretical work in the study of travel – for example, the role of metaphors, the gendered nature of urbanity, the significance of the 'post-tourist' perspective. It considers the social and cultural contexts in which our decisions to travel and our mental maps of tourism and the outside world are situated and how these provide the basis for making sense of tourist activity. The theoretical discussion is backed by more contextualised studies of the growth of cultural tourism, the performativity of tourist-related work, the heritage industry in sites on the margin and the role of the photo in the construction of the tourist experience. These studies give an insight into some of the most practical ways in which tourist sensibility is produced and maintained, not only at the level of actual tourist experience but also in the tourist sign economy and the cultural images of escape, freedom and relaxation.

In this book, Rojek and Urry bring together ᴄ   ᴏf the best-respected writers in the field to provide us with an original and stir   ·tribution to the sociological exploration of tourism, travel, culture anᵈ   ᵗion.

Chris Rojek is Professor of Socioloɢ   ᴨam Trent University, and **John Urry** is Professor of Sᴄ   ⱱersity.

TOURING CULTURES

Transformations of Travel and Theory

Edited by Chris Rojek and John Urry

London and New York

First published 1997
by Routledge
11 New Fetter Lane, London EC4P 4EE

Simultaneously published in the USA and Canada
by Routledge
29 West 35th Street, New York, NY 10001

Reprinted 2000

Routledge is an imprint of the Taylor & Francis Group

Typeset in Baskerville by Routledge
Printed and bound in Great Britain by
Biddles Ltd, Guildford and King's Lynn

British Library Cataloguing in Publication Data
A catalogue record for this book is available from the British Library

Library of Congress Cataloguing in Publication Data
A catalogue record for this book has been requested

ISBN 0–415–11124–2 (hbk)
ISBN 0–415–11125–0 (pbk)

CONTENTS

ILLUSTRATIONS

FIGURES

TABLE

CONTRIBUTORS

Carol Crawshaw Director of Tourism Studies, Dept of Sociology, Lancaster University, Lancaster, LA1 4YL, UK

Philip Crang Lecturer in Geography, University College London, 26 Bedford Way, London, WC1H 0AP, UK

Jennifer Craik Cultural Policy Centre, Griffith University, Brisbane, Australia

Eeva Jokinen Research Fellow of the Finnish Academy, Dept of Social Sciences and Philosophy, University of Jyväskylä, PO Box 35, 40351 Jyväskylä, Finland

Allan Liska Department of Sociology, University of Maryland, College Park, Maryland, 20742 USA

Celia Lury Senior Lecturer in Sociology, Lancaster University, Lancaster, LA1 4YL, UK

Sharon Macdonald Lecturer in Anthropology, Dept of Sociological Studies, University of Sheffield, Northumberland Road, Sheffield, S10 2TU, UK

George Ritzer Professor of Sociology, University of Maryland, College Park, Maryland, 20742 USA

Chris Rojek Professor of Sociology and Culture, Theory, Culture and Society Research Centre, Nottingham Trent University, Nottingham, NG11 8NS, UK

John Urry Professor of Sociology, Lancaster University, Lancaster, LA1 4YL, UK

Soile Veijola Research Fellow of the Finnish Academy, Dept of Sociology, PO Box 33, 00014 University of Helsinki, Finland

ACKNOWLEDGEMENTS

We are very grateful for the comments and advice of various colleagues and friends, either directly on the manuscript or more indirectly on the ideas contained here. These include Dede Boden, Ellis Cashmore, Gordon Clark, Carol Crawshaw, Jan Darrall, Tim Edensor, Bridget Fowler, Robin Grove-White, David Jary, Baz Kershaw, Mark Liniado, Celia Lury, Dean MacCannell, David McCrone, Sharon Macdonald, Phil Macnaghten, Richard Sharpley, Nigel Thrift and Patrick Wright.

1

TRANSFORMATIONS OF TRAVEL AND THEORY

Chris Rojek and John Urry

TOURISM AND CULTURE

Peoples, cultures and objects migrate. This book draws on the expansion of social science interest in mobility, in the mobility of peoples, cultures and objects. It is now clear that people tour cultures; and that cultures and objects themselves travel. It is this two-fold aspect that will be jointly addressed in the chapters that follow. We begin this chapter with an analysis of the complex connections between tourism and cultural change, inspired by Said's and Clifford's notions of 'travelling cultures' (Said 1983; Clifford 1992).

We will begin by interrogating the very category of 'tourism'. Is there such an entity? Does the term serve to demarcate a usefully distinct sphere of social practice? Where does tourism end and leisure or culture or hobbying and strolling begin? This book is based on the view that tourism is a term waiting to be deconstructed. Or as Marx might have said it is a chaotic conception, including within it too wide a range of disparate phenomena (Marx 1973). It embraces so many different notions that it is hardly useful as a term of social science, although this is paradoxical since Tourism Studies is currently being rapidly institutionalised within much of the academy.

One significant reason for the problematic status of tourism is that its meaning stems from its 'other', from the other term or terms with which it is contrasted. There are many of these, including travel, day-tripping, culture, excursion, voyaging and exploration. Its meaning constantly slides as its 'other' changes. This is shown in Buzard's (1993) analysis of the tourist–traveller distinction. He brings out that in the case of many different literary and academic writers during the nineteenth century the meaning of each term continuously slides under that of its other. Indeed more generally the very critiques of the role of the 'tourist', as found within many discourses surrounding 'travel', are in a sense part of the very nature of tourism as a complex set of social discourses and practices.

And yet at the same time it is believed by both the academy and the wider public that tourism does in fact possess a self-evident essence. People still want to 'get away from it all'. Yet interestingly this desire for contrast and escape is increasingly freighted with worries that the impetus for tourism is itself destroying the possibility of tourism. For example, it seems obvious to the public and to academic commentators that in the past three decades Majorca, to take but one instance, has been more or less destroyed by a engulfing process which can be unambiguously identified as tourism or mass tourism; or that the retreat to Miami Beach has developed threatening, crimogenic aspects which threaten the very safety of tourists. Lying therefore behind many claims in this field is a fairly simple-minded realism: that there are clear and identifiable processes 'out there' and these can be straightforwardly described by terms such as 'tourism' and 'travel'. Moreover, once they are so described they can then be explained through the use of conventional social science methodology, especially survey-type analysis (Krippendorf 1984).

It may be that this belief in the real essence of tourism is related to what can be described as a 'realist' search undertaken by tourists themselves for evidence that they really were in some particular place. This 'realism' of popular representation is associated with the role of photography. Crawshaw and Urry discuss how this produces a definite narrative and interpellation of the individual subject as a tourist in a particular place, engaging in apparently touristic activities (see Chapter 9).

One response to those who point to the problematic nature of tourism as a theoretical category is to seek to operationalise it. For example, tourism is often defined as involving stays of more than four nights and less than one year. But the problem with this is that it ignores whether these stays have in any sense the same significance to visitors. If they do not, then the investigator is placing together in one operational category quite different social practices, some of which might be merely that of weekly commuting. In what follows we shall presume that the variety of meanings is part of what we are seeking to identify and to explain. So while the collecting and analysis of the flows of visitors within and between countries, including the number of nights that they stay and so on, is crucially important data, we will not seek to reduce the tourism phenomenon to such an operational definition. Rather we will be concerned with unpacking the orientations that people bring with them when they engage in tourist activity and also with tracing some of the mythologies of escape involved when people go touring or dream of touring.

Another response to the problematic character of tourism is deliberately to abstract most of the important issues of social and cultural practice and only consider tourism as a set of economic activities. Questions of taste, fashion and identity would thus be viewed as exogenous to the system. Tourism on this account is treated as a set of economic factors, and individuals are viewed as bundles of given preferences. This is the standard treatment of tourism in the main textbooks (although less so in Shaw and Williams 1994). Again, the economic analysis of tourism provides crucial information for understanding the phenomenon. But it is limited. The number of hotels built in Berlin since the destruction of the Wall, or the average tourist expenditure by British tourists in Greece, tell us very little about the diverse qualities of tourist experience. In addition they carry the danger of reifying tourist experience so that thinking about tourism and developing tourist policy simply become a matter of reading and seeking to manipulate economic indicators.

Touring Cultures, by contrast, is premised upon the rejection of both positivist operationalisation and the strategy of economic abstraction. We will examine a wide range of phenomena which are characteristically viewed as 'touristic'. And we will engage with the diverse meanings actors attribute, intentionally or otherwise, to the activities which are conventionally deemed to be part of tourism. But this identification of 'tourism' is now particularly problematic because of recent discursive and social transformations. Until the past two to three decades there were a series of temporary frontiers erected between what we can loosely term tourism and culture (since the demise of the Grand Tour which, for the sons of the wealthy, combined the two; see Craik in Chapter 6). As we have argued elsewhere, during organised capitalism, tourism and culture were relatively distinct social practices in both time and space (Rojek 1993; Urry 1994a), so it was a reasonable tactical move to presume that they could be analysed separately from each other. There was differentiation of social practices, each presupposing their own modes of judgement, hierarchy and authority. Tourism as practice and discourse involved clear specification in time (the week and the fortnight) and space (the specialised resorts and spas). It particularly involved the centrality of clock-time to its organisation. This was seen not only in the week being the key time-period but also the significance of fixed mealtimes, high levels of time–space synchronisation, and a remarkable degree of time surveillance (see Urry 1994b). All of this presumed a clear boundary between tourism and culture; a grid-like distinction between the two. Indeed Ritzer and Liska in Chapter 5 argue that tourist sites had been increasingly 'McDisneyized', becoming places in which people seek tourist experiences which are predictable, efficient, calculable and controlled.

This grid-like construction of life was not without criticism and resistance. Elsewhere one of us has used the collective term 'Modernity 2' to refer to such categories of resistance (Rojek 1995). If Modernity 1 set down certain rules to live by and attempted to install a universal, binding 'order of things', as Ritzer and Liska show in Chapter 5, Modernity 2 sought to express the 'disorderliness' of life. Modernity 1 tended to emphasise that life could be organised around consistent and comprehensive rational principles, whereas Modernity 2 stresses the irrational consequence of rational actions and, more generally, the impossibility of 'planning' or 'managing' social life. The 'antinomian' tradition described by Thompson (1994) shows the deep roots of Modernity 2 in various traditions of religious dissent. Criticism and dissent were often expressed in political forms. Socialism, feminism and the civil rights movement can all be seen as examples of Modernity 2's rejection of the rigidities imposed under Modernity 1. But these movements rejected the existing order of things in order to achieve a qualitatively superior state of affairs. It was left to the poet Rimbaud at the end of the nineteenth century to express the anarchic kernel in Modernity 2 with his remark that life should seek to attain 'the complete derangement of the senses'. But despite the erosive effect of Modernity 2 on the dominant order of things, Modernity 1 proved remarkably resilient. In spite of the breaching of various boundaries, until very recently the rules of division (public and private life; work and leisure; home and abroad; male and female roles; popular pleasure and high culture) were regarded, in the final analysis, to be clearly drawn and understood by most in 'Western' societies.

It is these rules and the notion of the 'final analysis' which has now been shattered. Tourism and culture now plainly overlap and there is no clear frontier between the two. They cannot be kept apart. First, this is because there is a 'culturalisation of society', a de-differentiation between all sorts of social and cultural spheres which were previously distinct, as Craik shows in Chapter 6. Even the apparently separate economy has partly turned into an economy of signs; while the development of a post-modern cultural paradigm involves the breaking down of conventional distinctions, such as high/low culture, art/life, culture/street life, home/abroad, that had kept different social practices within different social/spatial locations (Baudrillard 1981; Harvey 1989; Lash 1990; Lash and Urry 1994).

Further, many border-maintaining distinctions and discriminations have been overwhelmed by cultural innovations which have swept across frontiers, including those historically exerted around and by the nation-state. Migration has brought many 'exotic', 'foreign' cultures into the cities of Europe, the Americas and Australia. The old colonial metropolis is having to come to terms with post-colonial conditions. As Lury demonstrates, both objects and people are increasingly mobile, and such mobilities are culturally encoded (see Chapter 4 below; Clifford 1992; as well as the literature on post-colonialism). The diffusion of peoples between cultures can no longer be understood through the employment of conventional notions of control and resistance. Instead, the notion of hybridity which brings to mind the organic binding of different cultural conventions and symbols is more appropriate. For example, the Irish Americans in the US have evolved a hybrid culture which is neither purely American nor Irish, yet is clearly indebted to both; the same is true of British Afro-Caribbeans and British Asians. Hybridity moreover exposes the conventional division between home and abroad as over-simplistic. From a 'Western' standpoint, living-in and travelling-in cultures must be seen as occurring in the context of unparalleled cultural diffusion and hybridity (see Gilroy 1993). There is no simple sense of the spatially and temporally distinct 'home' and 'away'.

Third, more specifically there has been the increasing culturalisation of tourist practices themselves and their profound impact on the range of 'toured' communities (see Morris 1995). Crang points to this in his discussion of what he calls 'the mediation of co-presence' (see Chapter 7). This culturalisation is most obviously seen in the growth of so-called 'cultural tourism'. For example, educational tourism and keep-fit/adventure tourism are explicitly marketed as improving the 'culture' of the tourist. One does not simply see more of the world by engaging in these forms of tourist activities, one also accepts the invitation to become a better person. Culturisation can also be seen in the increasing significance of signs to the design and marketing of tourism sites. Various commentators have demonstrated that tourist practices do not simply entail the purchase of specific goods and services but involve the consumption of signs. Tourists are semioticians (see Culler 1988; MacCannell 1989). Indeed it is sometimes claimed that the sign or marker is constitutive of the sight which, in a sense, cannot be 'seen' without the marker. And with the extraordinary proliferation of images and signs in the last few decades, this economy of signs has swept across and overwhelmed the signs typically consumed by the traveller while away, as Rojek discusses through the concepts of indexing and dragging (Chapter 3). And the signs derived from travel are routinely produced and circulated by all sorts of other culture industries. Indeed, as Rojek discusses, people are beginning to discuss the whole idea of virtual travel or cyber-tourism. The result is that the distinctions made under Modernity 1 between 'home and abroad', 'work and travel' and 'the authentic and the contrived' are further drained of popular authority (see MacCannell 1989; Frow 1991; Morris 1995).

Most tourism research has not sufficiently recognised these developments – although it has of course noticed the marketing and economic opportunities of cultural tourism (see Taylor 1994; Morris 1995; and Craik in Chapter 6, for recent exceptions to this criticism). Crang partly attempts to redress the balance by demonstrating the performative character of many kinds of tourism employment; and thus to show how the labour undertaken involves the mobilisation of culturally meaningful selves. He shows that much tourism employment involves 'cultural performance' (see Chapter 7 below; Kershaw 1993). However, he also demonstrates that this is very varied in its impact, depending upon the social definition of the settings; the spatial and temporal structuring and uses of those settings; the materials through which product provision is organised; and the identity politics played out through the interactions between employees and tourists (Chapter 7 below; Crang 1996).

In a number of ways then, this book aims to go beyond existing studies by demonstrating the following: that tourism is a cultural practice; that tourism and culture hugely overlap; that tourism as a cultural practice and set of objects is highly significant or emblematic within contemporary 'Western' societies organised around mass mobility; that tourism has largely to be examined through the topics, theories and concepts of cultural analysis, especially the current foci upon issues of time and space; that there should not be a specifically *social* science of tourism; that particularly significant in the analysis of culture will be the examination of the human senses, and especially the relative importance of the sense of sight; and that none of the supposed essences of tourism, such as the notion of 'escape', provides the kind of desired conceptual unity.

In the rest of this chapter we will consider some recent debates and theories relating certain of these claims, to tourism and the variety of human senses involved in the appreciation of place; to how cultures and objects and not just people travel or tour; and to the gendered nature of cultures and tourism practices and metaphors. There is a brief conclusion.

TOURISM AND THE SENSES

Issues of time and space are central to contemporary cultural analysis. But such a claim about the timed and spaced character of social phenomena forces us to confront how and in what ways we sense such phenomena. What senses are involved in the perception, interpretation, appreciation and denigration of other spaces? How do we sense what other places are like? How do senses work across space? How are other times remembered? Which senses predominate in different historical periods? Are there hierarchies of value between the different senses? (see Rodaway 1994 for his advocacy of a 'sensuous geography').

These are immensely complex issues relating to the history of Western philosophy and its particular fascination with the eye as the mirror of nature (Rorty 1980). Our initial claim is simply that the cultural analysis of 'tourist' social practices also necessitates analysis of these different senses, and in particular the privileging of the visual which appears to parallel the ocularcentrism of Western philosophy (Jay 1993). Crawshaw and Urry note that it is rather paradoxical that what Levin terms the 'hegemony of vision' appears to characterise the heights of Western philosophy and the depths of the Western holiday industry (see Chapter 9 below; Urry 1992b; Levin 1993; Gregory 1994: 404). In the history of the West, sight has been typically taken as the noblest of the senses. Arendt, for example, argues that 'from the very outset, in formal philosophy, thinking has been thought of in terms of *seeing*' (Arendt 1978: 110–11). Observation came to be regarded as the only sure basis of scientific legitimacy.

But in the twentieth century the denigration of the central role of the visual has developed, especially within French social thought. The dark side of sight has come to be particularly emphasised. Jay (1993) brings this out in his interrogations of Sartre, Derrida, Irigaray, Debord and especially Foucault. In Foucault's analysis there is the demonstration of how sight shifts from the primacy of the individual knowing eye, to its spatial positioning through especially the panopticon, and of the relationship of that social vision to the operation of power (1979). Such writers particularly bring out the complicitous role of vision in the mundane operations of power and control – it is no longer simply the source of enlightenment and science.

To some extent these debates parallel discussions in the 1920s and 1930s. Jokinen and Veijola note how Benjamin used the metaphor of the metropolis as a 'labyrinth' (Chapter 2 below; Benjamin 1973). Flânerie was the act not merely of intelligent wandering, but also of peeling away the blasé indifference to everyday life and the opening up of the senses. Kracauer (1995: 65–74) presented tourism as the organised bombardment of the senses. He argued that the commercialisation of tourism no longer enables people to savour the sensation of foreign places. Tourism no longer involves capturing a long-imagined sight.

This is in stark contrast with when Goethe travelled to Italy, which he viewed as a country he 'sought with his soul' (Kracauer 1995: 65). Indeed, reading Goethe's memento of his journey to Rome in 1786 one is struck by the extraordinary richness of his preparation (Goethe 1962). He read voraciously on all things Roman; he pored over the history and street plans of the city; he studied engravings of the significant buildings, and he collected woodcuts, plaster casts, etchings and cork models. Goethe's imagination immersed itself in the city, so that upon arrival he remarks that 'everything is just as I imagined it, yet everything is new... my old ideas have become so much more firm, vital and coherent' (Goethe 1962: 65).

For Kracauer even the tourist of the inter-war period was no longer like that. Rather, tourist senses are attuned to the pleasures of variety and oscillation. He writes that

> More and more travel is becoming the incomparable occasion to be somewhere other than the very place one habitually is. It fulfils its decisive function as spatial transformation, as a temporary change of location.... Travel has been reduced to a pure experience of space.
>
> (Kracauer 1995: 66)

Kracauer takes Rimbaud's comment about modernity and 'the derangement of the senses' and turns it into the main passion for travel. That sense of no longer being at home, of organised dislocation, is itself pleasurable (especially for the male tourist, as Jokinen and Veijola note in Chapter 2). Sights become staging posts on a journey. One no longer embraces them with one's soul. Rather, the tourist uses them to give shape to the passion of travel which would otherwise be shapeless.

Various chapters below describe aspects of the relationship between the senses and various tourist practices. Crawshaw and Urry show how the history of 'leisured' travel has been inextricably bound up with the modes in which the visual has been given objectified form, first through painting and the development of the 'landscape' (Barrell 1972; Berger 1972; Bryson 1983; Cosgrove 1985). This growth of 'scenic tourism' was of course further developed through the desire to fix images permanently; with the 'invention' of the photograph in 1839 (see Chapter 9 below, and Adler 1989, on the historical origins of 'sightseeing'). This contributed to the nineteenth-century transformation of nature into an object of the sightseer, into spectacle, as Green (1990) describes happening in the area around Paris.

And interestingly, the critique of the visual is similarly reflected within travel discourse in the ways in which the mere sightseer has come to be universally denigrated, as someone who is necessarily superficial in their appreciation of peoples and places (see Buzard 1993). Crawshaw and Urry discuss how the different senses can also be seen in the diverse effects that they have on the places that are travelled to (Chapter 9). Such places are subject to the inquisitive senses of visitors, especially that of the visual. Living in a tourist honeypot is akin to being a prisoner in the panopticon.

This relationship between the senses and how places are experienced is interestingly discussed by Stallybrass and White (1986: 134). They quote the House of Commons Select Committee of 1838 which argued that, because there were whole areas of London through which no thoroughfares passed, the lowest class of person was therefore secluded from the observation and influence of 'better educated neighbours'. Steadman Jones (1981) refers to the urban 'residuum' of unemployed and seasonal labourers who were literally submerged beneath the horizon in everyday life. It was argued that such classes would be transformed and improved once they became *visible* to the middle and upper classes, both through surveillance and through the inculcation of respectable and rational standards. There are some crucial parallels with the rebuilding of Paris and the hugely enhanced visibility, to see and be seen, that the grand boulevards developed during the Second Empire, as mediaeval Paris was destroyed (see Berman 1983). Jokinen and Veijola demonstrate that most models of the urban dweller were based on a mixture of fear and control; and especially the techniques of sustaining control by middle-class urban men when faced by the fear of the other, especially the sexual other (Chapter 2).

At the same time as the dangerous 'other' could now be seen in the nineteenth-century city, they were not to be touched (increasingly, of course, they were photographed; see Taylor 1994). Stallybrass and White (1986) argue that the notion of 'contagion' and 'contamination' were the tropes through which nineteenth-century city life was apprehended by the urban male. Since the 'promiscuity' of the public space was unavoidable, so it was argued that one should try to avoid touching the 'other'. Especially the male flâneur should not get too close to the dangerous women of the *street*. Can one not see an echo of this differentiation in the private members' enclosures and luxury spectator boxes in today's sports grounds? As before, the wealthy oversee the masses from positions of relative isolation and distance. There seem to be two dichotomies at work here: gaze/touch; desire/contamination. The upper classes mainly sought to gaze upon the 'other' (while, for example, standing on their balconies overlooking the 'other'). Young sons would often travel to crimogenic/ twilight neighbourhoods in order to gaze at the lowlife. Writing novels and newspaper articles and taking photographs also made the grotesque visible while keeping it at a safe distance.

But some (men) of course sought out the touch and feel of the other through crossing to the dark side of the city and engaging with the diverse charms of prostitutes, opium dens, bars and taverns. This was known as 'slumming'. Underprivileged areas and crimogenic zones came to be redefined as tourist sights. Rojek discusses some contemporary examples of the way that scenes of crime become culturally fixed as tourist sights (Chapter 3). Jokinen and Veijola remind us that, for Benjamin, it was thought that the prostitute in the great cities had come to possess the secret of the 'labyrinth'; and yet contemporary cultural analysis never considers that it could be the prostitute who is particularly emblematic of the modern condition (Chapter 2).

There was a further sense which was particularly significant in the nineteenth-century Western city; that of smell. It was the sense of smell which enraged social reformers, since smell, while, like touch, encoding revulsion, had a pervasive and invisible presence difficult to regulate (Porteous 1985; Stallybrass and White 1986: 139). Smells, sewers and rats played a key role in the nineteenth-century construction of class relations within the large cities. Stallybrass and White note that, as the nineteenth-century upper classes represented reference to their lower bodily functions, so they increasingly referred to the simultaneous dangers and fascination of lowlife: slum-dwellers, prostitutes, below stairs, the kneeling maid and so on. The development of new middle-class housing in growing industrial cities like London, Glasgow and Manchester was in part driven by the requirement to get away from the rank smells of the masses. Similarly, Shields maintains that the desire for fresh and clean air was a key factor in the construction of Brighton and other coastal resorts (Shields 1991; and see Corbin on 'the foul and the fragrant', 1986, and the 'lure of the sea', 1992).

Bauman takes this argument about smell even further. He argues that:

Modernity declared war on smells. Scents had no room in the shiny temple of perfect order modernity set out to erect.

(Bauman 1993: 24)

For Bauman modernity sought to neutralise smells by creating zones of control in which the senses would not be offended, as Ritzer and Liska show more generally in Chapter 5. Zoning has become an element of public policy. Planners have accepted that repugnant smells are an inevitable by-product of urban-industrial existence. For example, refuse dumps, sewage plants, industrial plants, are all spaces in which bad smells are concentrated. But they are typically screened-off from everyday life by being situated on the periphery of cities (Classen et al. 1994: 170–1). Tourist sights are generally distanced from bad or offensive smells, although those for poorer visitors are less separated. For example, the Indian Supreme Court ruled in 1993 that 200 factories should be closed down in the town of Agra because pollution was posing a threat to the Taj Mahal. It is not only the fine filigree work of the white marble tiles that is disintegrating; tourists were being driven away by the fumes of these industrial and chemical processes (see Edensor 1996). Similarly, the meeting places in most hotels are regularly sprayed with scents. Flowers are arranged to neutralise unwelcome smells and to endow the hotel experience with the quality of fragrance.

Bauman (1993) argues that smell is essentially subversive. Since it cannot be banished it reveals the artificiality of modernity. The grand project to create a pure, rational order of things is undermined. This is why Bauman submits that decomposition has 'a sweet smell'. Bad smells remind us that the world cannot be totally controlled. They confirm the post-modern condition since they encourage people to keep on the move and to be aware of contingency. Interestingly, though, our first awareness of smell is often accomplished by the eye and not the nose. Warning signs of bad smells, images of offensive smelling areas, are everywhere. The question of the visual and its ordering of everyday life is thus ever-present (as Jenks 1995a, 1995b shows).

Indeed in the twentieth century the transformation of this sense of sight through the widespread adoption of what Sontag (1979) calls the promiscuous practices of photography has been stunningly important. Crawshaw and Urry show that the visual sense has been transformed by the emergence of such a novel discourse (Chapter 9). It has democratised all forms of human experience (as Barthes says [1981: 34], making notable whatever is photographed); it gives a shape to travel (see Urry 1990: 137–40); it constructs a twentieth-century sense of what is appropriately aesthetic (see Taylor 1994); and it produces the extraordinary array of signs and images which constitutes the visual culture of the late twentieth century (Rojek and Turner 1993). As Heidegger says: 'the fundamental event of the modern age is the conquest of the world as picture' (1977: 134). Rojek describes how most tourist sites involve the conscious and unconscious 'dragging' of diverse elements from various files, especially those consisting of media signs and images (Chapter 3).

This visual culture has a number of crucial implications for the very distinction between popular and academic travel. First, academic work in many fields increasingly consists of producing and interpreting visual data. There are interesting parallels between academics and tourists in the ways in which they produce and interpret the 'visual', especially as the former increasingly deploy photographic, filmic, televisual and other multi-media material.

These parallels are even closer in the case of those very disciplines which involve travel as a key element of the research method, particularly geography and anthropology (see Crick 1989 on the latter). In the field of geography Gregory brings out the significance of the conception of the 'world-as-exhibition' for this emerging discipline, which appears to have developed on the basis of the visual representation of the world, through the world conceived of and grasped as though it were a picture, as landscape or map (Gregory 1994: 34). David Lodge's satire on the anthropologist of tourism in *Paradise News* brings out the essential parallels between academic and popular travel (Lodge 1984). It is hard to identify just what makes academic travel a special source of academic authority. Where does tourism end and so-called fieldwork begin? This lack of a clear distinction results from the immensely varied ways in which we now know tourists 'sense' the external world. Some of those senses involve the deployment of skills which parallel those used by the academic researcher. Semiotic skill is the most significant here, involving an ability to move forwards and backwards between diverse texts, film, photographs, landscape, townscape and models, so as to 'decode' information. Culler argues that, within tourism, objects are taken to be signs of themselves:

> All over the world the unsung armies of semioticians, the tourists, are fanning out in search of signs of Frenchness, typical Italian behaviour, exemplary Oriental scenes, typical American thruways, traditional English pubs.
>
> (Culler 1981: 127)

And academic work itself increasingly consists of travel to overseas conferences/other institutions where the conferees engage in academic tourism; and may use their travel experiences as part of their supposedly authoritative academic data. Clifford makes this argument rather more general when he claims that, in order 'to theorize one leaves home' (Clifford 1989: 177; and see Gregory 1994).

'CULTURES' TRAVEL TOO

So far we have concentrated upon some of the characteristics of what has been normally understood as 'tourism' as a set of specific social practices. We will now broaden the discussion to take into account wider-ranging features of 'mobility'. This is now a crucially significant generic topic within the social sciences.

First, there is the realist investigation of the flows or scapes which criss-cross national borders and which include money, capital, ideas, images, information, people, objects and technologies (Appadurai 1990; Lash and Urry 1994). What we normally understand as tourism obviously involves massive flows of people, images (via magazines, films, TV programmes, books, etc.), and, as Lury demonstrates in Chapter 4, objects. In a simple sense this means that travel/tourism is not on the margins of the academy. In a way it is symptomatic of an increasingly mobile society and almost comes to occupy centre-stage rather than being a marginal, peripheral activity (although of course many of the key 'modern' cities derived from the late nineteenth-century invention of the centrally important phenomenon of mass travel, as in the case of Paris).

Second, within cultural analysis, metaphors of travel, of narratives of home and displacement, of borders and crossings, have become exceptionally widespread. This is shown in detail by Jokinen and Veijola (Chapter 2; see also Wolff 1993). As they note, it is now almost impossible to escape from travel as metaphor. Such metaphors of travel destabilise fixed and ethnocentric categories of culture and especially of the supposed superiority of the culture of the West.

Braidotti, for example, employs the metaphor of the nomadic subject (Braidotti 1994 argues that the 'critical intellectual' should adopt a nomadic consciousness). Others talk of cultures being 'on the road' (a kind of 'Easy Rider' view of culture!). Clifford invokes the hotel lobby as a site of travel encounters. He argues for that chronotype, a setting of time and space in a particular form, in preference to those which imply the stasis of particular fixed points, such as the home or dwelling (Clifford 1992: 101). However, he also notes that this chronotype of the hotel is itself rather nostalgic and he goes on to recommend Morris's (1988) chronotype of the motel. The motel has no real lobby, it is tied into the network of highways, it functions to relay people rather than to provide settings for coherent human subjects, and it demolishes the sense of place and locale. More generally, Bauman (1993) suggests that both the 'tourist' and the 'vagabond' are plausible metaphors for post-modern times. Such 'characters' move through other people's spaces, they both separate physical closeness from moral proximity, and they both set the standards for happiness. Bauman suggests that the normal or good life has come to be thought of as akin to a 'continuous holiday'. Jokinen and Veijola however demonstrate the 'maleness' of most of these metaphors and provocatively suggest the examination of alternative female metaphors, including the prostitute, the babysitter and the au pair. They also show that certain 'male' metaphors can be re-written or coded differently. And if they are, as say the paparazzi, homeless drunk, sextourist and womaniser might be, then they no longer enjoy the positive valuation that they have typically enjoyed within the writings of male cultural theory (as in Bauman 1993; see Chapter 2 below).

A major reason for the actual and metaphorical significance of mobility is because cultures travel as well as people; and yet part of what is involved in the movement of cultures is the migration of objects and peoples (as migrants as well as tourists; see Robertson *et al.* 1994). This particularly relates to the current interest in post-colonial literatures and modes of analysis which especially focus upon the nature and consequences of various kinds of mobility. Such mobilities occurred during both the colonial period (and resulted of course in, *inter alia*, Orientalism; Said 1978); and the post-colonial period. Post-colonial societies possess necessarily impure cultures, resulting from both the particular set of indigenous peoples the colonisers chose to administer as one colonial territory; and the flows of colonisers who passed through that 'society' over the colonial period (see Gilroy 1993, on the Black Atlantic). Such societies are hybrid – resulting in part from varied patterns of mobility; and as such they do not possess a culture so obviously different from the kinds of culture that tourists consume, and are produced and reproduced by virtue of their mobility. Lury brings out the role of the mobility of objects in the development of 'superorganic' and 'superterritorial' cultures (Chapter 4). In this process travelling-in-dwelling and dwelling-in-travelling are more or less indistinguishable (see Clifford 1992). Such a culture of flows produces spaces of 'in-betweenness' inhabited by various types of traveller and tourist.

Thus the kinds of culture that result from such mobilities are more fragmented, hybrid and disjointed than conventional accounts of French or British or German culture would once have recognised. These cultures are impure and are being continuously re-invented. That 'Britain' does not possess a single culture is of course now widely understood. One consequence is that the 'culture' which gets produced and consumed by tourists may not be as obviously artificial or contrived as once was thought. It should not receive the denigration that tourism typically receives since all cultures are inauthentic and contrived, as Rojek demonstrates (Chapter 3). All cultures get remade as a result of the flows of peoples, objects and images across national borders, whether these involve colonialism, work-based migration, individual travel or mass tourism (Bhabha 1990; Clifford 1992; Gilroy 1993).

However, if this is the case it poses a major challenge for the traditional understanding of travel within the sociology of tourism. The dominant position is that tourism should be interpreted as a quest for authenticity (Krippendorf 1984; MacCannell 1989). The world of habitual life is so ordered and managed that authentic feelings are subdued or choked off. Through tourism we are said to have the chance of expressing real feelings. But if cultures travel they cannot be closed-off from other cultures. The admixture of elements and the unintended production of new cultural values are an inevitable consequence of movement. The traditional idea of a tourist culture which exists in clear contrast with the rest of the society becomes implausible. Indeed, as Venturi *et al.*'s (1972) discussion of Las Vegas makes plain, tourist sights are increasingly using extravagantly inauthentic accessories to attract tourists. Replicas of Egyptian temples; reconstructions of the Wild West or Victorian England; futuristic theme parks; Gaelic revival centres (Chapter 8) – all feature as magnets to lure tourists in. Indeed Ritzer and Liska argue that much tourism involves a search for the inauthentic, a search for those perfect simulations (Chapter 6). It is no longer enough for a tourist sight to be merely an 'action' place (Goffman 1967) or a place of dedicated relaxation. Now it must also distort time and bend space to produce the illusion of an extraordinariness of experience, or what Ritzer and Liska, following Baudrillard, term an ecstasy of experience (Chapter 6). The closer that life in the tourist resort comes to resemble the pure play form, the more will tourists flock to visit. Because tourist cultures travel, the ante is never fixed. As we get more reconstructions of Mediterranean villages or Mexican saloons in our shopping malls, and more Thai and Chinese restaurants in our city streets, so the tourist industry in the real Mediterranean, the real Mexico, Thailand and China, has to exert itself with ever more contrived representations of the apparent 'reality' of these places.

We will now briefly note some implications of the parallels between the travelling of cultures and the travelling of peoples. First, we have seen that cultures do not exist in a pure state, hermetically sealed from each other, and possessing a clear and distinct essence. Further, cultural participants do not simply, straightforwardly and unambiguously adopt a culture as such. Knowing a culture involves work, of memory, interpretation and reconstruction. And most significantly here it almost always involves travel. Edensor brings out the exceptional levels of mobility in 'traditional India', such mobility being central to the maintenance of the diverse cultures of that 'society' (1996). Such travel will occur to the culture's sacred sites (in the case of 'English culture', to Buckingham Palace, Anfield, the Albert Hall); to the location of central written or visual texts (Westminster Abbey, the Lake District as immortalised by the Lake Poets, Stratford-upon-Avon); to places where key events took place (Battle of Hastings, the Blitz, the Wars of the Roses); to see particularly noteworthy individuals or their documentary record (the monarch, 'Shakespeare', the Beatles); and to view other cultures so as to reinforce one's own cultural attachments (rest of Europe, former colonies which demonstrate the benign effects of Empire; see Urry 1995 for examples of most of these).

And in the case of many cultures, even that of well-established ones such as the 'English', the travel involved will entail the crossing of national frontiers. Indeed for some cultures the sacred places that have to be visited will be located in many different 'societies' and thus there will be even more work involved in reconstructing the sense of that culture. The importance of such patterns of mobility across borders is most marked in the case of diasporic cultures which entail the reconceptualisation of the very sense of what is a social group's 'heritage' (Hall and Zeppel 1990). Such cultures cannot persist without a great deal of travel; Clifford suggests these involve 'discrepant cosmopolitanisms' (1992: 108; and see Chapter 4 below on 'cosmopolitanism'). Modes of institutional commemoration across societal borders are crucial in attracting members from elsewhere and representing such a culture's often precarious achievements.

How people come to know and experience 'their culture' is an obviously huge and daunting issue that is beyond the scope of this chapter. However, we will briefly consider one of the key processes involved in how people do in fact experience their culture, namely through reminiscence. This has become a key issue in some of the debates about so-called heritage. Some of the central texts in British debates have been Wright's (1985) excavation of the nature of oldness in an old country;

Lowenthal's (1985) magisterial analysis of how societies regard their past; Hewison's (1987) tirade against the 'heritage-isation' of Britain; Samuel's (1994) robust attack on the 'heritage baiters' through delineating a different genealogy of 'resurrection-ism'; and McCrone *et al.*'s (1995) examination of the more positive role of heritage within the Scottish context (see Urry 1996 more generally on how societies remember their past).

One problem in this literature is the lack of research on exactly how history and heritage are in fact remembered by people (but see Chapter 8 below; and Crang, M. 1994). First, we do not know much about how people's popular memories, of a place, industry, or social institution, are initially stimulated, enthused, and then organised into a potential documentation of remembrance (see Hoggett and Bishop 1986 on how people 'organise around enthusiasms'). Of what media is that documentation comprised and what relationship do those 'documents' have to the places, events or activities that supposedly took place in some sense 'in the past'? How is the initial enthusiasm turned into a social practice? And how is such documentation converted into a commodified site, a site which captures a share of a particular market, because it represents some national, regional or local achievement? More generally, then, we can ask what are the conditions of existence of particular discourses and practices of heritage (see the examples discussed in Crang, M. 1994).

One of the few such studies is Macdonald's account of the establishment of the heritage centre of *Aros* on the Isle of Skye (Chapter 8). She describes the nature of Gaelic revivalism and how this is seen by young, upwardly mobile Gaelic-speakers as compatible with commercial enterprise. Setting up such a heritage centre is viewed by revivalists as a way of strengthening and not diluting Gaelic language and culture. The concept of 'cultural tourism' is employed to indicate tourism 'for the people' of Skye. And the account presented is an alternative to the romantic heritage account of Scottish history. So *Aros* partly develops out of Gaelic enthusiasm and the desire to tell a different story of the Highlands, but it is a story which is at the same time commercially profitable. Enterprise and heritage are seen as compatible (although see Corner and Harvey 1991a).

Furthermore, there are various possible readings of the same heritage. Extreme versions of the heritage-critique presuppose a somewhat condescending, uniform and one-dimensional reading of such sites (see Urry 1995, for discussion of north-west examples). These interpretations rest upon too simple a contrast between real history and false heritage, implying that those people who do not visit heritage sites acquire historical understanding through the reading and understanding of significant historical texts. This is obvious nonsense. In the case of Scotland, McCrone *et al.* (1995) argue that Scottish heritage is a significant element in the development of cultural and political nationalism. They researched the membership of the National Trust of Scotland who see the idea of 'heritage' in a very positive way, as involving a strong sense of lineage and inheritance. Heritage, for the members of the NT in Scotland, has an identity-conferring status. Even though most of the membership are politically Conservative, they distinguish between English and Scottish heritage and are strongly committed to the latter, which is a central enthusiasm in their lives. But again one should note the inauthentic character of many of these representations of heritage. To stay with Scotland for a moment, the run-up to the Scottish National Party conference of 1995 was marked by press reports that the Scots had rediscovered their national identity through the Hollywood film 'Braveheart'. The film takes cinematic liberties with the life story of William Wallace and uses the Australian actor, Mel Gibson, in the title role. Heritage cannot really be understood in isolation from the society. The capitalist core of society makes a certain commodification of memory and heritage inevitable (see Huyssen 1995, more generally on time and memory).

But this does not mean a uniform manipulation of the readings made by visitors. Even the most apparently unambiguous of museums or heritage centres will be 'read' in different and paradoxical ways by different groups of visitors. There is no evidence that sites are uniformly read and passively accepted by visitors. In other qualitative research conducted at the Albert Dock in Liverpool, Mellor (1991: 100) argued that people actively use such sites as bases for reminiscence: 'as the point of departure for their own memories of a way of life in which economic hardship and exploited labour were offset by a sense of community, neighbourliness and mutuality'.

In the following we suggest that 'reminiscence' is indeed a major 'practice' at such sites. Kershaw (1993) argues that reminiscence is not the same as nostalgia and indeed may offer considerable insight into recent history. He talks of it allowing a kind of collective democratisation of history memory. There is a 'reminiscence peak' in the more elderly who enjoy enhanced longer-term memory, and with the 'greying' of the population this kind of reminiscence becomes more widespread and socially influential. But his most significant claim is that reminiscing involves performance – both by those 'real' performers who are there to stimulate memories, and by visitors who have to work, often cooperatively, with others in order to produce memories. Kershaw thus emphasises the *performativity* of reminiscence which is by no means an apparently passive process of consumption (see Chapter 7 on performativity in the service industry). In some ways it is similar to the variety of other spatial practices which take place at tourist sites; these include walking, talking, sitting, eating, photographing and so on (see Edensor 1996). What then are the characteristic features of reminiscence as performance?

First, it involves a concentrated and not a distracted viewing of all kinds of objects and performances. There is a clear understanding that actors are performing; or that the objects on view have been placed in a simulated environment or are copies or fragments of the historical record. Just like an audience at a play, visitors are reflexively aware that what they see has been 'staged'. One effect of such reminiscing is the reawakening of dreams. And these can be personal (what one might have done, if only...); focused around the neighbourhood or locality where one was born or grew up; or focused on a broader collective interest, such as class, gender, generation or ethnic grouping. Seeing certain scenes or artefacts is to reawaken repressed desires and thereby to connect past and present (Buck-Morss 1989, and Chapter 2 below). It is also to remember how some collective dreams have failed or have faded from memory – while others have at least been partly realised (material abundance, educational qualifications, the opportunity to travel and so on). So while visiting museums and heritage sites is to experience an essentially artefactual history, it is not one which is necessarily received passively. To reminisce is collectively to effect a performance; and as Macdonald shows in the *Aros* heritage centre, performances are made possible because of the significance of small-scale, localised collective enthusiasms (Chapter 8). Craik also shows how certain literary locations provide sights for nostalgic reminiscence, a kind of starting-off point particularly for people's experiences of childhood (Chapter 6).

Finally here, we should appreciate that there are variations in the rate at which cultures travel, and in particular Rojek argues that there is a speeding up of images and signs at the end of the twentieth century (Chapter 3). Kracauer (1995) identifies the importance of 'the cult of distraction' in his discussion of tourism. Yet since he first dealt with these matters in the 1920s and 1930s it is obvious that the sheer density and velocity of signs and images has experienced a quantum leap. One effect is that places and cultures are instantaneously communicated around the world, both intentionally through place-marketing and more generally through the economy of signs (Lash and Urry 1994). Recent events in a place's history become rapidly historicised and made part of its past, such as the demolition of the Berlin Wall (see Shurmer-Smith and Hannam 1994: ch. 13). Other events become sensation sights which mobilise travellers to visit them and collectivise a larger audience of armchair travellers who watch the sensation unfold on their TV screens, as Rojek describes in the case of the O.J. Simpson trial (Chapter 3). Sensation sights give the impression of history being made before one's eyes, producing what Rojek terms 'collage tourism'.

Moreover, Virilio (1991) argues that the very representation of speed itself can distinguish one place from another. Virilio talks of the way that different places 'dazzle', seducing the visitor with astonishing displays of image and information, simulacra and spectacle, people and products. He talks of the over-exposed city without depth, and of buildings as sites for the circulation of people, information and images. These are places which appear full of 'instantaneous' time (Urry 1994b). Other places do not of course dazzle. They appear empty of time, slowed down, lacking speed. People, objects and images do not flow within them. There is almost a drudgery of place. Many English seaside resorts are often now viewed in this way. They were once places 'on the edge', up-to-date and modern (see Urry 1990 on Blackpool's modernity). Now they are often seen as left behind, empty or heavy with time (see Shaw and Williams 1996 for a wide-ranging assessment of the future of the seaside resort).

More generally Lynch (1972) famously asked: 'what time is this place?'. Elsewhere we have suggested that some places do attract visitors because they are almost timeless, they have (it seems) not been ravaged by time, or at least not by instantaneous or clock times. They represent what has been termed 'glacial time' (Lash and Urry 1994). Relph (1981: 31) talks of people having a growing attachment to places, to 'the feeling that this place has endured and will persist as a distinctive entity even though the world around may change'. Such places particularly invite visiting in order to stroll around 'as though one had all the time in the world'. Wilson (1992) says walking in such places is like walking 'out of time'. These are places which, as Sennett (1991) says, are 'full of time' or rather, we would say, full of glacial time. In commodified cultures, marking off these sights as replete with time becomes crucial, since the rest of society is experienced as increasingly instantaneous and placeless (Meyerowitz 1985).

But of course places are not all equivalently experienced by visitors. In the next section we will consider recent debates on the gendering of travel, an issue debated in various chapters below.

GENDERS AND TRAVEL

The question of gender raises interesting questions for travel and tourism. Wolff (1995) insists that vocabularies of travel are gendered. 'The practices and ideologies of *actual* travel', she asserts 'operate to exclude or pathologize women' (Wolff 1995: 115; emphasis in original). Morris (1988: 12) notes that the masculine tradition in travel literature casts the home as a blank and empty space and connotes travel experience with adventure and excitement. It is as if the home is the place of the mundane running order which keeps mind and body together, but 'abroad' is the place one looks for peak experience and real development. Jokinen and Veijola crystallise the point by arguing that the literature on travel and tourism is essentially based on the real and fantasised experiences of men (Chapter 2). Even post-modernism is an attempt to obscure the inequalities between the sexes in their access to travel and tourism and to the images and fantasies of such travel.

Historically speaking, one should be cautious in claiming an absolute segregation of travel experience between the sexes. For example, Jusserand's history of wayfaring in the Middle Ages confirms the Chaucerian perspective that pilgrims were 'a very mingled race' (Jusserand 1888: 350). Although female pilgrims were not as free as men to travel where they pleased, they were not banished from the pilgrim road. Also there have of course been a variety of enterprising female travellers: explorers, mountain and rock climbers and the redoubtable Victorian lady-travellers (Wolff 1995: 123–5).

Yet the dominant tradition in travel was and is palpably masculine (see Craik in Chapter 6). The first explorers often refused to take women on board because they were believed to bring bad luck and to distract the men from their task. Bourgeois culture evolved the home as the temple of femininity. Domestic life was radically segregated from the public sphere. Although women obviously inhabited public space, they did so under the protection of a chaperon. Women who attempted to roam the metropolis freely struggled with deep male prejudices regarding sexuality and space. These prejudices involved lurid accounts of the dangers to feminine virtues of unaccompanied wandering (although the role of Thomas Cook in providing the chaperoning of Victorian lady-travellers should be noted; Lash and Urry 1994: ch. 10). Public space was presented as being dominated by prostitutes, pickpockets, beggars and muggers. It is no accident that prostitutes were often described as 'women of the streets'. Respectable women who wished to explore and travel were often forced to adopt the character armour of the male (see Enloe 1989; Wolff 1995).

But Wilson (1992) contends that there are dangers in presenting travelling cultures simply in terms of a dominant male ideology. In her view modernity dissolves essentialist notions of gender. In Wolff (1995) and Morris (1988), women's travel experience is presented as male-dominated. Wilson argues that gender rules were and are much less clear cut. She maintains that the flâneuse is an evident category in nineteenth- and twentieth-century experience. Her analysis runs contrary to the orthodox feminist position that women are simply viewed as objects in travel culture. Instead she claims that women have played a more active role in viewing, observing and influencing standards of taste and performance in travel.

There is then a debate in feminist approaches to travel cultures and the experience of women. Wolff (1995), Morris (1988), Jokinen and Veijola (Chapter 2) and Craik (Chapter 6) all point to the segregation between the sexes. They deplore the close identification of women with the home and men with the limitless expanse of external space. The destabilisation and fragmentation associated with modernity is recognised. But its effect on gender relations is seen as limited. The 'restlessness' which is often regarded as a characteristic of modernism is conceptualised as the ability of men to escape from the commitments of family and home and to engage in sexual adventures. So modernity, with its emphasis on change, contingency and constant movement, becomes reinterpreted as the expression of phallocentric reason. Women remain excluded from travel and the metaphors of travel within cultural theory and analysis (Wolff 1995: 122). Against this, Wilson (1992) brings out the ambivalence in gender relations without denying structural and institutional inequalities between the sexes. For Wilson, modernity destabilises cultural relations so that gender categories are inherently ambiguous. Feminism is one expression of this. But within the masculine tradition there is also the recognition of ambivalence. For example, camp and campness are masculine ways of responding to the absurdity of the notion of absolute male superiority.

Travel and tourism can be thought of as a search for difference. From a male perspective, women are the embodiment of difference. For Wolff (1995) and Morris (1988) they are, as it were, 'imagined territories'. The activity of leaving home to travel involves for men sexual adventure, with 'finding a woman', as Jokinen and Veijola show (Chapter 2). The loosening of everyday ties and responsibilities opens the male self for sexually coded assignations (including gay travel, of course). Indeed holiday romances are a distinctive category of popular culture. The Romantic tradition in the nineteenth century explicitly related travel with the gratification of libido. Byron's adventures on the Continent were the object of fantasy for thousands of men from industrial cities.

The Byronic legend of the mobile, lusty lover remains highly durable. Added to it are the travel memoirs of Flaubert, de Nerval, Wordsworth and many other (male) nineteenth-century artists. The liberation that these men felt in travelling has a palpable libidinous connotation both for themselves and for their readers. The Victorian pornographer Frank Hankey, described by McLynn as 'the nineteenth century's Aleister Crowley', unconsciously revealed the male fascination with travel as a break from the stifling rules of civilised life and a release of unfettered male libido (McLynn 1990: 178). He asked the explorer and the anthropologist Richard Burton to return from one of his journeys into the 'dark continent' of Africa with skin stripped from a living female that he could use to bind books in his library (McLynn 1990: 202). This is a pathological request from a man who was, by all accounts, mentally unstable. Even so it touches part of the masculine tradition which regards travel as unbridled freedom for masculine aggression and sexual adventure; what Leed (1992) calls the 'spermatic journey'. Clift shows, in a study of representations in magazines for young people, that men on holiday are viewed as being concerned with obtaining 'sex without strings', while women seek 'romance' (Clift 1994). More generally, Craik shows how the literature of travel has consistently presupposed the operation of the male gaze, and thus of the pleasures associated with aggrandisement, uniqueness, exploration, and intrepidness (see Chapter 6).

Libidinous characteristics are certainly a prominent feature of mass travelling cultures. The promenade, the pavilion, the floral gardens, the esplanade, were and are spaces in seaside resorts that one went to in order to watch and to be seen. The beach became a place were nudity and semi-nudity were legitimised (see Shields 1991 on the beach as a 'pleasure zone'). The tanned female body became an ornament of holiday culture. For some men, it became a trophy. Many European seaside resorts developed and retain intensely sexual connotations, but in which female pursuit of the male body was also permitted. More recently the promise of the abundance of alcohol and welcoming flesh is used by many Club-type holiday firms in their marketing strategies (while the less enticing promise of skin cancer is just as cogently suppressed). Craik notes the recent development whereby women tourists seek out young male lovers (Chapter 6).

Yet while the culture of travelling is sexualised, it is not only sexualised. Issues of race, inequality and disability influence travel relations, often of course in ways which cross-cut relations of gender. In addition, the ways in which sexualities are expressed are many-sided. It is unsafe to see matters only in terms of the dominance of male power. Some of the most interesting questions arise precisely because of that dominance most men no longer see this relation as unproblematic. Actual gender relations in travelling cultures have a way of unfolding in ways which are not anticipated or predicted by theoretical categories. Craik, for example, talks of the increasing 'feminisation of the tourist gaze' (Chapter 6). The culture is marked by an 'as if' characteristic which bends and inverts sexual stereotypes as well as confirming them.

CONCLUSION

We have thus far considered a strikingly wide range of topics and issues in which a 'cultural analysis' is necessary to take further the examination of contemporary travel and tourism patterns, practices and metaphors. The following chapters examine some of these in more depth. They are organised in two parts.

In the first part a number of conceptual and theoretical topics are confronted in detail. These include: the role of metaphors of the modern, the urban and the traveller and their gendered nature (Chapter 2 as well as Chapter 6); the nature of tourist sites in the contemporary era and the role of dragging and indexing processes in the production of tourist sights (Chapter 3); the complex overlapping intersections between the movements of people and the movements of tourist objects (Chapter 4); and the significance of modern and 'post-tourist' perspectives (Chapter 5). We would argue that these subjects are at the cutting edge of conceptual and theoretical work in the study of travel. The social and cultural context in which our decisions to travel and our mental maps of tourism and the outside world are situated provide the essential basis for making sense of tourist and travel activity.

In Part II, four 'contexts' are examined to reveal rather more precisely some of the cultural processes which generate and stabilise tourist sites/sights: the growth and impact of cultural tourism and of the ways in which it should be studied (Chapter 6); the performative nature of work in much tourism-related employment (Chapter 7); the representation of history and heritage in a site away from the 'centre', 'on the margins' (Chapter 8); and the role and significance of photographic images in the construction and reproduction of tourist sites (Chapter 9). These chapters draw on issues from the general, and still developing, debate around modernity and post-modernity. They seek to convey an understanding of some of the most important practical ways in which tourist sensibility is produced and maintained. This applies not simply to the level of actual tourist experience but also, and crucially, to the tourist sign economy and the images of escape, freedom and relaxation which it produces.

In a parallel with Bauman's work on the disruptive effect of smell (Bauman 1993), de Certeau (1984) invites us to consider the mere acts of walking and wandering as possessing subversive qualities. In the 'McDonaldized', 'McDisneyized' world described by Ritzer and Liska (Chapter 5) the social control over movement seems to be ever-more restricted. Spatial distinctions are redrawn, redefined and policed in new ways so that walking and wandering may be relabelled as 'trespassing' and 'interloping'. The spectacular growth of tourism in the West during the post-war period reflects the tensions and conflicts involved in controlling movement. Package tours and organised visits to famous sites may seek to obey the requirement of 'orderly travelling', but their volume means that local people often interpret them as exerting a disruptive effect. The density of contemporary industrial life means that any mass transportation of large numbers of people will leave its mark on the cultural and economic infrastructure of communities. The desire to see new places and enter the closed-off spaces or 'back regions' of everyday life is unlikely to diminish. Thinking positively, this movement will continue to have important effects on the character of civil society. Notably it may demystify our notions of 'the other' in all of its manifold forms, revealing the strengths and limitations of our domain-cultural assumptions and bonds of association.

However, at the same time the growth of 'tourist wars' and conflicts which aim to harm tourists is only too evident. Recent cases include the kidnapping and murder of Western tourists by separatists in Kashmir, and the Irish Republican Army's stated aim to use bombing campaigns in London to damage the British tourist industry as part of a wider campaign to produce a united Ireland. Despite the strong cultural associations in the West between tourism and personal enrichment and social enlargement, we are not able to immunise ourselves from the wider cultural conflicts of everyday life when we go for our pre-travel jabs to protect ourselves against physical disease. Part of the transformation in the fact and theory of travel that has occurred over the last twenty years is that travellers and students of tourism have a greater awareness of the morphology and character of these conflicts. Our hope is that, by stressing the compelling links between culture and tourism, we will contribute to this awareness, but not at the expense of denying the sense of lightness and adventure that still – on some occasions at least – animates tourist activity.

Part 1
THEORIES

2

THE DISORIENTED TOURIST

The figuration of the tourist in contemporary cultural critique

Eeva Jokinen and Soile Veijola

INTRODUCTION

What originally caught our attention was the increased use of the figure of the tourist in contemporary writings on the modern/post-modern condition. The tourist seemed to appear everywhere, in every keynote paper at social scientific conferences, as a symbol of our allegedly post-modern era. But what was also surprising was that, in this context, little reference was ever made to the body of tourism studies, which are rich in depth and breadth (see the various chapters in this book).

We started to wonder. Are the tourist's new clothes due to the fact that the researchers and ethnographers of tourism have never produced anything worthwhile, and, in a manner of speaking, what *they* can reveal, the social theorists can reveal better? Or, more excitingly perhaps, has the tourist really become the emblem of our time?

We decided to look into this figure, the tourist, and into the context in which s/he is now playing the leading role. Our purpose is threefold. In the first place, we try to locate, illustrate and eventually rewrite the contemporary use of the figure of 'the tourist' (and her/his parallels) as the metaphor of the (post-)modern condition. Second, we study the effects of the use of this particular metaphor in the debate on the (post-)modern condition to see what kind of *space–time configurations* the tourist epitomises and what kind of subjectivities are embedded in this figuration. Finally, we invent alternative metaphors to that of the tourist, metaphors not based on *implicitly* sexed bodily and imaginary morphologies.

The notion of 'configuration' comes (to us) from the social historian and cultural sociologist Henning Eichberg. Configuration, here, is a local relationship of time, space and power. Eichberg has, for instance, reflected upon the changes in the configuration of a child's own room. How and when did the need for a room – a space – of the child engender; what kind of argumentation supported that need; into what kind of interrelations does this discourse place the bodies of the family members (Eichberg 1984). Configurations 'flow' through embodied subjects. Hence, the embodied subject does not draw her/his borders on to the skin. S/he extends and spreads into the space 'outside' the skin.

Particular spaces at particular times are specific configurations, mostly 'unconscious', but very powerful nevertheless. By asking what kind of space–time configurations the discourse about 'the tourist' epitomises, we try to find out what are the hidden boundaries of this particular metaphor.

The tourist, the flâneur, the stranger and the adventurer, are also metaphors, not just social figures with a more or less real history. When we speak about configuration, we refer to situated and moving figures in the spatial and temporal context which they invoke. An integral part of this context are the inter- and intra-subjective relations. Given our notion of subjectivity as an embodied flux in configurations, these relations are always embodied and, accordingly, sexed. Thus the context is unavoidably marked by one or the other sexed, bodily morphology – as Irigaray argues.

What we intend to do is to explore the morphologies of sceneries and landscapes which theoretical texts produce, in order to see how sexed subjects are able to move about them. In doing this, we will use, in ample measure, the concepts of the 'male imaginary' and the 'male imaginary morphology'. We use them to refer to Irigaray's thesis that the economy of the male imaginary supports the Western symbolic order: scientific theories, among other visible works of imagination, are based on images, fantasies and identifications whose roots in male experience remain unconscious. According to Whitford, what Irigaray finds when interpreting philosophy is 'the shape of the male body and the rhythms of male sexuality' (Whitford 1991: 150). For Irigaray, the imaginary always bears the marks of either the female or the male body and corporeal morphology informs both the symbolic and the social at every level (Whitford 1991: 55, 150).

The reader of *Touring Cultures* might, in the present context, wonder if modifications of the female/male imaginary have anything to do with the field we call the sociology of tourism, or, for that matter, with tourism itself. The discussion we develop may however be of use to a student of tourism since it deals with the notions of contemporary subjectivity, ethics, and time–space connections – all essential in understanding the sociological and the cultural phenomenon of tourism.

'We' and 'us', used in the text, refer to the writers, EJ and SV, rather than to people in general. Accordingly, what we offer is partial knowledge, produced by mixing Finnish authorship with mainly Anglo-American readership. Connoisseurs will soon notice that we do not even try to recite French thinkers in French. In other words, instead of trying to read all there is, in all languages, or, as its opposite, remaining in the symbolic order of our own native language, Finnish, our state of mind is that of constant translation, travelling between languages, dwelling – not quite comfortably, we would say – in the language-house of Western social theory.

FLÂNEURS (AND PROSTITUTES)

I was skiing this morning and started to wonder whether skiing could be conceived of as flâneuring. Me – a ski-neur? Thoughts flow freely when one is skiing, just like when one is walking. But what about the masses, then? In fact, it is about accurate to talk about masses in the place where I usually ski. This is the most popular skiing area in Jyväskylä, and in the rush hours people ski in queues. When playing with the thought, I notice that I, like a true flâneur, construct lives for my co-skiers – love at last sight! A young man passing me by in the daytime makes me wonder whether he is unemployed. A young woman, for her part, raises (unfeminist?) thoughts about her possible children. Who is taking care of them now? Or are they old enough to be at school? I see an old man who looks sad and wonder whether he has recently lost his wife. . . .

The flâneur, says Wilson (1992: 93), is a key figure in the critical literature of modernity and urbanisation. In literature, she continues, the flâneur is represented as an archetypal occupant and observer of the public sphere in the cities of nineteenth-century Europe: 'He might be seen as a mythological or allegorical figure who represented what was perhaps the most characteristic response of all to the wholly new forms of life that seemed to be developing: ambivalence' (Wilson 1992: 93).

The figure of the flâneur has survived modernity and urbanisation and is loitering in the literature which is called post-modern and post-urban. As Tester puts it: 'the figure and the activity [flânerie] appear regularly in the attempts of social and cultural commentators to get some grip on the nature and implications of the conditions of modernity and post-modernity' (Tester 1994b: 1). Still, one does not speak of post-flâneurs, does one?). Let us study two examples of the tying together of the figures of the flâneur and the tourist.

Bauman (1994) draws a schema in which the pilgrim epitomises the context of modern life, and the stroller, the vagabond, the tourist and the player, jointly offer a metaphor for the post-modern context. This monster, with four heads, is constantly in horror of being bound and fixed. S/he wants to keep options open. The styles, which were (in the modern context) practised by marginal people in marginal time-stretches and marginal places, are in the post-modern context practised by the majority, in prime time in central places. Loitering, flâneuring, is one of the currently prime-time practices in prime places (Bauman 1994: 27.)

Bauman uses the stroller synonymously with flâneur. He says that all strands of modern life seem to meet and intertwine in the pastime and in the experience of the stroller: being a stranger, taking other strangers as surfaces, seeing them and knowing of them episodically – without past and with no consequences. Perceiving the fleeting fragments of other persons' lives. Spinning them off into stories at will. The flâneur is 'the creator without penalties attached to creation, the master who need not fear the consequences of his deeds', says Bauman (1994: 27). The flâneur mocks playfully what he sees; he is a man of leisure.

The four types put together – the stroller, the player, the vagabond and the tourist – sing in a post-modern chorus, says Bauman. What they have in common is the tendency to render human relations fragmentary and discontinuous and militate against constructing lasting networks of mutual duties and obligations:

> They all favour and promote a distance between the individual and the Other and cast the Other primarily as the object of aesthetic, not moral evaluation; as a matter of taste, not responsibility.
>
> (Bauman 1994: 29)

One of Bauman's post-modern types is the tourist. The tourist symbolises the needs for safety, pleasure, the homely, the cosy (Bauman 1994: 29). In short, the tourist turns into a rather banal figuration in Bauman's hands. However, Bauman does not compare the tourist to the stroller, but to the vagabond: the tourist has a home, the vagabond does not. Neither does he suggest that the tourist would be a banal version of the stroller.

Urry, for his part, takes the figuration of the flâneur as the forerunner of the twentieth-century tourist, in particular of the activity now emblematic of the tourist: the democratised taking of photographs – of being seen and recorded and seeing others and recording them (Urry 1990: 138; and see Chapter 9). The role of the gaze connects flâneurs and tourists. The 'strolling pedestrian who is able to travel, arrive, gaze, move on, be anonymous in a kind of liminal zone' can, according to Urry, be seen as kind of a counter-tourist, who poetically confronts the 'dark corners' of a town or city, occupied by the dispossessed and the marginal, and experiences supposedly real authentic life uncluttered by dominant visual images of that place (Urry 1992b).

We will now consider the flâneur as sketched by Benjamin who is probably the most often referred writer on the flâneur, at least among cultural critiques. What was his flâneur like? What did he feel? Was he poetic? Mocking? Did he invent stories, experience episodes? Was he cool? Lonely? Was he intent on gazing, what was he gazing at?

> *In order to get an insight into the feelings of the flâneur, I took my pocket-Benjamin, 'On some motifs in Baudelaire', to a pub. But, as one can guess, there are some difficulties when masquerading as a flâneur if you are a woman, which I am. A bloke, who had spent half of his life in prison, sat down at my table (without asking, of course), and told me he could not even think of such bourgeois choices as working or living on unemployment benefit. He steals the money he needs for a living. That is why he has spent so much time in prison. However, he had been released once again, six weeks ago, and had been travelling around Europe by Interrail. Now he is back, but not at home, since he has no home. A vagabond?*

The flâneur is the central figure in (some of) Benjamin's studies, and flâneuring was, metaphorically, the way he worked. 'It is to him [Benjamin], aimlessly strolling through the crowds in the big cities in studied contrast to their hurried, purposeful activity, that things reveal themselves in their secret meaning... and only the flâneur who idly strolls by receives the message', as Arendt characterises Benjamin's notion of flâneuring (Arendt 1979: 12).

It appears that the flâneur exists in the context of crowds or masses; the flâneur is, on the one hand, different from the crowd (slower, more observing, idler), and on the other hand, he lives through the masses; he lives only from the masses. The flâneur is a man of the crowd as opposed to the man in the crowd (Tester 1994b: 3). In his essay on Baudelaire's poetry, Benjamin inquires into the relation between the flâneur and the masses. He deals with this theme through contemplation of shock and anxiety as motifs in Baudelaire's verses. Benjamin suggests that the crowd, though it does not serve as a model for any of Baudelaire's works, is yet imprinted on his creativity as a hidden figure. Benjamin also maintains that, metaphorically, 'it is the phantom crowd of the words, the fragments, the beginnings of lines from which the poet, in the deserted streets, wrests the poetic booty.' Here, in the footnote, Benjamin refers to the flâneur:

> To endow this crowd with a soul is the very special purpose of the flâneur. His encounters with it are the experience that he does not tire of telling about.
>
> (Benjamin 1973: 197)

Benjamin makes it clear in his essay that there is a connection between the masses and the reading public. The crowd was 'getting ready to take shape as a public in broad strata who had acquired facility in reading' (Benjamin 1973: 168). The crowd was to become a customer, to be painted in novels for the same reason as the patrons were portrayed in paintings in the Middle Ages: both gave life to a poet. There was no reason to despise the crowd.

Benjamin also reads those (early) writings of Marx and Engels which deal with the crowd, and notes that for them the crowd is something unsettling, unaesthetic, immoral. These descriptions lack the skill and ease with which the flâneur moves among the crowd, says Benjamin (1973: 169). He then situates and localises the flâneur in Paris; that is, in Baudelaire, or, at least, with the help of Baudelaire. Benjamin reads the famous poem by Baudelaire called 'A une passante' (To a Passing Woman), and comments:

> Far from experiencing the crowd as an opposed, antagonistic element, this very crowd brings to the city dweller the figure that fascinates. The delight of the urban poet is love – not at first sight, but at last sight.
>
> (Benjamin 1973: 171)

The crowd is a way of seeing things, too clearly almost, but it is also the generator of shock-type experiences, horror and catastrophe. 'It is precisely this image of big-city crowds that became decisive for Baudelaire. If he succumbed to the force by which he was drawn to them and, as a flâneur, was made one of them, he was nevertheless unable to rid himself of a sense of their essentially inhuman make-up' (Benjamin 1973: 174). Benjamin comments that Baudelaire becomes an accomplice of the crowds – even though he dissociates himself from them. Baudelaire becomes deeply involved with the crowds, only to 'relegate them to oblivion with a single glance of contempt' (Benjamin 1973: 174).

Benjamin says that Baudelaire found it fit to equate the man of the crowd with the flâneur. For Benjamin, it is hard to accept this view. The man of the crowd is no flâneur, emphasises Benjamin. The flâneur is calm, the man of the crowd is manic:

> There was the pedestrian who would let himself be jostled by the crowd, but there was also the *flâneur* who demanded elbow room and was unwilling to forgo the life of a gentleman of leisure. Let the many attend to their daily affairs; the man of leisure can indulge in the perambulations of the *flâneur* only if as such he is already out of place.
>
> (Benjamin 1973: 174)

He is already out of place.... Benjamin goes even further. He comments Baudelaire's piece 'A Lost Halo' and his diaries with the same motif: 'The man who wrote these pieces was no *flâneur*.... The luster of a crowd with a motion and soul of its own, the glitter that had bedazzled the *flâneur*, had dimmed for him' (Benjamin 1973: 195). Baudelaire was a disappointed man, believes Benjamin, and states that in order to exaggerate his disappointment Baudelaire creates, in his writings, a scene where even the most wretched prostitute praises the ordinary and safe life and acknowledges only money. 'Having been betrayed by these last allies of his, Baudelaire battled the crowd – with the impotent rage of someone fighting the rain or the wind' (Benjamin 1973: 195–6).

The phantasm of the crowd that lives of itself, ends in Baudelaire. In a way, in Baudelaire ends also the figure of the flâneur who lives of that crowd, calmly:

> In the flâneur, one could say, the idler (*Müssiggänger*) whom Socrates engaged as

his partner in discussion in the Athenian market place, returns. Only there is no longer Socrates and so he remains unengaged. And even the slave labour has come to an end which guaranteed him his idleness.

(Benjamin 1985: 51)

How is it possible, then, that the figure of the flâneur (and his successor, the tourist) has stayed alive, unengaged maybe, at least in the texts of cultural critics and sociologists? A great disappointment, a phantasm? What blows life into it?

One possible explanation for the long life of the theme of the crowd, and hence the figure of the flâneur, is its close connection with the motif of death. This paradoxically immortalises the flâneur. Blomstedt (1986) writes that death is one of Baudelaire's most fixed ideas. This motif is not secret, like the crowds, but explicit. In the crowd, one is not just totally alone, one has also lost one's private death. There is no privacy in the crowd: the eye looking at the crowd does not get a look back – the crowd does not see. The aura of uniqueness withers away; a general status of being deceased takes the place of death and life. Hence the immortality of the figure of the flâneur could be based on the fact that this figure catches, at least in Baudelaire's and Benjamin's texts, something of the anguish which is an elementary part of the post-modern, touristic experience.

Thus, how does the figure of the flâneur catch the anguish? By inventing stories. Imagining lives. That is, by flâneuring. The modern city produced a new scenario of social actors: the crowd, the bohemian, the detective, the policeman, the flâneur – and the sociologist (Turner 1994: 28). The existence of the flâneur, and other modern figures, is based on the mixture of fear and control (cf. Tester 1994b: 5). This mix can also be seen in the figure of the tourist. The tourist tries to cover her/his fears by touring.

In addition to the flâneur, Benjamin – and Baudelaire – presented a number of other figures of social life in their texts, all equally modern. Contrary to the flâneur, they have not been incarnated in theories of modernity and post-modernity, at least not as often. Modernity also makes visible a number of *female* city-dwellers. Among the most prominent ones are the prostitute, the widow, the old lady, the lesbian, the murder victim, and the passing unknown woman (Wolff 1985: 41–2). Take the prostitute, for example, who is one of the chief objects of Baudelaire's poetry. Benjamin thinks that with the rise of great cities prostitution came into possession of new secrets. 'One of those [new secrets] is the labyrinthine character of the city itself. The labyrinth, whose image had passed into flesh and blood in the flâneur, is at the same time colourfully framed by prostitution' (Benjamin 1985: 53).

Why, then, it is not common among sociologists and cultural critics to speak about the prostitute when they want to describe the (post-)modern condition? What could possibly be a more suitable figure to illuminate our living space than the labyrinth/prostitute? Or the lesbian, for that matter, the heroine of modernism? A lesbian who overcomes the gender and (according to Baudelaire) the death that always exists in the relationship between a man and a woman. Or, the Angel, Benjamin's personal cipher, 'this beauty coming from abyss,' as Buci-Glucksmann (1994: 43) puts it: 'as a constellation of multiple temporalities (family novel, scene of writing and history of class struggles), the Angel would allegorise that conflictual meeting-point between the "familiar" everyday and the "uncanny"...' (Buci-Glucksmann 1994: 45).

A flâneur is a man, by definition, or a woman dressed as a man. Women, instead, are part of the spectacle – flâneuring – among the curiosities of the flâneur's interest (Bowlby 1992: 8; Parkhurst Ferguson 1994: 28). Moreover, the figure of the flâneur seems to resist feminine aspects. The true flâneur contemplates from a safe distance, whereas window shopping, for example, a female variation of walking in the streets, presupposes too close connections and is, accordingly, defined as not-flaneuring (Parkhurst Ferguson 1994: 35).

Bowlby discusses 'the passante', Baudelaire's passing unknown woman:

> Amid the clatter and din of the street, there she is; or there she was, no sooner there than gone, vanishing, disappearing, here only in what is now the loss of her. But the poem brings her back: gone/there, *fort/da*, brings her back fixed and no longer fleeing, but fixed as one who flees, 'fugitive', runaway, 'tu fuis'.
>
> (Bowlby 1992: 9)

The poet/flâneur/sociologist has the power and the ability to picture/write the crowd, the passing woman, the prostitute, the lesbian. When the passing woman goes away, the flâneur makes her come back by imagining. *Fort/da*. While the mother is away, a baby boy throws a toy, and draws it (the fantasised mother, that is) back. What kinds of metaphors and figures would we have, in our sociological as well as our everyday vocabulary, had Freud paid attention to the doll to whom a baby girl was talking to when the mother was away? (Irigaray 1993: 97).

So far we have suggested that the popularity and lure of the figure of the flâneur might be based on its capacity to deal with ambivalence and death. Moreover, we find similarities in the moves of the flâneur and the male imaginary: controlling (the fear), distancing (from the motherly, the crowd, the cover, the *ursprung*), using women as the material of imagination, downgrading female tasks and duties. Later in this chapter we shall investigate further the tourist as an analogous metaphor of contemporary life and try to find out whether similar connections can be made there. But before doing that, we shall reconsider another classic.

STRANGERS AND ADVENTURERS

This dog, sitting on the pavement, looked me in the eye when I got off from the bus in Hakaniemi, and, suddenly, I felt we both acknowledged an encounter. I didn't try to guess what kind of a story s/he invented in her/his head of me, and the only idea I had about her/him was that Mika Waltari used to have that kind of dog, too. Corgies. 'Fugitive and ephemeral' though the gaze I exchanged with this particular corgi may have been, I was stuck for the rest of the day with a strange thought: a dog had seen me.

Many contemporary notions of the contemporary subjectivity and identity, epitomised by the travelling man or the man of leisure, wear the boots of two ancient sociological figures invented by Simmel (1950, 1959). The protagonists are the *stranger* and the *adventurer*. Both capture the general idea of leaving the consistency of everyday life and replacing it with something more 'fugitive and ephemeral', something more akin to the modern or post-modern 'condition'. Something more 'ambiguous', to say the least.

Elementary to the stranger as a 'sociological form' is the unison of fixation and wandering; the stranger is 'a *potential* wanderer: although he has not moved on, he has not quite overcome the freedom of coming and going' (Simmel 1950: 402). The stranger's position in a group is 'determined, essentially, by the fact that he has not belonged to it from the beginning.' Nearness and remoteness are organised into a specific form of interaction: 'he, who is close by, is far' and 'he, who also is far, is actually near' (Simmel 1950: 402). This 'fundamentally mobile person' comes into contact with everyone, 'but is not organically connected, through established ties of kinship, locality, and occupation, with any single one' (Simmel 1950: 404).

Of course, what is noteworthy when studying tourism is that the stranger 'often receives the most surprising openness – confidences which sometimes have the character of a confessional and which would be carefully withheld from a more closely related person' (Simmel 1950: 404). The stranger, thanks to his formal position in the group, is hence free 'to experience and treat even his close relations as though from a bird's-eye view' (Simmel 1950: 405).

Despite the stress Simmel lays on our particular, formal relation to the 'stranger', he states that the other figure, the adventurer, is 'the extreme powerful example of the ahistorical person, of the man who lives in the present. On the one hand, he is determined by no past . . . on the other, the future does not exist for him' (Simmel 1959: 245). What then is the adventurer's relation to the world?

> Adventure has the gesture of the conqueror, the quick seizure of opportunity regardless of whether the portion we carve out is harmonious or disharmonious with us, with the world, or with the relation between us and the world. On the other hand, however, in the adventure we abandon ourselves to the world with fewer defenses and reserves than in any other relation.
>
> (Simmel 1959: 248)

For Simmel, the perfect adventure was the amorous one, although the degree of balance between 'conquering force' and 'victory and triumph' on the one hand, and 'unextortable concession' and 'favor by fate' on the other, both required by the adventurous form of experiencing, are only conjoinable in men. For women, the two poles of conquest and grace stand closer together; in men, they are much more decisively separated (Simmel 1959: 251, 252). This is why 'as a rule, a love affair is an "adventure" only for men; for women it usually falls into other categories. In novels of love, the activity of woman is typically permeated by the passivity which either nature or history has imparted to her character' (Simmel 1959: 251). A woman is not able to borrow the conquering force of man for the moment of adventure, whereas a man can borrow the passivity and grace of woman needed for his adventure.

Le look le plus cool: I

We will now inquire into the ways of how the grounding metaphors discussed above have contributed to engendering 'the tourist'. In order to do this, we shall analyse certain contemporary writers who have used the figure of the tourist in their discussions of modernity and post-modernity. It should also be noted that we shall not present the arguments of these writers in full, but rather some examples from their texts, and analyse them with respect to the hierarchies and relations of time and space, home and travel, subjectivity and sexual difference. And what we are after are the discourses and their unconscious and unmarked conventions.

Dancing through Frisby's reading of Simmel's adventure, we notice the crucial role of adventure in modern leisure: adventure, including amorous adventure, is identified with escape, it illuminates the 'motif of the attempt to escape from the mundane everyday world', other motifs being sociability, travel and fashionability. For Frisby, the adventure is ambiguous in its encapsulation of 'the experience of modernity as immediate presentness and its promise of an eternal presentness' (Frisby 1992: 133). '[T]he most general form of adventure is its dropping-out of the continuity of life'; 'something alien, untouchable, out of the ordinary'; 'an island in life which determines its beginning and end according to its own formative powers' (Simmel, cited in Frisby 1992: 132.)

For a thicker description of adventure today, we turn to Rojek's *Ways of Escape*, which he ends with the following:

> the restless dissatisfaction and desire for contrast which often colours our leisure and travel experience reflects modern values. We are never convinced that we have experienced things in our 'free' time fully enough; we are always dully aware that our experiences could be better; no sooner do we enter 'escape' activities than we feel nagging urges to escape from them. . . . The ephemeral, the fugitive and the contingent describe our experience of leisure just as they are at the heart of the phenomenon of Modernity.
>
> (Rojek 1993: 216)

And in his more recent *Decentring Leisure*, Rojek evokes the nature of restlessness:

> Nothing seems worthwhile but rather... everything seems worthwhile. Hence making one life or leisure choice as opposed to another seems to be completely arbitrary. . . . Leisure becomes a hectic move from activity to activity. It is dominated by a consciousness which emphasizes the discontinuity of experience.
>
> (Rojek 1995: 157)

There seems to be no such thing as the eternal adventure, as a permanent dwelling 'between conquering force and unextortable concession' (Simmel 1959: 251). *No sooner do we enter than we feel nagging urges to escape.*

Rojek also questions the whole notion of 'an integrated personality', which could be haunted by previous restlessness, and asks: 'What about the dimly felt, the unconscious, the transparent, the aspects of leisure which are so obvious that they do not even figure as objects of inquiry?' (Rojek 1994: 11). But he stops short of investigating this 'unconscious' and settles for restating the 'nagging' questions of the contemporary subject, who has the urge to exit everything that lasts from now until almost the next moment. Rojek repeats:

> No sooner do we successfully enter an escape enclave – a space of social life where life seems to have struggled free from normal routines – than we want to escape from it. There always seems to be somewhere else that we want to go.
>
> (Rojek 1994: 8)

Thus, according to these descriptions, the contemporary condition seems to be one of constant oscillation, both temporally and spatially. As soon as you enter, you want to exit, then re-enter and re-exit again. Back/forth, back/forth. *Fort/da*. The rhythm and mobility described above could, when considered in the feminist psycho-analytical frame, be read as that of male sexuality, which makes men 'establish limits, boundaries, punctuation in time'. 'When the little boy says *fort* (gone), he is rejecting in order to grasp, introjecting the mother in some sense. It is difficult for the imaginary to accommodate the thought of a "becoming without breaks", continuity of jouissance rather than punctuation' (Irigaray, according to Whitford 1991: 160, 162).

Are the experiences of strangeness and adventurous, then, by definition, situated in a *fort/da* movement, between (culturally and geographically) distant places and home? Are they shaped by an imaginary morphology of the male symbolic order, based on determinate and mutually exclusive forms: either abroad or home, leisure or work, light or dark, straight or curved, active or passive, adventure or science, one or many, limited or unlimited, male or female . . . ? According to Irigaray, the conceptualisation of experience is also, namely, an ontological matter: it designates the objects as well as allocating the subjects in the world (Whitford 1991: 54). Do we want, or are we even able, to represent ourselves as subjects with the images of this discourse? Should we ride along with a movement marked by disconnection, throwing and pulling back, or start looking for other kinds of exchanges, relations and modalities between equal sexed subjects? In other words, should we 'borrow signifiers' (Irigaray 1985a: 71)?

In Bowlby's words: ' "we" [is] a community of (masculine) readers invoked for the occasion of sharing in, recognising, this as a commonplace experience, and the appeal to whom is a further reinforcement of the generalisation of the scene' (Bowlby 1992: 11; see also Jokinen and Veijola 1994).

Le look le plus cool: II

Bauman proposes that the stroller, the vagabond, the tourist and the player 'offer jointly the metaphor for the postmodern strategy moved by the horror of being bound and fixed' (1994: 26). We will now consider whether Bauman's figures have anything in common with the adventurer and/or the stranger. But before doing so we will make two preliminary reservations concerning Bauman's general framework in this particular text. First, it is an overstatement to say that the majority of people in the prime time of their lives and in places central to their life-world go about being vagabonds, tourists, strolling and playing games. There are a number of social worlds – kitchens, for example, or hospitals and factories – in which many people spend their prime time and which are far better equipped for other kinds of 'styles' than, say, strolling. Second, a nice counter-argument is raised by Arto Noro (1995) when he writes that, even though atomistic social figures – figures who have no commitment to any social world that would be coded by an objective aesthetics – remain, quite truthfully, mere 'tourists', it would, nevertheless, be an antisociological move for a cultural critic to consent to such an individualistic concept as the model of a post-modern man. According to Noro, this view would miss various (new) social bonds and forms of collective behaviour. 'We are many times "tourists" in the modern world, but not always, not in all social worlds' (Noro 1995: 7).

We now move on to the social figures which Bauman launches as representatives of contemporary life. What are the strange adventures of the tourist like?

> [T]he tourist is on the move...he is everywhere he goes *in*, but nowhere *of* the place.... The tourist moves *on purpose*.... The purpose is new experience; the tourist is a conscious and systematic seeker of experience, of a new and different experience, of the experience of difference and novelty – as the joys of the familiar wear off and cease to allure. The tourists want to immerse in the strange and bizarre element...They choose the elements to jump into according to how queer, but also how innocuous, they are...the strange is tame, domesticated, and no more frightens; shocks come in a package deal with safety. This makes the world...obedient to the tourists' wishes and whims, ready to oblige; but also...pleasingly pliable, kneaded by the tourist's desire, made and re-made with one purpose in mind: to excite, please and amuse...what the tourist buys, what s/he pays for, what s/he demands to be delivered...is precisely the right not to be bothered, freedom from any but the aesthetic spacing.
>
> (Bauman 1994: 29)

Let us take a breather here, and ask: what seems to be the element that the tourist likes to *jump into*? What appears to be the *strange and bizarre element* that is kneaded by the tourist's desire, which exists for no other reason but to *excite, please and amuse*?

A critical, feminist mind might answer: the (exotic) body-matter of women, of course, poor women of the third world who do not bother the tourist; meaning, they do not demand reciprocity, dialogue, or a subjectivity of their own (this by the way does not imply that the women at home would have the privilege to *bother* the tourist). Moreover, according to Bauman:

> the tourist has a home...for the pleasure to be unclouded and truly engrossing, there must be somewhere a homely and cosy, indubitably own, place to go to when the present adventure is over or if the voyage proves not as adventurous as expected. 'The home' is the place to take off the armour and to unpack – the place where nothing needs to be proved and defended as everything is just there, obvious and familiar.
>
> (Bauman 1994: 29)

Everything is just there, obvious and familiar. Is it really? We would say that the space–time configurations of a home – just like the power relations of family members – are never just there. They need to be practised, repeated and performed. Besides, as Douglas has stated, home starts by bringing a space under control (Douglas 1991: 289). As every housewife knows: even carpets need to be kept on the floor. In passing, we also reject the idea that tourists simply are there as permanent, fixed identities, just when practically everybody else seems to be elaborating on the situationality, relationality and performativity of all identities.

Bauman further maintains that:

> Homesickness means a dream of *belonging*; to be, for once, of the place, not merely in.... The value of home in the homesickness lies precisely in its

tendency to stay in the future tense forever. It cannot move to the present
without being stripped of its charms and allure.

(Bauman 1994: 32)

When read within an Irigarayan framework, this homesickness seems to have no
space for 'metonymic co-existence' (Whitford 1991: 177–85), without opposition and
substitution, no space for (loving) exchange between those who share and take care of
a home together. Keep the carpets on the floor, if nothing else. In fact, the figure of
the tourist described above seems to fight, not only homesickness, but a more severe
problem – that of a 'borderline personality'. The tourist sounds like an autoerotic
subject who cannot love anyone or let himself be loved, 'except by a maternal
substitute who would cling to his body like a poultice – a reassuring balm,
asthmogenic perhaps, but nevertheless a permanent wrapping' (Kristeva 1986: 251).
Indeed, this 'permanent wrapping' or 'maternal substitute' needs no 'particular
building, street or landscape' (Bauman 1994: 29–30). She is *just there.*

'(W)hen tourism becomes the mode of life … the possibility of the home-dream
ever coming true is as horrifying as the possibility of it never becoming real', writes
Bauman (1994: 32). Rojek, when reading Maffesoli, confirms the thought: '[I]n the
condition of postmodernity, a life permanently lived in intense emotional solidarity
would at best be self-deceiving and at worst totally suffocating' (1995: 152). Bauman,
for his part, confirms the previous horror and suffocation:

> Homesickness, as it were, is not the sole tourist's sentiment: the other is the fear
> of *home-boundedness,* of being tied to a place and barred from exit. … The
> tourist's favourite slogan is 'I need more space'. And the space is the last thing
> one would look for at home.
>
> (Bauman 1994: 32)

And the space is the last thing one would look for at home. According to Irigaray (see Whitford
1991: 159–60), the pole of home/woman/body, in the male symbolic order, is space,
in contrast to time and the temporalisation of space, which belong to men. Small
wonder then that Bauman's protagonists never look for space at home. Home *is*
space. Home is mother, matter and origin.

Once is not enough – recycle!

Sexual and sexed relationships between and in-between women and men in concrete
social worlds are not discussed in Bauman's (or other tourist-user's) texts. The tourist,
for instance, is never seen sauntering from place to place with his family; he is never
of a certain age and certain education; he is never sought out by another vagabond,
with a baby in her arms; he is never the other half of an old, crippled, American
couple, stumbling and tumbling over the ruins of Pompeii, the goal of their lifetime
saving and dreaming. Instead, the figure of the tourist is drawn out by merely alluding
to abstractions derived from an interplay of male and female morphologies. Hereby
the dominant male symbolic order (structuring and structured by the male imaginary)
is performed, repeated and supported by the sociological discourse.

The more we think of the four types of 'the post-modern personalities' – the
stroller, the vagabond, the tourist and the player – the more tempted we are to deal a

new hand from a completely different pack of cards: to re-metaphorise and multiply Bauman's metaphors with a sensibility, on the one hand, to sexed subjectivities and, on the other, to concrete social worlds (Noro 1995). In our transferral/translation, the corresponding metaphors of 'post-modern strategies' would be (in the order of appearance):

the stroller	–	the paparazzi
the vagabond	–	the homeless drunk
the tourist	–	the sextourist
the player	–	the womaniser

We have already laid down our sextourist card on the table. Now let's see how our remaining hand matches with that of Bauman's.

> for a stroll as one goes to a theatre... (in the crowd but not of the crowd), taking in those strangers as 'surfaces' – so that 'what one sees' exhausts 'what they are', and above all seeing and knowing of them episodically... rehearsing human reality as a series of episodes, that is events without past and with no consequences... the fleeting fragments of other persons' lives the *paparazzi* spun off into stories at will – it was his perception that made them into actors in the plays he scripted, without them knowing that they are actors, let alone the plot of the drama they play. The *paparazzi* was the past master of simulation – he imagined himself a scriptwriter and a director pulling the strings of other people's lives without [sic!] damaging or distorting their fate.... he was the creator without penalties attached to creation, the master who need not fear the consequences of his deeds, the bold one never facing the bills of courage. The *paparazzi* had all the pleasures of modern life without the torments attached.
>
> (Bauman 1994: 27)

For the paparazzi, '(t)he ultimate freedom is screen-directed, lived in the company of surfaces, and called zapping' (1994: 28).

Second:

> It was the free-roaming *homeless drunks* that made the search for new, state-managed, societal-level order imperative and urgent.... the movements of the *homeless drunks* are un-predictable; unlike the pilgrim the *homeless drunk* has no set destination. You do not know where to will he move next, because he himself does not know nor care much. The *homeless drunkenness* has no advance itinerary – its trajectory is patched together bit by bit, one bit at a time. Each place is for the *homeless drunk* a stopover, but he never knows how long will he stay in any of them; this will depend on generosity and patience of the residents, but also on news of other places arousing new hopes.
>
> (Bauman 1994: 29)

Third, the player/*womaniser*:

> The point is to guess the moves of the adversary and anticipate them, prevent or pre-empt – to stay 'one ahead'. The *womanizer's* world is the world of risks, of intuition, of precaution-taking.... Time in the world-of-a-*womanizer* divides into a succession of games... Each *womanization* is made of conventions of its own;

each is separate 'province of meaning' – a little universe of its own, self-enclosed and self-contained. Each demands that disbelief be suspended at the entry.

(Bauman 1994: 32)

Further:

> Each *womanization* has its beginning and its end. . . . one must make sure that the *womanization* has also a clear, uncontested ending. It should not 'spill over' the time after; as far as the later *womanization* is concerned, no *womanization* played before must handicap, privilege or otherwise determine the partners of *womanization* – be of consequence. . . . To make sure that no *womanization* leaves consequences, the *womanizer* must remember (and so must his partners and adversaries) that 'this is but a game'. An important, though difficult to accept reminder, as the purpose of the *womanization* is to win and so the *womanization* allows no room for pity, compassion, commiseration or cooperation. . . . 'we are grown up people, let us part as friends' demands the *womanizer* opting out from the *womanization* of marriage, in the name of the gamesmanship of future, however merciless, *womanizations*.

(Bauman 1994: 32–3)

Although the accounts and descriptions match both with the original and the translated types, the fact that the sex of the social figure, after re-metaphorisation, becomes manifest, makes them less alluring and tempting to identify with. When the sexed nature of these social figures is rendered explicit, the illusion that they represent humanity in general is destroyed; the universal 'post-modern self', which we found presupposed in Bauman's original gallery, is shattered.

We do not, by any means, claim that Bauman would find the descriptions and accounts of the 'post-modern life strategies' good and preferable, any more than other cultural critics do. At the same time, neither he nor the others appear to take the trouble of investigating the symbolic and social orders which their vocabularies and their descriptions of forms of experience support, and in which these vocabularies and forms of experience prevail and dominate. Thereby they retail that which they seem to criticise, leaving other kinds of vocabularies, experiences and orders unsymbolised, unrepresented, unthought (Irigaray 1985a). Actually, when reading Bauman's accounts of the 'post-modern ambivalence', the mentality described is beginning to sound rather a cool way out from all kinds of problems of a more personal and intimate kind. It is not only home that is left behind – but also the relations between people who make the home.

Dying is the most difficult task, leaving home the saddest

The metaphors launched by the writers quoted above are not simply 'bad'. Rather they are the product of the symbolic order and of a certain discourse in which we unavoidably exist as sexed subjects. However, in our Western culture, (sexed) subjectivity is, according to Irigaray, not an equality of a two-term dimension but primarily a male condition; the function of women is to provide the supporting body-matter for men. Is it, then, even possible to think of metaphoric figurations of subjectivity which are *not* constructed by the movement of back and forth, by penetrating and conquering, by constantly leaving the space of maternal/feminine body? In other words, can a female subjectivity be symbolised between women-among-themselves; or, even, as an amorous and fertile exchange between the two sexes?

Nevertheless we are not willing to give up Simmel's classic figurations. The stranger and the adventurer may have been incorporated into images which we find exclusively and implicitly male as models of 'contemporary condition', but, at the same time, we recognise the importance of a continuing and sustained rethinking of 'all the categories that structure our thought and experience' (Whitford 1991: 165).

We will now study the stranger and the adventurer with the help of a new figure; not a 'powerful' metaphor such as the tourist or the player, but a powerless one, that of a babysitter. The babysitter evokes images of a woman, that is an adolescent, a nurse perhaps. Could the babysitter subtend, in a critical way, 'the most powerful example of... the contemporary essence', the implicitly sexed (male) tourist?

'Observer, philosopher, flâneur – call him what you will...', wrote Baudelaire (Bowlby 1992). So far, nobody has called him the babysitter.

Bauman writes about 'strangers' of whom 'we know too little to engage in any but a most shallow and perfunctory interaction....The "strangeness" of strangers means precisely our feeling of being lost, of not knowing how to act and what to expect, and the resulting unwillingness of engagement' (Bauman 1993: 149). Indeed, from the point of view of a babysitter, for the moment put in charge of a totally strange baby, one does not quite know *what to expect* and *how to act*, but the refusal to *engage* with the baby would result in an outcome even worse for all parties concerned. There is really not much space or time to be *shallow* or *unwilling* about and around the baby.

> The most striking and off-putting trait of strangers is that they are *neither* neighbours nor aliens. Or, rather – confusingly, disturbingly, terrifyingly – they are (or may be – who knows) both. Neighbourly aliens. Alien neighbours. In other words, *strangers*. That is, socially distant yet physically close. The aliens within physical reach. Neighbours outside social reach. Inhabitants of no man's land – a space either normless or marked with too few rules to make orientation possible. Agents and objects of an intercourse which for that reason is doomed to remain disconcertingly erratic, hazardous, with no assurance of success. Intercourse with the strangers is always an incongruity. It stands for the paucity or incompatibility of the rules which the non-status or confused status of the stranger invokes.
>
> (Bauman 1993: 153–4)

As for a strange home, it may very well be marked *with too few rules to make orientation possible*, even though the basic pattern may be familiar. The *status* of a babysitter is certainly a *confused* one since she has command, but only for one night. But for the babysitter who is a stranger in a strange home, everything is not *just there*. For her, the *obvious and familiar* at home is at the same time manifest and a question mark, foreseeable and potentially misleading. She sees the home and the family with 'the stranger's eyes'.

Bauman proposes to describe '(t)he confused, ambivalent sentiments aroused by the presence of strangers... as *proteophobia*... dislike of situations in which one feels lost, confused, disempowered' (1993: 164). With a strange baby, one feels, many times, *lost, confused, disempowered* – especially when the baby, seizing the *opportunity*, so to say, suddenly snatches the tablecloth or your eyeglasses, or refuses to communicate. Nevertheless, it is also possible to feel 'recognition and wonder' (Braidotti 1994: 83), affinity and abandonment, with the strange baby, *with fewer defences and reserves than in any other relation*. One can always speak or sing to the baby, as the little girl may speak or sing to her doll.

> We receive happiness not only from the other: the fact that we do receive it from him is a blessing of destiny, which is incalculable. In the proudest, most self-assured event in this sphere [adventure] lies something which we must accept with humility.
>
> (Simmel 1959: 252)

A baby is a stranger. A strange baby is an adventure. Peaceful moments with a strange baby are, at best, 'fugitive and ephemeral'. The weak metaphor of the babysitter is, to our mind, proper to express the contemporary condition. When babysitting, she is near and far away at the same time. She is in a familiar surrounding (we all know a home, don't we?). At the same time she does not know where the salt is. She usually knows the language, but the baby does not. Nevertheless, they have a language, that of touching, singing, holding, caressing. The metaphor of babysitting unites and separates, as all good metaphors do.

PILGRIMS AND NOMADS

I guess I should be enthusiastic about sport, being a Finn, but when I watch Susanna Rahkamo and Petri Kokko compete in ice dance, it is not nationalism that brings tears to my eyes. Nor is it Valse Triste of Jean Sibelius to which they often skate, or the fact that despite speaking Finnish (the dominant language of a marginal nation obviously wishing to remain monolingual) this couple is, for once, allowed to beat their competitors – who know/speak French as their mother tongue!

More than their being Finnish, my being touched has to do with the ultimate talent of these two, in speaking the metonymic, bodily language of ice dance, together with someone else, in figurations that might be said to resemble a female imaginary, which, as we know, is largely yet to be symbolized. A woman and a man, two skateurs, in an amorous exchange, in which there are two terms, two sexes forming a fertile and ingeniously mobile couple, both in spirit and in body, embracing and fertilizing each other. This is 'an energy produced together and as a result of the irreducible difference of sex. . . . The loss of boundaries does not lead to a fusion in which one or the other disappears, but to a mutual crossing of boundaries which is creative, and yet where identity is not swallowed up' (Irigaray, in Whitford 1991: 167).

I am not surprised to read, in today's morning paper, that the gala in the honour of Rahkamo and Kokko filled all the seats in Helsinki ice hall – 'mostly mothers with their daughters'.

As we have witnessed, for Bauman, the stroller, the vagabond, the tourist and the player offer jointly a metaphor for the post-modern strategy. As for modernity, Bauman finds the pilgrim the most fitting metaphor. We will now consider the figure of the pilgrim in more detail, beginning with Adler's analysis. She argues that 'many of the cultural uses of travel lately receiving attention are so traditional as to be found at the very core of Christian ascetic culture' (Adler 1992: 409). She further claims that 'the use of travel as a religious ritual far transcends the narrow sense of pilgrimage proper, to encompass all geographical movement bound up with cultural invocations of "ultimate reality" and with the deliberate construction of supremely valued forms of subjectivity' (Adler 1992: 408).

What kinds of spaces do the pilgrim-tourists penetrate into – or withdraw from? What kinds of embodied subjectivities do they promote? Adler finds two different orientations or ideal typical orientations toward movement within the early Christian ascetic world: flight from the world expressed in repeated geographical relocations (*anchoresis*) and disciplined stability. Anchorites fled the world and their times to the spiritual freedom and purity of wilderness spaces, conceived of as timeless and socially empty. According to Adler, 'the religious romance of the desert "anchorite" is best understood as part of a comprehensive folk romance of free space and individual rebellion – of geographically expressed flight from sinful society and morally degraded times into space narratively figured as asocial and timeless' (Adler 1992: 409).

Ascetics voluntarily divested themselves of the comforts and securities of a known place in a kin-based society. They sought to 'die to the world' in order to recreate themselves out of nothing in the middle of nowhere. Geographical movement away from home and its securities was seen as essential to the creation of a new self (Adler 1992: 410). Temptations should be left behind, one ought to flee them, concretely and literally.

What temptations? Temptations of a home? What are they? Nearness and safety? Devious mother-bound temptations which prevent men from becoming men. Men? We shall return to this question after mapping the geography of our field of investigation in more detail.

The morphology of the male subject was clearly existent in this early monastic theology of anchoresis. The female matter was to be penetrated as well as projected out of one's own body. Actually, the whole body was to be killed, to be completely certain of dying to the world. As Adler phrases it: '[A monastic theology of literal flight] was linked to modes of subjectivity that came to self-consciousness through disciplined confrontations with the demonic, the uncanny and the foreign on the borderlands of settled community' (Adler 1992: 412).

However, there was simultaneously another monastic theology at work, that of stability. This theology found the impulse to move as a temptation to be avoided! One was, instead, to explore the interior (mental) space. A moral critique of movement, says Adler, linked the ascetic's temptation to change places with other sinful passions, 'from fornication and gluttony to vainglory and avarice' (Adler 1992: 412). This was, in effect, the first systematic Christian psychology, which laid 'the rhetorical groundwork for later organized efforts to stabilize and settle wandering holy men and women' (1992: 12). According to this discipline, the monk was to remain at his station, 'fleeing' only metaphorically, into the interior, mental space, by becoming the watcher of his own thoughts.

The 'monastic contemplative was to rivet one's body to one spot in order to still, for purposes of observation, a spinning inner world of experience, an undisciplined slipperiness of thought' (Adler 1992: 413). This kind of monk did not move, and killed his temptations by attempting to concentrate on them, mastering his unconscious, the (M)other/matter. In Adler's words, '[w]here a theology of literal flight implied a conception of evil as external, and of literal evasion as the best defense against it, a monastic theology of stability implies a very different construction of the ascetic subject: the demonic is within, rather than external to, the self, and defense against it entails inner "splitting", self-observation, and self-reflexive inner conversation and combat' (Adler 1992: 413–14).

Accompanying this stable discipline of self-observation was the cultivation of mourning as a permanent emotional orientation. 'The immobilized, immured, self-observing, self-examining, self-subjective subject is also a mourning, sorrowful, tear-drenched subject, whose soul is to be softened and prepared for cultivation by weeping' (Adler 1992: 414). Hence, the interiority is a space of loss, punitive self-examination, and mourning. It resonates with absence and renunciation. Adler concludes: 'I simply want to stress that discourse about movement in external (geographical) space and constructions of internal (psychological) space have been closely linked from the very beginnings of Christian tradition' (1992: 19).

Adler further suggests that we should, as researchers, be sensitive to the extent to which movement in itself (or the inhibition of movement) has figured as a performed theology, a dance, a play of a figure against a background. Accordingly, one could suggest that the movements of flâneurs, tourists, sociologists, philosophers and so on are performed disciplines, dances, plays of the figures, against backgrounds (the matter).

Free your mind and the rest will follow

Elsewhere, Adler writes extensively of holy women, of 'female long-distance ascetic travel' (ascetic movement) as well as of 'cloistered female bodies' (the theology of stability; Adler 1994). Let us look first at the travelling holy women. Adler's study is based on the texts written by the contemporaries of holy women, mostly men. Depending upon the motives of a particular writer, '(t)he movements of these women were glossed as a sign of sublime humility, raising them above the weakness of their sex and legitimizing their rule over men, or as a veritable scandal which disqualified them from any claim to sanctity' (Adler 1994: 7). One of the examples given of how to raise above female gender is the life of Melanie the Elder who lived in the fourth century, a Roman noblewoman who journeyed to the Eastern Mediterranean and returned to Rome at the age of sixty. Melanie had lost her husband and two of her three children in her early thirties, and decided to leave for an ascetic long-distance journey. (It is appropriate to say 'she decided', because she was extremely rich.) She became a much praised ascetic, and received ritual homage and loud acclaim on her return:

> Melanie who, according to narrative tradition had as a young woman turned her back on her relations and abandoned her son to be raised by others, earning merit as a 'virile soldier' of Christ in the East, returned West in the very image of sacred Motherhood, transferring spiritual 'wealth' and honour to her materially rich and powerful family.
>
> (Adler 1994: 29)

Her long journey (with an enormous party) merited her public glorification and raised her above the common status of her sex. Adler writes that Melanie and other elite women like her 'not only acted out a freedom of movement normally unavailable to their sex, but penetrated space conceived as morally "virile" (the deserts of the hermits) and became, to some extent, honorary males' (1994: 64).

How is it possible that females get 'raised above their sex' by penetrating morally virile spaces, whereas their male counterparts tried to reach 'self-consciousness through disciplined confrontations with the demonic, the uncanny and the foreign on the borderlands of settled community...' (Adler 1992: 12; see above)? Females seek out morally virile space, males demonic space? Interestingly, holy men and women were also tourist attractions: other wanderers visited them. In fact, there were strict norms about hospitality to other pilgrims. Our suggestion is that female ascetics achieved their glory partly by meeting – hosting and visiting – virile male pilgrims.

But not all females were lucky enough to gain glorification from their wanderings (and lose their sex). There is another narrative, on the side. Some of these female ascetics were cursed because they penetrated (sic) holy places and spoiled their atmosphere. Adler comments:

> Women were perhaps the first travellers to become conscious of an irony now familiar in the discourse of modern tourism: The traveller presses longingly toward a pure and holy ('unworldly') site which holds out the promise of personal transformation, knowing all the while that the purity and power of the space is corrupted by contact with travellers like herself. At best, she can hope to be the first, and the last, of her kind.
>
> (1992: 68)

The only one of her sex? Like Virgin Mary?

It was Good Friday yesterday so I went to church to listen to Stabat Mater *by Giovanni Battista Pergolesi.* 'Stabat mater dolorosa, juxta crucem lacrimosa, dum pendebat filius.' *A mother is standing at the crucifix of her son – says the chorus – crying; she is full of grief. Having read my Kristeva (at least the part of* Stabat Mater*), I expected to be crying there too. I was certain that all of my own feelings of loss and pride would burst out. But I was recoiled by the tone of the tunes. They were almost glad. By joining the grief of the mother, all of them – the chorus, the alto, the soprano, the listeners – would get rid of the grief of the mother whose son had been murdered.* Fac me plagis vulnerari, cruce hac inebriari, ob amorem filii. *All others, they wanted to get drunk with his wounds and the crucifix!* Via mater*!*

Julia Kristeva writes that young Pergolesi was dying of tuberculosis when he wrote *Stabat Mater.* 'Man overcomes the unthinkable of death by postulating maternal love in its place – in the place and instead of death and thought', notes Kristeva. She suggests that we think of such love as a surge of anguish at the very moment when the identity of thought and living body collapses: 'It is only "normal" for a maternal representaion to set itself up at the place of this subdued anguish colled love' (Kristeva 1986: 176–7). '*No one escapes it. Except perhaps the saint, the mystic or the writer...*' (177, italics added).

Saints, mystics and writers escape the anguish called love which is 'normally' substituted by representations of crying/loving mothers. Following Adler's texts about the early monastic texts, we have seen how holy males could win the ur-anguish by 'dying to the world'. This, according to our reading, means 'killing the body', neutralising the unconscious, the temptations of nearness and warmth (be they in the desert or within oneself). As we also have learned, one way for a female ascetic to do this was to 'rise above her sex', to become an androgyne. Is it possible for a woman to become a saint? We have one more story left.

Most ascetics of the ancient world were poor, unlike Melanie the Elder, whose journey we joined earlier. Adler presents to us male heroes of asceticism who wandered alone, took up remote stations, and sometimes seemed to merge with animal existence. They went almost, or completely, naked. They were often praised as the most radical renouncers of worldliness, and therefore as the truest of monks. Ascetic literature does not offer parallel female heroines of ascetic vagabonding (Adler 1994: 73). Female holies could not do that. Neither were there any female pillar saints. Saintly women, by contrast, were more likely to draw attention insofar as they 'buried' themselves alive. Stability was a characteristically female ascetic virtue, and so were the extremes of cloistering. Strict cloistering (burial alive, strict inhibition upon movement or going out) was an ascetic ideal far more associated with women than with men. Even when men were 'cloistered', the rules were less strict. Adler writes: 'The cloister itself, with its thick walls and few entrances is a metaphor for the body, attracting interest precisely to its sealed openings or orifices' (1994: 89).

When thinking of yourself, you have no time for others

After having cloistered ourselves in argumentation, which seems to suggest that there is no way 'out', nor 'in', for a female subjectivity, we remember that writing is also one kind of a way. There is a growing body of feminist writing that either creates new figures or recreates old ones in order to make things look different. *If* we presume that the imaginary morphology of the male body misses categories of *her* space–time, makes them unthought and unthinkable, these new figures try to create possibilities of how to think women's space and time. We shall now take a look at such a figure, which is also, constantly, on the move. This figure is Rosi Braidotti's *nomad*, her own version of the Deleuzian 'nomadic becoming' (see Chapter 1, pp. 12–13).

The notion of 'nomadic subjects' might be a suitable theoretical figuration for contemporary subjectivity, and feminist subjectivity in particular, says Braidotti. Accordingly, we are no longer speaking of figures, but figurations: a figuration refers to 'a style of thought that evokes or expresses ways out of the phallocentric vision of the subject' (Braidotti 1994: 1). Consequently, nomadism is for Braidotti a theoretical project and a praxis – which emphasises the bodily roots of subjectivity: location, differences and the blurring of boundaries, rather than universality, unity and the burning of bridges. The nomadic subject is a myth, a political fiction – which might be more effective than theoretical systematisation:

> Though the image of 'nomadic subjects' is inspired by the experience of peoples or cultures that are literally nomadic, the nomadism in question here refers to the kind of critical consciousness that resists settling into socially coded modes of thought and behavior. Not all nomads are world travelers; some of the greatest trips can take place without physically moving from one's habitat. It is the subversion of set conventions that defines the nomadic state, not the literal act of traveling.

> (Braidotti 1994: 5)

We feel, nevertheless, uneasy about this characterisation. Why should one be on the road all the time, be the road literal or symbolic? We recall the feelings of a tired mother: she wouldn't mind if everything stayed in its place, say, for at least five minutes. But, luckily, Braidotti assures us that the nomadic scheme is sober. 'It entails a total dissolution of the notion of a center and consequently of originary sites or authentic identities of *any* kind' (1994: 5). If there is no centre, is there penetration? If there are no originary sites, are there places such as homes to be killed either? Are there any more tired mothers who lack the energy to move at all? Let us hope not.

When inventing alternative metaphors for epitomising the contemporary condition, we are tempted to follow Braidotti's suggestion to use 'nomad' as a way of thinking *as if*:

> [N]omadic becoming is neither reproduction nor just imitation, but rather emphatic proximity, intensive interconnectedness.... Nomadic shifts designate therefore a creative sort of becoming; a performative metaphor that allows for otherwise unlikely encounters and unsuspected sources of interaction of experience and of knowledge.
>
> (Braidotti 1994: 5–6)

We feel it is pertinent to follow Braidotti here since there is absolutely no other way to think 'differently' (in our language house) than to say: let's imagine that.... Let's proceed *as if* my frames of reference were true (or at least the best ones). This is the method we have practised in this chapter: rethinking ideas as if the major discourses in Western thinking were based on the imaginary morphology of the male body (see Veijola and Jokinen 1994). If this works, what possibilities does it open up for women?

The effectiveness of this kind of nomadic strategy, it is useful to remember, is to be judged by *the space* it creates, the possible space–time, reflection, dwelling and espacement of the female subject (cf. Whitford 1991: 155). According to Braidotti, what is politically effective in the political practice of 'as if', 'is not the mimetic impersonation or capacity for repetition of dominant poses, but rather the extent to which these practices open up in-between-spaces where new forms of political subjectivity can be explored. In other words, it is not the parody that will kill the phallocentric posture, but rather the power vacuum that parodic politics may be able to engender' (Braidotti 1994: 7).

Wolff has argued that 'just as the practices and ideologies of actual travel operate to exclude or pathologise women, so the use of that vocabulary as metaphor necessarily produces androcentric tendencies in theory' (1993: 224). However, when read through Irigaray, Whitford, Kristeva and Braidotti, many aspects of the vocabularies of the apparently 'banal and hegemonic model of the tourist or traveler' (Braidotti 1994: 24), as a male fantasy, can be reworked, in order to make men reclaim the body and stop immobilising women as space, home and matter.

If you don't go you can't return

Before ending this section, we will metaphorise a particular nomadic becoming, a female figure, whose 'crises and adventures' have led her to choose trajectories formerly reserved for men only: the trajectories of travelling abroad. She is notoriously absent from the travel and leisure theories (as well as from the sociology of work, for that matter), and she is not the prostitute, the lesbian, the hysteric or the murder victim, but the *au pair*. (People rarely pay attention to what *girls* do.)

An au pair is, most often, an adolescent girl (for instance, from a country like Finland) who travels away from home to do domestic work for a year in a household in a foreign country (preferably Paris or London). She has usually been warned (by fathers, friends and feminists) against becoming an au pair since its hazardous nature is common knowledge. Still, young girls want to leave, perhaps they have to leave – to free themselves from fathers, mothers, possessive boyfriends. This is, after all, a relatively acceptable way for a girl to get on the road. What else is relevant to be taken into account in this figure? The au pair enters – not only a foreign culture, a foreign locality, a foreign family, but also – a foreign language. In more than one sense, she has left all her homes/houses, in order to enter a totally strange symbolic order, a configuration of a foreign culture/language/household. Either she adapts herself to it – or she is sent back home.

Now could this kind of an 'exit' epitomise the theoretical notions with which we are interested in the present framework, namely, those of travel/home, space/time, language/subject?

As Braidotti puts it, 'I chose to become a nomad, that is to say a subject in transit and yet sufficiently anchored to a historical position to accept responsibility and therefore make myself accountable for it' (1994: 10). In this connection, she also reveals her enchantment with monolingual people: 'those who were born to the symbolic system in the one language that was to remain theirs for the rest of their life...people comfortably established in the illusion of familiarity their "mother tongue" gives them' (1994: 11). Braidotti, however, consoles herself (1994: 11) with the notions of Lacan ('all tongues carry the name of the father and are stamped by its register') and Kristeva ('the state of translation is the common condition of all thinking beings').

But Braidotti, a cosmopolitan philosopher/feminist, is not the only one who is 'structurally displaced in between different languages' (Braidotti 1994: 12) – so, too, is the au pair. In the au pair, Braidotti's idea of the nomadic becoming as 'emphatic proximity, intensive interconnectedness' finds a real-life counterpart: taking care of a strange baby, a strange *foreign* baby.

One familiar gesture remains, though. The totally strange foreign baby babbles as babies do and is taken care of by the au pair, in the mode of feminine 'spacing' (Bauman 1993: 145), in a 'signifying space, a both corporeal and desiring space' (Kristeva 1986: 209) of a 'maternal space', characterised by 'monumental temporality, without cleavage or escape, which has so little to do with linear time (which passes) that the very word "temporality" hardly fits: all-encompassing and infinite like imaginary space' (1986:191). 'Love for an other...the slow, difficult and delightful apprenticeship in attentiveness, gentleness, forgetting oneself' (Kristeva 1986: 206).

(A Filippino housemaid working abroad is, of course, another story completely. All nomads and vagabonds cannot choose the length and 'style' of their stay.)

SEXED SUBJECTS

I take a break in writing this article and watch a documentary on the American artist, Louise

Bourgeois. I hold my breath when she starts to caress a sculpture of hers and describes it as 'a disoriented figuration emerging... hanging, not knowing left from right... waiting for something, not knowing what'. Well, I breathe again, doesn't that epitomise a female figuration in the process of becoming! But, then again, I realise that if there is no centre from which to separate right from left, there is no situated knowledge either. Metaphors, as well as facts, are stubborn things.

If the house/home distinction can be used as a spatial metaphor for language/ symbolic distinction, we might summarise the previous discussions with the help of the distinction and look at what kinds of epistemological subjects we have constructed, in what kinds of houses do they live in the discourse, and in what kinds of homes they live in the symbolic.

We shall now pick up the three Janus-faced metaphors, produced in the previous sections (paparazzi/flâneur, sextourist/stranger/adventurer and au pair/pilgrim/ nomad), for further scrutiny. Leaning on Irigaray's presupposition that '[e]pistemology is subtended by the subject of enunciation' (Whitford 1991: 48), we construct a table of the three corresponding epistemologies.

We do not wish to make a totalising claim that the figures of the paparazzi, sextourist and au pair would be the predominant types or models of our times and the post-modern identity. But neither do we claim that they are mere exceptions in the real world, in its images, representations and symbolic orders. In contrast, they are situated and sexed readings and positionings of the figuration of 'the post-modern tourist'. One could, of course, argue that all the metaphors we have invented here are mere social roles and temporal positions, and can be occupied by anyone of any gender, age or race. Still, it is not just anyone, at random, who takes care of a totally strange baby – who is encouraged or allowed to do that. Nor is it just anyone who exploits totally strange bodies – and is financially capable and socially allowed, even encouraged, to do that. Nor is it just anybody who has the money, resources and urge to hunt the secret hiding places of celebrities across the borders. 'If not me, then somebody else', as an ethical statement (see Table 2.1), means different things for each individual tourist.

Table 2.1 Sexed subjectivities

	paparazzi/flâneur	*sextourist/stranger/ adventurer*	*au pair/pilgrim/ nomad*
space–time configuration	fort/da, gaze	fort/da, penetration	with, in-between, exchange
temporality	historical, linear	historical, linear	monumental, cyclical
travel–home	hierarchic, spatial	hierarchic, spatial	'messy'
subjectivity	subject–object/other	subject–object/other	subject–subject/other
ethics	'if not me, then someone else'	'if not me, then someone else'	'if not me, then someone else'
rationality	instrumental	instrumental	caring
embodiment	gaze/camera	gaze/penis	touch, mouth, hands, ear

One way of looking at the matter is to picture all of these subjects as taking part in and co-producing a specific Western, capitalist, male symbolic order, which is built on a specific imaginary as well. Given the premise that 'Western thought is informed by an imaginary which in turn has the morphology of the male body', and 'this level of "essentialism"...subsists in the most deconstructive thought' (Whitford 1991: 103), every discourse including that of social theory should constantly 'analyse its own conditions of existence'; at least if it does not want to 'repeat the founding gesture of exclusion' of the maternal-feminine, maternal genealogy, women-as-subjects and the female body (Whitford 1991:103). As Bowlby says:

> The woman in the street is not the equivalent of the man in the street, that figure of normal representativeness, and her sexually dubious associations give to her stepping out a quality of automatic transgressiveness that is also the chance of her going somewhere different.
>
> (Bowlby 1992: viii)

We will now picture our configurations for the very last time.

One cannot ski without leaving a trace

The job of a paparazzi is, roughly, to 'reveal the truth' about the rich and the famous. His usual method of collecting data is to follow a celebrity to a place where s/he (usually she) thinks nobody has followed her, and to get a photo of her naked body: the extent of exposition of flesh corresponds to the money the paparazzi gets. He sells to anyone, for as good a price as he can. What a paparazzi needs is a set of good cameras, a valid passport, a quick car – sometimes even a helicopter or a boat – and a fluency in languages that are the hard currency when small-talking one's way into places at high-class tourist resorts.

What a paparazzi does is to turn private relations between people, as well as private parts and proportions of their bodies, into public knowledge, gossip, and – preferably – scandals. He cuts naked or half-naked bodies out of contexts (vacationing with family members, friends and lovers). He is solely interested in capturing a scene in which the activity and its background – licking a princess's toes, for example, on the beach or on a sailing boat – conforms with the images attached to the life of the rich and the beautiful, images that 'travel well' across continents and symbolic orders. These scandalous scenes reinforce our images of power, inequality of wealth, sexual roles, and sexual orientations.

As for the object of this violently penetrating gaze, she is definitely a silenced part of this discourse. She does not speak, she is only spoken about. (Occasionally the number one target, Princess Di, protests and declares she feels she is being raped by the paparazzi. With what consequence? The announcement is immediately published all around the world, together with a photo in which Diana hides her face – whereby even the tip of her nose becomes scandalous.) The paparazzi, the enunciator, for his part, is happy to remain anonymous in the streets.

The paparazzi, a social figure between extreme privacy and extreme publicity, epitomises the fleeting and impersonal contacts in public life and the quick seizure of opportunities so often referred to in critical theories. He conquers not at first sight, but at last sight. (Thereafter he is out of sight.) He embodies the invisible gaze, the look from anywhere, the all-encompassing eye (many a hiding place has been found in a tree or on a roof). He does not need to talk or listen to his target, to get involved, he merely documents, 'objectively', with his modern, high-tech equipment. In his profession, '[t]he ultimate freedom is screen-directed, lived in the company of surfaces, and called zapping' (Bauman 1994: 28). The paparazzi is a male post-tourist: a (post-)modern figuration producing 'objective', situational truth and knowledge – at the flick of a switch.

The forest gives what the forest has

The sextourist criss-crosses the globe to get sexual and emotional satisfaction with the help of women (to a lesser extent, men) of another ethnicity; often to avoid social and moral consequences in his own culture. Some sextourists return to the same places many times, but, on the other hand, 'other places beckon, not tested yet, perhaps more hospitable, certainly able to offer new chances. . . . If natives cease to amuse, one can always try to find the more amusing ones' (Bauman 1994: 29).

To all practical purposes of a theory, the sextourist is, by definition, a man. (By definition but not by term, which, not surprisingly, masks the sexual division implied in the phenomenon.) If international sextourism had to do (only or mainly) with women's economy of desire, there would, most probably, be no such institution (even if there are individual women and groups of women out there practising sextourism). As a worldwide, institutionalised phenomenon, sextourism deals with the male imaginary and, consequently, stands out as a solid support of the masculine symbolic order.

In the framework of a critical social theory, what is the language-house of the sextourist like? Or, in the words of Deleuze and Guattari: 'How to become a nomad and an immigrant and a gypsy in relation to one's own language?' (Deleuze and Guattari, cited in Kaplan 1990: 360–1). Is the sextourist 'a gypsy of his own language' – if we were to imagine, for a moment, his own language as the unsensual (as is often claimed) and guilt-ridden sexuality and body culture of the Western culture? No, the sextourist is no gypsy since his 'immigrance' – sextourism – does not estrange him from his own language. His language is, and continues to be, the master's language and he, home and abroad, speaks it from a singular position of interlocution without providing a position for an equal partner of another sex. By speaking his own language in new places he turns continents, cities, neighbourhoods and women into the 'body-matter' of prostitution. The printed version of this 'body-matter' is, then, called (the 'universal' language of) pornography.

The figures of the sextourist and the paparazzi resemble one another in that their travelling is repressive repetition in search of the perfect climax/the perfect shot. Neither is interested in the encounter, as such, with the other/strange. Only the proofs or the personal pleasure of that 'mismeeting' count. As a counter-argument, one could point out that the sextourist often buys sexual services which place him into the object-position, the position of 'woman'. He may, for instance, pay to be tied up and whipped (with the vacuum cleaner turned on), as foreplay to (his) sexual satisfaction. This, however, does not mean that the sextourist would experience his humiliation as-woman. Nor does this make the woman, whom he pays to do the whipping, act as-man: only like-man. This performance may be compared to

Irigaray's view of male writers who 'are interested in feminine identity and their identity as feminine or women'. They are 'in practice trying to colonize the space that might be women's... [t]hey are still within the same hom(m)osexual economy' (Whitford 1991: 50).

The truth which a foreign woman performing sexual services produces out of her experiences and power relations with the sextourists does not affect her positioning, neither in the discourse nor in the practise of sex business. No matter what the prostitute says to make her client reach his climax, 'the distinction between speaking like a woman and speaking as a woman is vital, since to speak as a woman implies not simply psychosexual positioning, but also social positioning' (Whitford 1991: 49). The employee of the sextourist is merely a powerless she. The only subject of enunciation, the only epistemological subject, is the sextourist himself – among-other-sextourists.

One could also argue that the sextourist is not an ethical or moral subject who is responsible for the abuse of Third World women, since 'everybody does it' (Bauman 1993: 242). 'No one but the tourist is so blatantly, conspicuously dissolved in numbers, interchangeable, depersonalized.' Indeed, in defence of the sextourist it can be said that the vast pornographic literature of sexual encounters presents him as he/it, as a third person statement. Just like '[i]n the discourse of science and knowledge, apparently no one is responsible' (Whitford 1991: 49). In the sex business, no man – himself – is responsible. 'There is sextourism' masks the 'I's ('eyes') of men (cf. Whitford 1991: 49).

Indeed, being a tourist more generally can be defined as having or taking no responsibility for the social situation one is a part of.

No child is so bad that he is not welcome at home

What kind of an epistemological subject is the au pair, then? Given that subjectivity is possible only as a place of interlocution in a discourse, as 'the ability to respond to the speech of the other speaker' (Whitford 1991: 39), the subjectivity of the au pair seems to be, in a double sense, questionable. If, within her 'own' symbolic order and language, she-as-a-woman is not a subject, but imprisoned in language, then a free subjectivity in a foreign language should be even more impossible. Then again, is it?

There is one difference, though. In a foreign home and in a foreign language-house – that is, in a foreign symbolic order – the au pair is legitimately and consciously *only a visitor* in language; just as women as speaking/enunciating, individual subjects are only visiting the language of the male symbolic order. In this sense, she is a 'proper' tourist. But, like the tourist, she can see her situation with the stranger's eyes: for her, her subjectivity in language is no more transparent. The au pair sees the language at work, the language which she operates and which operates her; which she figures and is figured by. Word by word, utterance by utterance, she wins her subjectivity in a foreign language by speaking and positioning herself as the subject of enunciation, an interlocutor in a conversation.

In a way, in the foreign symbolic order, she is a 'stranger' and an 'adventurer' who has to speak and enunciate in order to exist as a subject and not as one of the Others who 'do not have... "personal" identities – they derive identity from the classes to which they "belong" – or, rather, to which they have been assigned' (Bauman 1993: 149).

In the foreign language-house, when babysitting a foreign baby, the au pair knows the relations of power in a foreign household, in a foreign heterosexual marriage, embodied and materialised in the space–time configuration of the family/home/ house. The au pair is not one of her kind. Meeting other au pairs from all over the world on their day off, she engages herself in parole, in jouissance, the economy of which 'is that of the between-subjects, and not that of the subject–object relation' (Irigaray, cited in Whitford 1991: 45). In parole, in laughter and conversation with other women who are in a similar situation, she is granted a position of a subject, an enunciator. When among-themselves, even the Filipino babysitters are subjects – although their parole, perhaps, consists of both crying and laughter.

In a simulation of social theory, the au pair is a post-modern – female – pilgrim in a foreign language, who lives the contradicting ambivalences of her situation without having command over them. Or to make up yet another, post-modern, proverb, *The au pair is at home in the strange – the post-modernite is a stranger at his home.*[1]

Not all those in the boat are fishermen

The 'post-modern tourist', whose forms of experiencing we have been tracing in this chapter, seems to fall gradually out of the sphere of leisure, drop off his leisurely outfit, garment by garment, and re-emerge in the sphere of work, trade, re-dressed in a three-piece suit. He emblematises the modern professional at work: someone without reliable solidarities and loyalties grounded in shared long-term relationships. His job is to travel, and part of his salary consists of his own tourist adventures.

The professional is a kind of modern vagabond, a software specialist with a large computer company, perhaps, who flies across continents tutoring well-paying clients; or maybe he is a stockbroker, well paid for being a 'player'. One more applicable figure emerges: that of the congress tourist, the conference hopper. We, too, know, having hopped in and out of a few of them ourselves, that the configuration of a congress is a telling, modern combination of both spheres, leisure and work. The intellectual of the airport is there, the university guesthouse, the congress hotel, the well funded workshop retreat, the friendly host, the nightlife in town afterwards, and, inevitably, the early waking hours in the morning. . . . Less romantic than 'vagabonding' or 'pilgrimage', perhaps, because of all the paper work – and the necessity of charming others (cf. Lodge 1984).

Indeed, as 'vagabonding' is an attractively masculine image, free and independent, the conference hopper – smiling, charming, seducing and filling in his dancing card with names for future congresses and lecture circuits – comes a lot closer to the 'prostitute' and has, therefore, threatening, feminine connotations. (Not to mention the lack of 'immediate presentness' of an adventure, destroyed by the long months of preparations of performances to be given in another time and place.) Rather, we guess, one prefers to think of oneself as a tourist, a vagabond, a post-modern personality who is merely putting a post-modern 'life strategy' into effect.

However, to return to this 'paperwork', we will appropriate Haraway's notion that '[t]he only way to find a larger vision is to be somewhere in particular' (Haraway 1991: 196). In the previous sections, we wanted to experience and exchange realistic accounts of sexed social figurations instead of the universal, solipsistic constructions of the male imaginary, such as the post-modern tourist. In other words, we wanted to think the unthought, by inventing models and domains for creative and fertile co-parenting (romancing, double-syntax) between female and male subjects. We also wanted to invent representable and effective female symbolic orders.

For the sake of consistency, we shall give this article an ending in a 'concrete, sexed, social world'. Let us conjure an image of the Finnish sociologist, Jussi Vähämäki, with his colleague Arto Noro, standing side-by-side on a boat at sea; both being devotees – not tourists – of the social world of recreational fishing. Vähämäki describes 'the world of fishing and philosophy' as 'the art of excluding women' (Vähämäki, no date). 'Women break friendships and companionships, they turn friends against each other. . . . "Woman" is the body of the social contract, its material and nourishment: the fish.'

> The Fish, the woman, the offering, the one who binds the brothers together, gives them nourishment and a feeling of existence, lights their faces, warms them up, and, while burning, takes with it the excess, all that is indivisible and leading to quarrel and dispute. . . . Do we choose the offering because she is a woman, or because we are afraid of perishing in hunger and in fighting without an offering? Can any object calm us down and stop the pack of wolves, as the structuralist believes?
>
> (Vähämäki, no date)

Vähämäki answers his own question: 'The structuralist has, unfortunately, never tried to soothe a crying child.'

We have been trying to soothe a crying child. This is what babysitting, or dreaming, or cultivating one's thoughts, or writing social theory – whatever metaphor one finds appropriate – is about. Images of 'reflection', 'possession', 'seizure' and 'revealing' are, to say the least, not adequate enough when conceptualising the imaginary, symbolic and bodily existence of both sexes.

Our children are not (just) our own, any more than our thoughts are. We have agreed with Irigaray in suggesting that it might help to add daughters to various Holy Trinities: of religion, theory and society (Whitford 1991: 141–2). Not only daughters (and brides), it needs to be said, but also real – unburied – mothers, real sisters, real wives, real lovers, real women. But, first, women need to be able to occupy subject positions in discourse. Writing the babysitter/au pair into a metaphorical and concrete being is one way of bringing the maternal-feminine into discourse, of giving symbolic form to the feminine, trying to coin the signifier instead of borrowing it.

Can the babysitter's/au pair's knowledge as woman's knowledge, then, 'anticipate and perhaps assist the birth of a new social order' (Whitford 1991: 170) in theory, society and culture? All we can give as an answer, at the moment, is another question posed by Whitford and Irigaray (Whitford 1991: 188–9): 'Who can tell in advance which reworking, which creation, is going to crystallize a potential shift in the collective vision and make a new configuration possible?'

ACKNOWLEDGEMENTS

We wish to thank the following colleagues for commenting earlier drafts of this article, both critically and constructively: Leena Eräsaari, Risto Eräsaari, Asko Kauppinen,

Arto Noro, John Urry and Marja Vehviläinen. The proposition to investigate the increased use of the metaphor of the tourist was made by Tapio Aittola.

NOTE

1 The sub-headings in this chapter are from the ads of MTV (Music Television), as well as from a collection of 'Finnish Proverbs', translated into English by Inkeri Väänänen-Jensen (Penfield Press, 1990). Both 'styles' or 'types' of knowledge production present ways of thinking of 'our' condition in a nutshell.

   Social theory is a third way of knowing and communicating that knowledge. It, too, has a tendency to crystallise complicated phenomena into buzz words and slogans: post-modernisation; massification; great narratives are dead; what shall we do after the orgy?

   At the end of the day, the old Finnish proverbs provide much more up-to-date accounts of our era than the two other alternatives.

3

INDEXING, DRAGGING AND THE SOCIAL CONSTRUCTION OF TOURIST SIGHTS

Chris Rojek

INTRODUCTION

A tourist sight may be defined as a spatial location which is distinguished from everyday life by virtue of its natural, historical or cultural extraordinariness. Urry (1990: 11) argues that tourist sights are predicated in a binary opposition between the ordinary/everyday and the extraordinary. This opposition is culturally constructed. In Western culture a number of spatial locations and objects exist which signify extraordinary qualities and seem to command us to visit them at least once in our lifetime: the Eiffel Tower, the Pyramids, the Taj Mahal, the Grand Canyon, Sydney Harbour, Niagara Falls and the Statue of Liberty are all good examples. More generally the urge to travel to witness the 'extraordinary' or the ' wonderful' object seems to be a deep urge in all human cultures.

In ancient times, the Seven Wonders of the World exerted a powerful fascination for travellers. These were the Great Pyramid of Giza, the Hanging Gardens of Babylon, the Statue of Zeus at Olympia, the Temple of Artemis at Ephesos, the Mausoleum at Halicarnassus, the Colossus of Rhodes, and the Pharos at Alexandria (Clayton and Price 1988). Similarly, *The Travels of Sir John Mandeville*, which appeared in the fourteenth century, recounted distant wonders and habits of life that inspired travellers to leave home and see for themselves.[1] The book was hugely popular and immensely influential. It is authenticated as the only travel book in Leonardo da Vinci's library; Columbus consulted it for information on China before his voyage; and it was among the volumes in Frobisher's cabin anchored in Bantry Bay in 1576. Yet in fact most contemporary authorities regard the book to be a clever fake. Some suggest that Mandeville's account was a composite of many travellers' tales. Others allege that even if the book is genuinely the work of one man, the longest journey he ever made was from the library to his writing desk![2]

Mention of the mythical is unavoidable in discussions of travel and tourism. Without doubt the social construction of sights always, to some degree, involves the mobilisation of myth (Barthes 1957). As a social category 'the extraordinary place' spontaneously invites speculation, reverie, mind-voyaging and a variety of other acts of imagination. There is ample evidence in the history of travel to suggest that sights have produced a discursive level of densely embroidered false impressions, exaggerated claims and tall stories.[3] Adams (1962) points to an entire history of travel lies and travel liars. Of course, it is enormously difficult to disentangle this tradition of deliberate fabrications from our ordinary perceptions of sights. No culture is, as it were, falsehood-proof. Yet the peculiarly shifting and fragmented character of modern culture perhaps makes us more likely to disagree about the character of what Schutz called 'paramount reality' and, by extension, 'paramount falsehoods'. I shall return to this point in the penultimate section of this chapter.

At this stage of the discussion I want to establish the proposition that myth and fantasy play an unusually large role in the social construction of *all* travel and tourist sights. There are several reasons for this. In the first place, travel sights are usually physically distant from our ordinary locale. The remoteness of the sight requires abandoning our everyday life routines and social places and physically entering new areas. The physical movement to new places and situations obviously invokes the unfamiliar. This, in turn, invites speculation and fantasy about the nature of what one might find and how our ordinary assumptions and practices regarding everyday life may be limited. At the same time, there is an internal, psychological level to travel which must be addressed. This refers to our knowledge of the culture of tales, symbols and fantasies which surround a given sight. That is, speculation and journeying to an inner world in which the travel sight is imaginatively explored through cultural metaphors, allegories and fabrications. Spatially speaking then, travel experience involves mobility through an internal landscape which is sculptured by personal experience and cultural influences as well as a journey through space.

Second – and closely related to the first point – the cultural significance of sights engender representational cultures which increase the accessibility of the sight in everyday life. In theory one might speak of an index of representations; that is, a range of signs, images and symbols which make the sight familiar to us in ordinary culture. The process of indexing refers to the set of visual, textual and symbolic representations to the original object. It is important to recognise that representational culture is not a uniform entity. Rather one might speak of files of representation. A file of representation refers to the medium and conventions associated with signifying a sight. As examples of files of representation relevant to tourist culture one might point to travellers' tales, printed texts (travel flyers, brochures, as well as novels and poems such as Joyce's 'Dublin' in *Ulysses*, Proust's 'Paris' in *Remembrance of Things Past*, Wordsworth's poetry of the Lakes), dramatic and cinematic traditions ('Russia' in Chekhov's plays, 'the West' in Sam Shepard's plays or John Ford's films, 'New York' in the films of Martin Scorsese), and television ('America' as portrayed in *Cheers*, *Roseanne* and *Miami Vice*, 'Australia' as portrayed in *Neighbours*, or 'England' as portrayed in *EastEnders*, *Peak Practice*, *Upstairs*, *Downstairs* and *Coronation Street*). Metaphorical, allegorical and false information remains a resource in the pattern of tourist culture as an object of reverie, dreaming and speculation. In the social construction of sights this information can be no less important than factual material in processes of indexing. Thus the visitor to Dallas may frame the site by indexing cultural items from representational files of the Kennedy assassination and incidental knowledge from representational files relating to the Ewing family, as portrayed in the television series *Dallas*. It should not be assumed that either the factual or the fictional have priority in framing the sight. Rather, sight framing involves the interpenetration of factual and fictional elements to support tourist orientations. One should add that indexing operates on conscious and unconscious levels. The emerging sociology of tourism and travel has not really got to grips with the role of the unconscious in colouring sights. As an aside one might observe that there might be a basis for seriously questioning the post-modern proposition that it is no longer possible to refer to 'collective subjects' in everyday culture. More specifically, there is much in how our ordinary consciousness of tourist sights functions which suggests that we draw on a collective fund of unconscious symbols, images and allegories.

This brings me to the third point. Since the concept of indexing refers to a range of representations, it follows that everyday tourist perceptions typically consist of a combination of elements. Because these elements often draw on glamorous representations which are portrayed in guide books, movies and TV shows, it follows that sights are often anti-climactic experiences. Standing before the Sphinx in Cairo, or the Sydney Opera House, one may feel that the sight is not as breathtaking as one had been led to believe. The sky is not the right colour or the building materials look more weathered than in photographs. Although the tourist literature tends to emphasise feelings of satisfaction and fulfilment, it is worth noting that tourism can also end in disappointment and a feeling that one's expectations have been deceived (see Chapter 9 on this in relationship to one's photographs).

In trying to explain the complex feelings that one experiences in tourism it is helpful to think in terms of the dragging of elements from files. The term dragging refers to the combination of elements from separate files of representation to create a new value. Selections of images, symbols and associations are drawn from representational files to create new values for the sight. This is accomplished through tourist marketing, advertising, cinematic use of key sights and travellers tales. Dragging operates at both conscious and unconscious levels. As an example, consider the *Schindler's List* tour that has operated in the Polish town of Krakow since 1994. Spielberg used Kazimierz, the Jewish quarter of Krakow, as the setting for his film. The tour purports to allow the tourist to visit the places in *Schindler's List*. Tour guides frame the history of the area in terms of set-pieces from the film. For example, in the course of the tour one is shown the spot 'where they caught the boy who ran away and shot him and he just dropped down' (Bolger 1994: 24). This is an example of the process of conscious dragging. Cinematic events are dragged on to the physical landscape and the physical landscape is then reinterpreted in terms of the cinematic events. Because electronically generated images are so pre-eminent in framing our perception of territory and history, the tourist generally has little resistance to this version of 'reality'. In this respect, the *Schindler's List* tour also illustrates the unconscious dragging process. For the orientation of the tourist is typically defined in terms of the index of representations derived from the film. Most tourist have 'seen' Kazimierz before actually being there through the images and narrative of Spielberg's film. A reserve of sights in the mind of the tourist precedes the physical exploration of the sight. This is an example of how imaginary places have a direct influence on the structure of physical space. Here one should note that the area only became a significant tourist spot *after* the film was made. The film, so to speak, *made* Kazimierz an extraordinary place, a place worth visiting.

However, this process of *making* the sight involves several anomalies. To begin, much of the action portrayed in *Schindler's List* took place, not in Kazimierz but in the Podgorze ghetto on the other side of the river Vistula and in the nearby Plaszow concentration camp. In addition, both the film and the tour portray the camps in terms of the exclusive persecution of the Jews. Catholic Poles are presented either as willing accomplices or helpless bystanders of Nazi barbarity. In fact more than two million Catholic Poles died in the Second World War, and the Plaszow camp was half Jewish and half Polish.

The *Schindler's List* tour provides examples of how distortion, and also myth and fabrication, operate in the social construction of tourist sights. To some extent today's tourist is perhaps not so different to the credulous readers of Sir John Mandeville in being seduced by tales and images which falsify sights. Except, of course, that our range of representational files permits a much wider field of dragging and indexing. Still, as with Mandeville's critics, the notion of a privileged reading of tourist sights must be regarded with scepticism. This challenges one of the main assumptions in the literature on tourism, namely, that tourism is primarily motivated by a quest for authenticity. If sights are always pot-pourris which utilise elements from a variety of index files at both conscious and unconscious levels, how can one speak of an authentic experience of the real place? Some commentators allege that the notion of privileged reading is incompatible with electronic culture (Baudrillard 1983; Meyerowitz 1985). They argue that the character of popular culture has changed and that we need to devise new ways of reading it. This is a crucial argument in understanding sight construction. I shall return to this at greater length in my examination of sensation sights and the conclusions which derive from this.

At this point I want to disassociate myself from the proposition that there has been an apocalyptic change in popular culture. Uneasiness with the notion of authenticity has, of course, been a prominent feature in the analysis of modern culture for a long time. For example, Benjamin's discussion of aura suggested that the mechanical reproduction of 'original' objects fatally corrupts our sense of the authenticity of the object (Benjamin 1973). As the world fills up with duplicates of the original it becomes more difficult to believe in the uniqueness of the original. The reproduction is just as good and just as real. Long before Meyerowitz or Baudrillard, Benjamin was pointing to the corrosive effect of modern communication systems upon our understanding of place, identity and difference. Buck-Morss (1989) argues that modern and post-modern characteristics are inherent in industrialisation. Thus the surrealist movement fashioned a sensibility to the world which is palpably post-modernist yet which, nonetheless, preceded post-modernism by half a century. Post-modernist sensibilities are also evident in Romantic and Symbolist poetry and art in the nineteenth century. This is why many critics argue that Blake, Baudelaire, Verlaine, Rimbaud and Redon remain contemporary figures. Buck-Morss's point is that it is erroneous to claim a break between modernity and post-modernity. But her discussion also raises central questions of experience and epistemology as they apply to visual culture and travel activity.

Somewhat against current fashion, I argue that there has been an over-emphasis in the tourist literature on questions of experience and being (MacCannell 1989; Urry 1990). Ontological matters are obviously crucial to the study of why people travel, but questions of epistemology are also central. How we pattern tourist experience and what rules we use when we engage in 'escape' activity are much more important than is generally recognised. The pleasure and excitement that we feel in touring are partly related to the switching of rules practised in our domain cultures with contrasting rules. The contrast itself is pleasurable. Long ago Kracauer speculated that the phenomenon of tourism could not be understood without the cult of distraction

(Kracauer 1995). The pleasure of changing things and switching routines impels the tourist to travel. The logic of Kracauer's argument is that tourism approximates to a state of pure mobility. It is not the authenticity of sights that lures us on but rather the hunger for ever-new distractions. These ideas have been revisited, albeit in rather different form, in the recent work of Virilio (1977, 1991). He emphasises that velocity is a potent source of attraction in contemporary culture. The dissolution of space through speed caters to our desire for stimulation without demanding that we make serious important personal commitments. Travelling from sight to sight is an end in itself. What we see when we stand before a sight ultimately means less to us than the restless movement. I will return to these arguments in the conclusion.

SIGMUND FREUD VISITS THE PARTHENON

Although I have referred to a discursive level in respect of the social construction of tourist sights, it is apparent that the influences at work are multi-layered. Freud gives a glimpse of the psychological complexity of the processes involved in a short memoir which deals with tourist memory (1984). In his forties he achieves a long-cherished dream to visit the Parthenon. Once in Athens he is shaken by his sense of disbelief when he finally sets eyes on the Acropolis. The sight of the Parthenon is magnificent. It takes his breath away. But he is quite unable to believe that it really exists. Freud's explanation for this curious doubt is typically psychoanalytical. He remembers his father recounting stories of the wonders of Ancient Greece to him when he was a boy. These stories captivated him and left a deep impression on his unconscious. At the same time he recognised that as the son of a poor man he was unlikely to ever have enough money to visit these extraordinary places and see them for himself. Fate decreed that these extraordinary sights were to be banished from his experience. They would exist for him only in the realm of his imagination. He therefore repressed them except as objects of imagination and, in orthodox Freudian fashion, stoically got on with his life in Vienna. In Freud's judgement his sense of disbelief was entirely a matter of psychological repression. That is, a product of the unique circumstances of his life.

Yet disbelief is a far more common response to tourist sights than Freud's account suggests. We often experience a sense of anticlimax, disbelief or incredulity when we set eyes on a long-imagined sight. Following the vocabulary of psychoanalysis we might call this *tourist denial*. However, while the term is quite evocative, there is no need to resort to the logic of psychoanalysis to explain this reaction.[4] The analysis of culture offers more fertile ground.

Many critics of modern culture have argued that mass society is pre-eminently a sign culture.[5] But perhaps this has always been so. Bakhtin (1968), Burke (1978) and Stallybrass and White (1986) clearly convey the importance of *representation* in the rituals of everyday life in pre-industrial Europe. Religion and superstition furnished the pre-industrial mind with a shared theatre of angels, demons and other phantoms of the imagination. Folklore traditions extended them in distinctive, localised ways. However, for its part the rise of mass culture is associated with the vast multiplication of the institutions devoted to communication and the growth of modes of representation. Indeed, today any account of popular culture which fails to include the effect of television, film or print media on popular consciousness would be regarded as intrinsically flawed. As Baudrillard (1983) and many other commentators have stressed, ours is a time in which the density of the sign world has been augmented to such a degree that it may be impossible to determine where fact ends and fiction begins. However, it is again necessary to exercise caution in holding that this is a sudden change in the nature of modern culture.

The analysis that follows argues that sights can finally be demarcated from the sign cultures which surround them. Indexing and dragging processes can be exposed to reveal how sight fabrications occur. To this extent the analysis opposes several features of post-modernism. In particular, it rejects the arguments of Eco and Baudrillard that we now live in a condition of hyperreality in which it is impossible to separate fact from fiction. At the same time the analysis suggests the processes of indexing and dragging are now chronic in media culture so that distorted and fabricated readings of sights are now corollaries of normal tourist experience. The fictional is undoubtedly inherent in the presentation and cultural meaning of sights. However, it does not follow from this that reality can no longer be revealed or that all forms of fiction are of equivalent value. I will return to these points in the conclusion.

CULTURAL CONTROL AND PHANTASMAGORIA

As is well-known, a powerful tradition in the sociology of culture emphasises the control aspects inherent in mass culture. Adorno and Horkheimer (1944) refer to 'the culture industry' which is said to dominate popular consciousness and to promote mass obedience and conformity. Marcuse (1964) likewise argues that the culture industry is a key element in producing 'one dimensional society', a society organised around mass consumption in which political opposition is stifled. This tradition was adopted and modified by the Birmingham School of Cultural Studies (Hall and Jefferson 1975; Hall et al. 1980; Clarke and Critcher 1985). These authors placed greater emphasis on the sources and effects of resistance in society. Social actors are portrayed as effective practical critics and opponents of dominant forms of control.

What has perhaps been less thoroughly explored in the sociology of culture and tourism is the tradition of research stemming from the writings of Benjamin.[6] In part this reflects the hermetic status that was wrongly assigned to Benjamin for most of the post-war years by Anglo-American commentators. Deprived of English translations of his *Arcades* project[7] – that dense, many layered analysis of the rise of consumer culture in industrial Paris – Anglo-Americans resorted to the scatter of papers and articles assembled in retrospective collections. Benjamin emerges from these pages as a fragmentary, uneven and elusive thinker. However, as more of Benjamin's oeuvre becomes available to English-speaking readers, the underlying coherence and richness of his thought stands revealed (see Chapter 2; Buck-Morss 1989; McCole 1993).

However, one aspect of Benjamin's work is particularly significant for the cultural analysis of tourism. In the notes and reflections collected for the *Arcades* project between 1927 and 1929, Benjamin repeatedly characterises the culture of capitalism as a 'phantasmagoria'. Although never rigorously defined, this term loosely refers to the dreamworld of commodity capitalism. Two elements are fused in his mind with regard to the concept. The first is the Surrealist reading of the fantasy content of everyday life. Like the Surrealists, Benjamin sees capitalist culture as suffused with the direct expressions of the unconscious. Wish fulfilment and repression are integral to capitalist processes of exchange and distribution. The market is not only the showplace for commodities, it is also the material register of our inner fantasies and dreams. Following this, it can be argued that tourism is a concentrated instance of the phantasmagoria of capitalism. In tourism, escape experience is packaged in an intensely commodified form. For example, we are told that paying for a trip abroad will enable us to 'get away from it all'. The beach, the hotel, the casino, the ocean, the mountains and a variety of other tourist motifs are presented in the advertising materials almost as clinics of oblivion where we can check-in and then check-out from the cares of everyday life. However, it is too limiting to view tourist experience wholly in terms of the commodity. Interwoven with a commercialised escape discourse is the presentation of the distant and the remote as 'the other'. At least some of the sirens calling us here are of pre-capitalist origin. Perhaps one can posit curiosity about what lies beyond one's immediate realm as an innate feature of human beings. Be that as it may, there is no doubt that a desire to view or engage in contrary or antithetical forms of life is also a powerful motivation in tourist experience.

The second element in Benjamin's discussion of phantasmagoria is the Marxist insistence on dialectical analysis. He insists that the phantasmagoria of capitalist culture can be deciphered. He speaks of the process of deciphering in terms of both an 'awakening' and a 'remembering'. But to what are we awakening? What are we trying to remember? At the heart of Benjamin's discussion of the phantasmagoria of consumer culture is the concept of aura. The closest he comes to a definition is his remark that aura is 'the unique manifestation of distance' (1969: 148). However, from his general discussion we can see that the term 'distance' carries a dual meaning.

In the first place it refers to physical distance. The aura of an object is manifest by its magnetic power to attract us to leave our homes to see it for ourselves; what can be termed the *St Thomas Effect*. St Thomas disbelieved in the resurrected Christ until he had laid his hands upon the wounds and the body. Benjamin appears to suggest that, like St Thomas, we must occupy a physical relation with the auratic object before we can genuinely believe in its authority. Tourists do not quite have to lay hands on an object in a tourist sight to verify its reality. For one thing, these days the sights are usually policed by too many security guards to permit this. More generally, our cultural knowledge of the other relies heavily on trust relations. In this respect there are grounds for believing that trust relations in a society based upon electronic systems of communication have a propensity to be rather low. The discussion on sensation sights (61–8) is partly intended to substantiate this proposal. Nonetheless, even allowing for the presence of low trust relations in everyday life, it remains the case that most tourists feel that they have not fully absorbed a sight until they stand before it, see it and take a photograph to record the moment (see Chapter 9).

The second sense of distance is more esoteric. It refers to Benjamin's belief that auratic objects compel us to make an inner journey, a journey which peels away our ordinary layers of consciousness to reach a deeper level of realisation. The term 'realisation' refers to both self-understanding and an understanding of the relation between the self and culture. In other words, the 'inner journey' reveals something about the self and the place of the self in the wider cultural order. Benjamin's discussion of aura is predicated on the assumption that culture is organised around hierarchical principles of authority and order. Auratic objects are located at the apex of society. He submits that they convey uniform meaning in the host culture. For example, in Thailand the Emerald Buddha remains an object of universal veneration which requires one to adopt physical attitudes of obeisance in viewing it. One cannot point one's fingers at the Buddha or sit with one's legs pointing at it. Guards are on hand at the Imperial Palace in Bangkok to prevent any offensive or impolite behaviour. But what makes these practices difficult for Western tourists to comprehend is their unfamiliarity with Thai culture. For them the Emerald Buddha is simply another tourist sight. Benjamin's discussion of the decline of aura suggests that auratic objects inevitably become disembedded. The authority structures associated with them loosen. The increase in the density and velocity of representations of an auratic object weakens its auratic power and radically decentres its meaning. What makes Benjamin insist on this process?

First, mass reproduction increases the accessibility of the object. Why should we want to travel thousands of miles to see something that we can view in the comfort of our living room on television? The evaporation of physical distance eliminates the sense of remoteness which is the essential requirement in perpetuating the authority of the auratic object. Through ease of contact via mass reproduction, the object becomes just another found object in the showplace of mass culture.

The second point is that duplication denies the principle of unique manifestation upon which the object's authority is ultimately founded. Of course, representational culture inevitably dilutes the principle of unique manifestation. For example, Jusserand (1888) and Rowling (1971) describe what might be referred to as a 'medieval culture industry' in which trinkets, drawings and other tourist paraphernalia representing holy places were avidly consumed by pilgrims. But Benjamin, who was born in 1892 and committed suicide in 1940, belonged to a generation in which the rise of film and phonographic modes of communication seemed to promise the replacement of a limited visual, representational culture with one of mass reproduction in which images of auratic objects expand at an exponential rate. Central to Benjamin's analysis is the concern that mass reproduction is uncontrollable. The universe of determinate linear meanings and allegorical representations gives way to cultural pandemonium in which objects and representations cease to be authoritative. Indexing and dragging processes are the primary mechanisms in tourism which produce this. By encrusting the original object with secondary images, values and associations, these processes make us lose sight of the original meaning of the object. It becomes, as it were, co-opted to fulfil temporary, immediate personal or cultural interpretations. Secondary commentators frequently describe Benjamin's analysis of contemporary culture as 'troubled' or 'disturbed'. This is because the weakening of aura dilutes the possibility of transcendence and reduces lived experience to the condition of meaninglessness.

The third point is that the technology of mass reproduction acts upon the original object to extend or treat its meaning in various ways. Distorted representations of auratic objects such as the Statue of Liberty, the Crown Jewels or the Taj Mahal, participate in the general corruption of the hierarchical order upon which the authority of the object is situated. Mass culture makes the representation closer to everyday life than the original object. *Ipso facto* the object's place as a talisman of paramount reality is problematised (see Chapter 4).

Benjamin's sociology, then, depicts a culture in crisis. He argues that mass reproduction obliterates hierarchy and authenticity. Counterfeit objects are the common currency of cultural exchange. Everyday life is no longer typically negotiated in simple representational forms by reference to the relationships between representations and original objects. Representational files are multiplied, and with this arises the multiplication of opportunities for indexing and dragging. For Eco and Baudrillard representational culture attains a complex condition of self-referentiality in which meanings are typically negotiated in terms of the relation of representations to other representations. External reality is, so to speak, reduced to an incidental importance. Representations are more immediate and accessible than reality. The artificiality of modern culture continuously emphasises the ultimate meaninglessness of traditional quests for authenticity. Elsewhere, Benjamin suggests that the motif of the collector might be appropriate to comprehend the character of mass culture (Benjamin 1979). As Benjamin himself shows (1979: 349–86), high culture produced Eduard Fuchs, the astonishingly tasteful, learned collector of objects who turned his collection into a mosaic of beautiful meaning. But mass culture reduces the ordinary consumer to the position of an addicted consumer of reproduced objects, packaged events and other manipulated stimulants. Although Benjamin never abandons his belief that this situation is retrievable, he also emphasises its destabilising effects on the body politic. Social life is infested with a quality of chronic naivety which involves us in perceiving everything that we see as equally true or equally false. Benjamin and his colleagues in the Frankfurt School had reason enough to worry that this state of affairs made the masses susceptible to the rhetoric of the demagogue. But other writers have pointed to the rise of a couch-potato mentality. That is, a life-orientation which is predicated in the general withdrawal from active participation and relating to the outside world as a detached succession of spectacles which have nothing to do with one's own life except as objects of voyeurism (Debord 1983; Lasch 1984).

Benjamin's journey into the interior of mass culture and the psyche of the modern citizen is richly suggestive. His discussion of the waning of aura helps to contextualise the feelings of scepticism or indifference that we have in much tourist experience. In particular, it sheds light on that feeling of 'so what?' that sight-seeing often produces in the tourist. It is also a useful tool to explore the rise of the cyber-tourist who travels via the Internet from sight to sight without ever leaving home (Feifer 1986). For already in Benjamin's work one can infer the proposition that representations are independent of their physical referents, and are self-referential. In other words, the indexing and dragging processes which surround a sight have independent, self-generative cultural meanings. With respect to tourism, Benjamin's work implies that 'being there' no longer involves actually visiting a sight. Indeed, from the perspective of current representational technologies, it might be argued that the development of virtual reality produces opportunities for technically more thorough examinations of sights than can be achieved by physically travelling to them (Shields 1995). For example, computer technology enables one to magnify features of the sight, to penetrate the surface of the exterior, to examine the sight from all angles and, in general, to have a wider range of 'views' than ordinary sight-seeing allows. Indexing and dragging also render distant sights omnipresent in Western culture. Seeing images and distortions of the Eiffel Tower, the Statue of Liberty, the Leaning Tower of Pisa and so forth are mundane consumption experiences that are available to us in any shopping mall. In these respects the St Thomas effect in sight-seeing will become less important. Benjamin's analysis of the decline of aura would appear to be vindicated.

At the same time though this analysis is over fifty years old. It is asking too much to expect it to provide a perfect fit with today's conditions of life. In respect of the manipulation of the masses, Benjamin's theory is especially old-fashioned. More specifically his work seriously underestimates the extent to which fragmentation, differentiation and now de-differentiation typify ordinary social conditions (Lash and Urry 1994; Rojek 1994). In addition he presents the options facing mankind in the age of mass reproduction too starkly, as lying between the struggle to achieve transcendence and the retreat into meaninglessness. Fragmentation, differentiation and de-differentiation have opened up new social spaces in which meaningful association and identity-formation can flourish.

In tracing the decomposition of mass society in the post-war period, Maffesoli (1995) refers to the rise of neo-tribes. By this he means those social collectivities organised around limited, temporary affective unions who form and recognise bonds in the midst of general social conditions of anonymity and disembeddedness. Maffesoli has in mind social collectivities attached to brand names such as Rebok, Wrangler, Apple-Mac, Calvin Klein, Greenpeace, National Trust and other fashionable elements in commodity culture. Here the individual recognises collectivity with others in terms of lifestyle values. This amounts to a virtual collectivity in which social identity is expressed and recognised without necessarily wanting direct contact with others who express the same values. In other words this form of collectivity recognises association by practising a controlled approach of disassociation. That is, our association with others is essentially treated as a symbolic matter. The identity relation ceases to be comfortable precisely when others recognise association by wanting 'to get to know us'. Similar neo-tribal, virtual collectivities are organised around cultural products. For example, to enjoy Tarantino's films *Reservoir Dogs* or *Pulp Fiction* is not simply a matter of admiring a particular cinematic genre. It is also to express a modish, open, ironical lifestyle which differentiates the members of the neo-tribe from more established groupings. The same can be said about an attachment to the music of contemporary composers such as Michael Nyman, Philip Glass or Gavin Bryars, or the work of painters such as Jeff Koons and Damien Hirst.

Similarly, in tourist experiences we may campaign with others to preserve a local beauty attraction, but this attachment does not necessarily carry over into other political or cultural associations. Indeed, one might describe the virtual collectivities organised around cultural products and tourist sights as *pulpy*. That is, the attachments are basically superficial and have the propensity to be reconfigured in response to the opportunities of contingency. In consuming this experience neo-tribes recognise that their attachments can be pulped and reconstituted to form other temporary attachments elsewhere. Mobility rather than continuity is the hallmark of this psychological attitude, and restlessness rather than anxiety defines this emotional outlook. As Kracauer suggests, we are constantly aware of the urge to move on and to avoid unnecessary involvement (Kracauer 1995).

Another important difference between Benjamin's critical account and the analysis of the Frankfurt School as a whole, is that it is today less convincing to portray the consumer as the victim or terminal of commodified indexing and dragging processes. As is well known, a general weakness of the Frankfurt approach is its tendency to exaggerate the powerlessness of the consumer. With new communication technologies the individual is clearly an active participant in indexing and dragging. Personal computers with e-mail facilities enable the individual to combine elements from fictional and factual representational files. The practice might be described as *collage tourism*. That is, fragments of cultural information are assembled by the network user to construct a distinctive orientation to a foreign sight. Some commentators have thus referred to 'post-tourism', by which is meant a playful, ironic, formally individualised attitude to sight-seeing (Feifer 1986; Urry 1990). Post-tourists have no interest in attaching themselves to a guided tour or tour group. However, they will readily treat these social formations as part of the sight-seeing experience. They may even voluntarily and, of course, ironically play the part of being a mass tourist. This is because for the post-tourist, the sign economy surrounding a sight constitutes a kitsch tourist attraction which – in a society where indexing and dragging processes are chronically practised – is an unavoidable accessory to the sight (see Rojek 1993: 175–9 on the differences between tourism and post-tourism).

In the rest of this chapter, I focus less on theoretical arguments and pay more attention to the character of the contemporary tourist experience. A legitimate criticism of the existing literature in the sociology of tourism is that it is light on empirical examples which enable the reader to evaluate the power of the theoretical analysis. The empirical examples to be considered here relate to 'sensation sights'.

SENSATION SIGHTS

Elsewhere, I have argued that Black Spots constitute a significant tourist attraction (Rojek 1993: 137–45). I used the term Black Spot to carry a dual meaning. In the first place it refers to the marker of a death site. For example, cemeteries which contain the remains of celebrities are important tourist attractions with a specialised tourist literature.[8] Monuments such as the Lincoln Memorial in Washington or Nelson's Column in Trafalgar Square also belong to this category. The second meaning of the term refers to disaster sites and sites of notable deaths. Examples include the Auschwitz death camp, the killing fields of Cambodia, Dealey Plaza in Dallas where John F. Kennedy was assassinated, the forecourt of the Dakota Building in New York where John Lennon was murdered, the crash site in Cholame, California where James Dean died, the Viper Room on Sunset Boulevard where River Phoenix took a drug overdose and the pavement outside where he died, and Kurt Cobain's suicide site in Seattle.[9] In all of these sites of death, tourists leave messages. Some consist simply of random notes or graffiti. Others are part of complex rituals of role-playing and remembrance. For example, on the anniversary of her death, Marilyn Monroe's grave at Westwood Cemetery off Wilshire Boulevard is visited by Marilyn look-alikes as women – and men dressed in drag – come to pay their respects. Similarly, on the anniversary of his death, members of the James Dean Fan Club, dressed in period costume and driving renovated 1950s cars, retrace the exact route of his last drive (Rojek 1993: 142). On Dean's chrome memorial in Cholame valley, someone has scratched: 'Live fast, die young and have a good looking corpse'.

This discussion was vulnerable to the criticism that it failed to give the appropriate historical perspective to the understanding of so-called Black Spots. After all, since

Chaucer's time we have records of pilgrims travelling to death sites and relics. Furthermore, tourists have always visited sights of famous battles such as Waterloo and Gettysburg. To be sure the Viennese social critic Karl Kraus fulminated against the practice (Kraus 1920). In his article 'Tourist Trips to Hell' he attacked an advertisement in the Swiss newspaper, *Basler Nachrichten*, which invited tourists to take an excursion by car to the First World War battlefield of Verdun where 1,500,000 French and German soldiers died. Kraus asks rhetorically:

> What does it mean this most gruesome spectacle of bloody delirium through which the nations let themselves be dragged to no purpose whatsoever, compared with the enormity of this ad. . . . You understand that the goal is to make the tourist trip pay, and the tourist trip was worth the World War.
>
> (1920: 72–3)

Leaving the question of history to one side, it now seems necessary to introduce a further distinction to the concept of the Black Spot. In my original discussion I referred to contemporary sights of major disasters as Black Spots. Examples would include the Zeebrugge ferry disaster of 1987 in which 193 people drowned when the *Herald of Free Enterprise* went down; and the town of Lockerbie over which Pan Am Flight 103 exploded in 1988. I will categorise them as being analytically distinct from Black Spots as sensation sights. These are places in which violent death has occurred, or where abduction, chase or siege is occurring, or has recently occurred, and to which sightseers travel both physically and through reverie. As ongoing or recent major dislocations of life-routines, they permit much higher levels of voyeuristic participation than travelling to cemeteries or monuments. The process of gazing at the events involves either on-the-spot observation or TV viewing. Sensation sights involve mind-voyaging, reverie and fantasy-work. They concentrate the collective consciousness by interrupting collective life-routines, and focus it on external space which is invested with extraordinary meaning. As I have already stated, this may involve physical travel to the sight.

But it is the fantasy-work, reverie or mind-voyaging that I am particularly interested in here. For it suggests that indexing and dragging processes occur within the home. And further, collage tourism is a typical practice for anyone exposed to contemporary media communication flows; that is, it is not just the specialised activity of surfers and users of the Internet. Domestic space already permits interactive tourism via mind-voyaging, piecing together different aspects of reports on a sensational event. Through TV and radio we can practise collage tourism at home which replaces the necessity physically to visit the sight. We can manipulate the meaning of sights by dragging on different file indexes and combining elements to create meanings which differ from broadcast reports of the sensation. Moreover, this activity is practised as belonging to the ephemera of televisual mass culture. It enables us to participate in the cult of distraction as engaged actors without leaving the security of our houses or apartments. Sociologically speaking, sensation sights become a social space for temporarily affirming identity and the expression of intense collectivity in the face of violent disruptions of collective life routines.

Debord and other writers have referred to the rise of the society of the spectacle (Debord 1983; see also Plant 1992, Chaney 1993). By this they mean a society in which staged events, such as international sports fixtures, festivals, processions,

CHRIS ROJEK / 64

national rituals and fictional dramas, permeate popular consciousness. For Debord and his associates, spectacular society is noteworthy because it points to the replacement of a perceived sense of paramount reality with organised myth and manipulation. Sensation sights share some common features with spectacle. Most notably, they interfere with ordinary collective life-routines by focusing consciousness on a documented external event. There is an important sense in which the sensation and the spectacle is not recognised as real unless it is documented or reported by television, radio and the other branches of the media (Meyerowitz 1985). Broadcasts of sensational or spectacular events provide the basis for mind-voyaging, reverie and fantasy-work. To this extent the notion that there are common characteristics between sensation and spectacle spaces is validated.

But the two also differ in three respects. First, sensation sights refer to the interruption of ordinary collective life-routines by reason of a natural disaster, social outrage, crash or act of aggression. Bombings, massacres, murders, hijacks, explosions and suicides are well documented examples. Thus, the sight is a focus for popular consciousness because a real-world calamity impinges on the habitual life-order. In this sense they are not staged events. However, of course, media communication of the event may involve techniques of staging and editing.

Second, unlike spectacle, sensation sights do not occur – nor are they presented – as 'breaks' from everyday life-routines. Rather, they belong to the ordinary information flow in advanced sign societies. That is, they are carried by the same media networks that represent external social life to us. In so far as they interrupt our ordinary collective life-routines, they do so as dramatic variations to our daily menu of news and events. One inference of this is that we have high tolerance to sensational events.

Third, sensation sights are corollaries of societies which reproduce low trust relations and high levels of affective neutrality towards others. This point can be extended via Bauman's concept of contingency (1992, 1993). He argues that contemporary social relations develop against a backcloth of uncertainty and unpredictability. The relations we have with our partners, our employers, our welfare providers, are inherently prone to sudden and unexpected change. Uncertainty and unpredictability reflect the accelerated pace of change in contemporary social relations. New technologies, new fashions, new styles of life and new social values seem to engulf us in a whirl of ever-changing mental and physical stimulation (see Beck's 1992 discussion of the 'risk society', as well as Chapter 2 above).

Simmel also commented on the tendencies towards acceleration and uncertainty (Simmel 1907). He contended that the psychological response to this state of affairs was twofold. The first general reaction is that people become more agitated, anxious and nervous about immediate conditions and the future. They become preoccupied with what might go wrong in social relations, or harmfully over-excited by stimuli. He referred to this as the *neurasthenic* attitude in modern life. The second general reaction is the cultivation of indifference. Individuals withdraw from new stimuli and treat events in the external world as remote from their narrow sphere of interests. They cease to care about the plight of others and fatalistically dismiss the possibility of changing the world for the better. Simmel referred to this as the *blasé* attitude. Neurasthenia and indifference reflect the recognition that everyday conditions can no longer be trusted or controlled. Today's workplace may become a vacant lot next year; the house or apartment that we expect perpetually to appreciate in value may suddenly become a millstone of negative equity; and the spouse that we marry may in time sue us for capital in the divorce courts.

Consciousness of these risks figures in our ordinary monitoring of self and other relations. Dragging processes can contribute to tourist denial by emphasising sight elements that are peripheral to the calamity. Once these elements are dragged from the periphery to the core of our perception they contribute to our sense of the unreality of the sights being displayed in front of us. In this context external calamities which leave scores dead, or sieges in which armed forces confront a fugitive, cease to be matters which impel us to engage emotionally with perceived suffering. Instead we focus on them not primarily because we identify with or care very much about the victims but because they are momentarily 'in the news'. They dramatise humdrum routines by magnifying the sense of calculable dislocation in routine self-monitoring processes. They contribute to the cult of distraction.

Crashes, natural disasters, assassinations and bombings, as sensational items of news, vividly express the collapse of routine and the triumph of the unexpected or the unpredictable. Consciousness of the contingency of modern life is, of course, amplified by telecommunications. They have an automatic tendency to distance events from us. Hence we relate to the figures on the screen that are typically interviewed as participants in sensations – survivors of crashes and bombings, assailants, police staff, medical workers, attorneys and so on – but they seem divorced from our immediate web of relationships. Moreover, because sensational news is carried by the same information flow which brings us soap operas, police dramas, comedies and so forth, there is an irresistible tendency for events in the real world to merge with fictional data. This is perhaps one reason why our memory of sensational real-world events tends to be short-term. Something which stops us dead in our tracks on one day is relegated to the back lot of obscure and half-remembered events within a few months. It is something that we vaguely recall seeing on television; but we have the same difficulty in remembering exactly what happened or when it occurred as we do in recalling the last episode of a soap opera. Of course, by dragging different sight elements from associated file indexes, we can also participate in fabricating and softening sight meanings.

Moreover, dragging contributes to our general immediate sense of popular culture being composed of specious, artificial constructs. The breakthrough event in establishing sensation sights as part of the staple information flow was the Vietnam war. This was the first major conflict to permit detailed live coverage of warfare. Indeed audiences were so saturated with up-dates, sound-bites, specials and other journalistic devices of the conflict that they developed the impression of witnessing events in Vietnam *as they happened*. The horrors of war became part of the ordinary information flow into Western homes. Subsequent international conflicts, such as the Falklands War, the Gulf War and the ethnic bloodbath waged in former Yugoslavia, had tighter official restrictions imposed on what could be broadcast. The Vietnam war was a catalyst in extending public access and voyeuristic entry into the domain of private life. Of course, the erosion of barriers of intimacy and reserve is rooted in deeper historical processes. These refer to the dialectic between processes tending towards increasing surveillance (Foucault 1979, 1981) and processes tending towards greater informalisation (Wouters 1986). Nonetheless, Vietnam was a watershed in what television was allowed to freely broadcast to the public. It paved the way for live coverage of events like IRA bombings, the Waco siege, the Oklahoma bombing, and the capture of Shoko Asahara, leader of the doomsday cult *Aum Shinrikyo* in the foothills of Mount Fuji, all examples of recent sensation sights. These events concentrate a certain kind of touristic consciousness. They are objects for mind-voyaging and reverie and they provide resources for collage tourism.

The example that I will examine in greater detail here is the trial of O.J. Simpson. There are several reasons for selecting this example. In the first place it was a richly documented media event. Researchers have access to a large and growing archive of print and video material. If sensation sights involve the mobilisation and concentration of the collective *mentalitie*, then the Simpson trial is unquestionably one of the outstanding sensation attractions of recent times. Blanket television coverage has allowed the TV audience to drag representational elements together and create new values which may consciously conflict with broadcast meanings and values. By the same token, the trial supplied TV audiences with ready-made elements to produce collage effects.

Second, it has become part of the established tourist itinerary in Southern California. Thousands of people have left their homes to tour the sight. The sensation sight is in fact composed of three distinct areas: the house at 875 South Bundy Drive in Brentwood, California, which is Nicole Simpson's townhouse and also the scene of the murders; the O.J. Simpson mansion at 360 North Rockingham Avenue, from where Simpson fled to escape arrest; and the Los Angeles Criminal Courts Building which was the scene of the trial. Throughout the trial, both Nicole Simpson's townhouse and the O.J. mansion were protected by temporary green fences to provide an additional barrier between the sight and the sight-seer. In fact, the fence has been reappropriated as a makeshift tourist marker. For example, a flyer distributed in the student refreshment area of the UCLA campus in August of 1994 described the two homes as 'the most popular tourist attractions on the West Coast' where 'you may personally *gaze* and *gawk* at the famous O.J. Murder Homes'. The flyer described the green fence as 'a foolish attempt to discourage the myriad looki-loos, tourists, tabloid reporters, gawkers, thrill-seekers and paparazzi who have come to celebrate the O.J. Love Tragedy'. The green fences are isolated as an infallible way to identify the actual sights.[10]

Third, the flight of O.J. and the subsequent trial were both carried live by television. The intensive television coverage provided sensation-tourists with an unusually systematic number of opportunities for access and vicarious participation through indexing and dragging processes. This was supported by the publication of cheap comics which represented O.J.'s story and Nicole's story in cartoon form and allowed the man in the street to decide for himself what actually happened. Each story is presented from the viewpoint of the main protagonist, so that two mutually incompatible versions of reality are presented at once: O.J.'s story and Nicole's story. Each version is treated as equally true. It is left to the reader to decide what really happened or to drag elements from the O.J. and Nicole files to produce their own reading. The iconography of the trial was further extended by the production of T shirts and car stickers which expressed messages of solidarity with or antipathy to O.J.'s plight (see Fig. 3.1). The signs of the case seemed to have been divorced from the proceedings in the court room and reappropriated in popular culture.

The known details of the case can be summarised in a few words. O.J. Simpson is

Figure 3.1 O.J. T Shirts

widely regarded as the greatest American football player of the post-war era. His social ascent from a black neighbourhood in San Francisco to celebrity status in Hollywood was widely regarded as one of the outstanding recent confirmations of the American dream. After retiring from professional sport, Simpson carved out a lucrative and high profile career in film acting. In June of 1994 Simpson's estranged wife and her friend Ronald Goldman were found stabbed to death in the driveway of her townhouse. Simpson was questioned by police and denied any involvement. He was released without charge. However, police investigations gradually uncovered inconsistencies in his story and also unearthed a history of violence in the marriage. Simpson anticipated arrest charges and fled from his home in a car driven by a friend. The dramatic motorway chase was filmed by TV cameras and ordinary programme schedules were interrupted. Simpson was shown with a pistol at his head. Eventually Simpson voluntarily surrendered himself into police custody and, in the course of time, was submitted to trial for double murder. He was found not guilty and was freed.

The first point to note is that there is nothing unusual about a well-publicised murder case seizing the public imagination and acting as a focus for mind-voyaging, reverie, dragging and sensation-tourism. In 1869 Flaubert complained that the reception of his novel, *L'Education Sentimentale*, was eclipsed by press coverage of the Kinck murder case. All of France was captivated by the arrest, trial and execution of Jean Baptiste Troppmann for the frenzied murder of Madame Kinck and her children.[11] Sight-seers explored the scene of the murder and thronged outside the courtroom. 'The success of Troppmann', observed Flaubert in a letter to Georges Sand in 1871, was a symptom of 'the mental disorder of France' (quoted in Christiansen 1994: 56). The Troppmann case can hardly be said to have been the first example of sensation-tourism.[12] It is probable that mind-voyaging, dragging and sensation sights were corollaries of the rise of print culture. For print culture enabled the abstract concept of a 'national' audience to have a direct, immediate and uninterrupted impact upon the organisation of personal and local consciousness. Other 'nation-building' agents, such as fiscal policy, public health control, formal education and the law, lacked the variety, topicality and continuous penetration of the media. As the modern world came into being it became increasingly impossible to escape the media.

To some degree, the expansion of print culture presupposes the growth of the metropolis. For it was only in cities that the media could find a concentrated literate marketplace for their products. The expansion of media culture and the social construction of sensation sights are therefore connected with the growth of metropolitan lifestyles. Benjamin (1969) certainly equates the rise of phantasmagoric cultural forms with the expansion of the metropolis. He presents the urban streets and the consumer showplaces of commodity culture as a labyrinth of meaning in which different cultural elements are fused together to create rumours and gossip. This is effected by the density and velocity of social contacts. Telecommunications, of course, led to an exponential increase in density and velocity by producing the means for a 'global' audience to watch events as they unfold. In addition, the axis of rumour and gossip is transferred from the city street to the living room.

The Simpson case is rich in the phantasmagoric mixture of representational codes. This erodes our sense of watching a 'real' event which, in turn, reinforces the low trust assessments that we make about the proceedings. What is the cause of this low trust response? To begin with, the Simpson trial was staged in the midst of growing cynicism about the legal process in California. The acquittal of four Los Angeles police officers, who had been captured on videotape beating Rodney King, sparked the worst riots in the city since the 1960s. This was followed by the acquittal of Damien Williams of the attempted murder of trucker Reginald Denny, despite video evidence showing Williams smashing a brick on Denny's head and dancing a victory jig. Williams's lawyer claimed that his client was innocent, and that even if he wasn't innocent he didn't mean to do it. Next came the trial of the Menendez brothers who were accused of murdering their parents to claim a $14 million inheritance. Their defence developed an 'abuse excuse' which alleged that the parents had sexually abused the boys in childhood. Both trials ended in a hung jury, and retrials are pending. Finally, came the allegations that Michael Jackson had sexually abused a 13-year-old boy. Jackson avoided trial by reaching a multi-million dollar out-of-court settlement.

Public faith in US justice was therefore at a low ebb when the murders of Nicole Simpson and Ronald Goldman occurred. Simpson's subsequent arrest and trial provided the conjunction of a number of representational codes which complicate our sense of ever finding out the truth.

The Simpson case was a focus for mind-voyaging and reverie in popular culture. Mentally speaking, we travelled to the sight almost on a daily basis. The media has developed a set of representational files which form the basis for collage tourism in the home. We drag elements from files to construct our own framing of events. The index of files liberally utilises typifications of social actors: the racist policeman, the sexist athlete, the alluring female prosecuting lawyer, the slick, highly paid defence attorneys, the inscrutable judge, have all figured in the course of the trial. In the O.J.

case we employed them to mediate our readings of the trial. Sensationalising the main players inoculated us against accepting the official views of what really happened. In any case, these views appeared arbitrary and were ultimately not accepted as sufficiently persuasive to support a guilty verdict. Sensation sights support the generation of popular speculative and detective work. Collage tourism provides us with a sense of being an eye witness to the trial. But the collage is essentially a play form so that exaggeration and fabrication are part and parcel of reading the trial.

CONCLUSION

Some years ago Meyerowitz argued that modern society is dominated by television culture. Several consequences followed from this condition. The most important referred to place. Meyerowitz proposed that television culture erodes our sense of place. Communities that used to be organised around production are replaced by users and groups organised around the consumption of information and entertainment flows. The remaking of these cultures is not dependent upon personal contact between individuals but upon the continuous exposure of the individual to a television screen. Solidarity has ceased to be a matter of situation. It has become a matter of signs. Meyerowitz's (1985) argument is that watching no longer carries over into recognising place or community. For him, solidarity derives from place. Television culture has undermined our sense of embeddedness. The result is a global visual culture based upon superficial and diverse information flows rather than a culture organised around collectively agreed and reaffirmed values and beliefs. While these values and beliefs might be cultivated at local levels, it is the global level which sets the overall discursive and practical context of social interaction. Baudrillard develops the point. In his sociology, visual culture employs various strategies of simulation which destroy our sense of paramount reality (Baudrillard 1983; and see McLuhan 1967, 1973). For Baudrillard and, to a lesser extent, Meyerowitz, it has created a huge refugee camp in which viewers, disassociated from place and community, are caught up in global indexing and dragging processes which no one controls. Images of home and abroad, the mundane and the exotic, order and disorder, are jumbled up in a neutral flow of ever-changing images.

A logical implication of this argument is that tourism might be expected to decline as our belief in authenticity is corroded by TV indexing and dragging. Why travel if external sights have been stripped of their aura and if telecommunications allow us to practise collage tourism in our living rooms? Why risk being mugged in Miami, New York, Berlin, London, Rome, Rio or Moscow, when one can explore them from representational files in the safety of one's home?

These questions have already been asked by Feifer in her study of the history of tourism (1986). She contends that tourism will not wither away. Indeed, she argues that the rise of kitsch culture has already produced new 'post-tourist' orientations and stimulations. Urry extends this line of thought (1990). He proposes that the post-tourist sensibility responds to irony, playfulness and anomaly. According to this position, the plastic Eiffel Towers sold in the Paris gift shops around the 'real object' are as interesting to the post-tourist as the thing in itself; the tourist throngs that get in the way of one's camera when filming the Sydney Opera House or the Statue of

Liberty are as much part of the post-tourist gaze as the tourist attractions which bring them forth.

This is an elegant solution to the paradox that tourism is growing at a time in which the effects of simulation have eroded our distinctions between elite and popular, reality and fiction.

Contrary to expectations, people have indeed not stayed at home. Tourism now accounts for 7.5 per cent of world trade and is expected to be the world's largest industry by the year 2000. Just as obviously, the post-tourist orientation only applies to a minority of these travellers. It is reasonable to propose that most of us raised in television cultures are adept at playing with indexing and dragging codes. However, it does not follow that we travel in order to experience kitsch and simulation in packaged form. For example, most people who attend the *Schindler's List* tour in Poland believe that they are being exposed to a hidden part of history. They do not approach the experience as the chance to participate in fabricated codes and dragging processes. They are in search of traces of real events. Moreover, while many presentational aspects of the tour are distortions, the death camps in Kazimierz were all-too-real. Remembering them elicits important effects for citizenship practice today. To reinforce an argument made in the introduction, the convergence of reality with illusion is very far from being a *fait accompli* with regard to tourist sights. This is not to deny the rise of post-tourist sensibility. Nor is it to attribute a meliorist function to heritage tourism.[13] Rather, it is to propose that post-tourist sensibility is developing in a context in which the commodification of tourist experience remains the most obvious fact about the experience of travel for pleasure. Indeed, it is so obvious that it leads many commentators to believe that commodification is the only important thing about tourism. The consequence of this is that the effect of universal electronic forms of visual culture upon our perceptions is too readily dismissed as an epiphenomenon.

To close this chapter, the following are some methodological principles with which to analyse the social construction of tourist sights arising from the foregoing analysis:

1 All tourist sights rely on distinctions which demarcate them as extraordinary places. The demarcation process is reinforced by representational codes and routines of sight-seeing.

2 The demarcation between the extraordinary and the ordinary is a cultural process. Following Crawshaw and Urry in Chapter 9, there may be some cultural universals in respect of what is thought to be extraordinary. Thus, the 'natural' majesty of the Himalayas or the 'essential' power of Niagara Falls might draw tourists irrespective of their specific cultural backgrounds or prejudices. However, the relation of the tourist to the sight is also always culturally detailed and mediated.

3 Televisual culture has undermined the distinction between the ordinary and the extraordinary. Representational codes of tourist sights have reduced the aura of these places. Indexing and dragging processes in TV culture elicit collage tourism as an ordinary feature of domestic experience. Tourism is not a break or escape from everyday life. Rather, it provides a plane of cultural difference in which everyday life routines are contrasted and developed. The return to the familiarity and order of everyday life is the prerequisite of enjoyable tourist experience.

4 The quest for authenticity is a declining force in tourist motivation. Indexing and dragging problematise the proposition that sights have a single or original meaning. Switching codes of patterned behaviour is, in itself, a source of attraction for the tourist. The desire to keep moving on and the feeling of restlessness that frequently accompanies tourist activity derive from the cult of distraction. Pure movement is appealing in societies where our sense of place has decomposed and where place itself approximates to nothing more than a temporary configuration of signs.

5 In developed televisual cultures, culture itself will increasingly be a tourist attraction. Heritage centres and back regions of workplaces already attract tourists in large numbers (MacCannell 1989; and see Chapter 7 below). Sensation sights are another tourist form which is entirely dependent upon cultural determinations.

Taken together, these principles suggest that the tradition in the study of tourism which insists on examining tourism and travel in terms of ontology is faulty (Krippendorf 1984). These accounts focus on questions of being. They present tourism as an attempt to get away from oneself or to be a different self. Commodity cultures place strong emphasis on accumulating new possessions, change and fashion. So the desire to become something different by hopping on a plane is quite understandable. However, as all tourists know, the inescapable fact about travel is that you take yourself with you. The principles outlined above suggest that tourism must be primarily approached in terms of epistemology. It is the contrast between our domain-cultural assumptions and the practices of different cultures that attracts us. Of course, questions of ontology cannot be cleanly separated from questions of epistemology. The reason for laying stress on epistemology here is in part because it has been neglected by most commentators in the field.

A final important procedural point that follows from the discussion refers to how we should study tourist practice. With one or two exceptions it has been standard practice in academic study to treat tourism as distinct from ordinary life routines (see MacCannell 1989; Urry 1990). The discussion here suggests that *drift*, as opposed to division, is a more appropriate characterisation of tourist attitudes and practices. Indexing and dragging are intrinsically play forms. They allow us to stretch conventional shared meanings and disrupt our consciousness of order. This is a source of pleasure. We develop indexing and dragging skills as part of our socialisation in televisual culture. Tourism involves switching these skills to a new cultural plane. This is a source of pleasure. Difference – even if it is artificially constructed – is an immediate source of curiosity. But few of us 'go native' and exchange our domain-cultural attributes for newly encountered forms. Instead we drift back to our domain routines and habitual life-orders.

If this is correct, then the appropriate way to study the tourist experience is to treat it as developing towards a condition of pure mobility. Velocity is finally more important as a priority of tourism than arriving. Perhaps this accounts for the strong urge to keep on the move that we often encounter almost immediately after arriving at a long-dreamt-of travel destination. How deeply can we capture a sight? How far can we go into what it really means for ourselves and what is authentic about it? Even for post-tourists, there are strong pressures to reduce sight-seeing to a check-list activity. For example, by visiting the sight of the Sphinx, or of Raffles Hotel in Singapore, we satisfy ourselves that they exist, but we can only be present with them for a short time before succumbing to the cry of new places and surrendering them to our memory and imagination. Yet our tourist world is shrinking. The cry of new places is answered by tourist companies and the industrial–bureaucratic support complex of modernity. If the search for difference is widely presented as a tourist attraction, it is obvious that cultural differences are being negated. The new types of difference that emerge are hard to identify and require too much time to decode. In these circumstances the seductions offered by phantasmagoric forms of escape through collage tourism may prove to be irresistible. Yet if we surrender to the clamour of artificially induced differences, in what sense can we be said to travel? If the social construction of tourist sights is primarily shaped by forms of indexing and dragging which are driven by commercial imperatives, where 'on earth' is there left to go?

ACKNOWLEDGEMENTS

Many thanks to John Urry, Ellis Cashmore and Stjepan Mestrovic for commenting on an earlier version of this chapter.

NOTES

1 The *Travels* are first recorded in Europe between 1356 and 1366. They were originally written in French but, by 1400, translations were available in every European language. The author claims to have been an English knight who travelled from 1322 to 1356. In that time he claims to have seen service with the Sultan of Egypt and the Great Khan.
2 If the *Travels* are a fiction, they have proved to be a useful one. Mandeville has figured as a useful rhetorical device in inspiring subsequent travellers. The *Travels* are also acknowledged to question the moral and cultural superiority of Europe. To this extent, the book can be read as a liberating text.
3 The 'Contents' of Adams's (1962) book on travel liars is instructive in this respect. It divides travel liars into various types: false topographers; fireside travellers; fantastic memorialists; plagiarists; prejudiced travellers; and travellers who were denounced in their own time only to be vindicated later.
4 Of course, this is not to discount the value of psychoanalytic explanations, but only to suggest some alternative responses.
5 For example, see Baudrillard (1983), Meyerowitz (1985), Vattimo (1992).
6 Benjamin never wrote at length about travel or tourism. But his work on *flânerie* and the labyrinth reveal a deep fascination with the cultural significance of mobility and difference.
7 I understand that a translation is currently underway.
8 See, for example, Anger (1975, 1984); Herman (1982); Culbertson and Randall (1986, 1991).
9 Walking tours and hearse tours to these sights are widely available. See my description of the 'Deathstyles of the Hollywood Rich and Famous' in Rojek (1993: 224, note 4).
10 Hence a barrier designed to repel activity actually contributes to the attractions of the sight. Ethnographers might be interested in the full text of the O.J. tourist flyer distributed in August 1994:

DIRECTIONS TO O.J.'S MANSION

By Sam The Paparazzo

SAM THE PAPARAZZO shall give you both *verbal* and *map* directions to O.J. Simpson's mansion and Nicole's beautiful town house located in exquisite Brentwood, CA, just minutes from *you*. The two homes are the most popular tourist attractions on the West Coast! Now you may personally *gaze* and *gawk* at the famous O.J. Murder Homes, and at the same time contribute to the 'fish-bowl' life of O.J. and his hapless, tormented children and relatives. Wow, those ex-socialites are under the scrutiny of society's microscope!

Verbal directions to O.J. Simpson's Brentwood Mansion, 360 North Rockingham Avenue, Brentwood, Calif. 90049:

* Take the 405 Freeway to Sunset Blvd., which you want to travel west-ward on (toward the ocean). You will pass Barrington, Bundy Dr. and Carmelina. Start looking for Cliffwood Ave. The very next street after Cliffwood is the one you want to turn right on. Turn right on Bristol Ave. Take Bristol to Highwood St., which is the next cross-street, and turn left on it. Turn right on Rockingham, which Hollywood dead-ends into. After passing Parkyns Street, drive very slowly and look on your right. O.J. Simpson's mansion is the one with the temporary green fence erected around it. The exact address is 360 North Rockingham Avenue, on the corner of Ashford Street, in Brentwood Park. The green fence is a ridiculous attempt to discourage the myriad of looki-loos, tabloid press, gawkers, thrill-seekers and paparazzi who have come to celebrate the O.J. Love Tragedy. But it certainly won't keep you away! Happy Gawking!

Verbal directions to Nicole Simpson's town house, 875 S. Bundy Drive 1:

* Take the 405 Freeway to Sunset Blvd., at which you want to travel west-ward on (toward the ocean). You will pass Barrington. Turn left on South Bundy Drive. Hint: you want to go down the hill, not up. On Bundy, you will pass San Vicente Blvd. and Montana Ave. Look for Gorham Ave., and start driving very slowly (many tourists are coming in from all over the world to look at Nicole's town house, so you will probably be driving slow anyway). Look on your right-hand side after passing Gorham Ave. The exact address is 876 South Bundy Drive 1. It has an ironic gate. Nicole's town house is near the corner of Bundy and Dorothy Avenue. The town house has a temporary green fence around it, as well as a sign on the gate directed at the media: 'Please Respect Our Privacy,' courtesy of the Brentwood Homeowner's Association. The green fence is a foolish attempt to discourage the myriad looki-loos, tourists, tabloid reporters, gawkers, thrill seekers and paparazzi who have come to celebrate the O.J. Love Tragedy. But it certainly won't keep you away! Happy Gawking!

The British are not immune from this type of sensation tourism. The home of the alleged mass murderer, Frederick West, at 25 Cromwell Street, Gloucester, became a scandalous attraction in 1994. Neighbours of West were reported to charge tourists an entrance fee to their homes to allow people a better view of West's back garden, where many bodies were found by the police.

11 Troppman was accused of murdering Madame Kinck and her five children. Most of the victims had been attacked with a knife and an axe. Madame Kinck was six months pregnant. She was believed to have been buried alive. Troppmann was a singularly mysterious figure. Doubts were expressed by prosecutors during his trial that he acted with others in the murders. If he had accomplices he never revealed them. Although on the block, his last reported words were 'Tell Monsieur Claude that I persist!' In the moment when the blade fell, he twisted his head and sank his teeth into the hand of one of the executioner's assistants.

12 The macabre fascination of Charles Dickens and other Victorians with 'the Newgate Gallery' of public executions is a matter of recorded fact. Porter (1994: 153–4), in his admirable history of London, notes that the first permanent gallows was constructed in Tyburn in 1571, although Smithfield, Tower Hill, Newgate and Execution Docks were well established public hanging sites. Executions were often occasions for holidays and merry-making. Apprentices were given a 'Tyburn Fair' holiday. The procession from Newgate to Tyburn (now the site of Marble Arch) lasted for about two hours. The carts carrying the

condemned stopped at taverns along the way. Tyburn gallows was demolished in 1783 and executions were moved to Newgate. The last public beheadings took place outside Newgate in 1820, when the five Cato Street conspirators were executed. However, it was not until 1868 that public hangings were abolished in Britain.

13 Many of the heritage sights that have emerged in the post-war era are little more than calculated exercises in phantasmagoria (see Rojek 1993: 146–60).

4

THE OBJECTS OF TRAVEL

Celia Lury

I recall, over a decade ago, seeing 'UCLA' T-shirts all over the Pacific. What did they mean? I don't know. Or the New Caledonian Kanak militant in a Tarzan T-shirt I also saw, or the Lebanese militiamen wearing Rambo I recently heard about? Is this a fetishization of other cultures, of the elsewhere...or is it a way of localizing global symbols, for the purposes of action? Again, I don't know. Both processes must somehow be at work.

(Clifford 1992: 114)

INTRODUCTION

In the study of tourism, the emphasis has, until recently, been placed on an analysis of the movement of peoples to places, a movement variously conceptualised in terms of individual motives of escapism, the need for adventure, a desire to partake of the tourist gaze, or a socially ordered quest for authenticity. Tourism has thus been considered in terms of people travelling to places, or perhaps more specifically people travelling to places as cultures in a mapped space. This notion is made explicit in the recent advertising claim: 'Sicily. Tourism is culture'. There is in this approach a presumption of not only a unity of place and culture, but also of the immobility of both in relation to a fixed, cartographically coordinated space, with the tourist as one of the wandering figures whose travels, paradoxically, fix places and cultures in this ordered space. This is an understanding of cultures as situated, through an ordering of space, in places; as sites to be travelled to, around and through; cultures as the object of detours; cultures as places to visit and come back from, perhaps with some memento, an object or image that symbolises those places, those cultures – the photograph, the postcard, the souvenir.

In the last few years, however, there has been an increased interest in travelling cultures, in portable or mobile cultures, in cultures in motion, detached from specific places, a concern with, precisely, 'touring cultures' (see Chapter 1). One of the most influential critiques of the earlier approach, and thus an important contribution to the project of 'moving' cultures, is Clifford's discussion of 'Travelling cultures' (1992). He problematises the fixity of the opposition between dwelling *and* travelling, commonly assumed in much previous anthropology and comparative cultural studies (and, by implication, tourism studies). He also suggests that there has been an erasure of the activities of 'cosmopolitan intermediaries' in the privileging of the study of specific cultures as localities and the adoption of 'the field' as a methodological device to set limits on the object of study (Clifford 1992: 100).

A related indicator of the privileging of dwelling is shown by Clifford to be the typical representation of the native-in-place as the authentic or emblematic representative of a localised culture. So, just as he encourages a shift away from the bounded notion of the field and a recognition of the criss-crossing of space and place, so Clifford looks forward to a re-interpretation of the informant, a move away from the informant as a situationally representative cultural figure (as either a cultural type or unique individual). However, he does not wish to see the automatic replacement of the native-in-place as informant by the intercultural figure of the traveller, since that would be to invert the strategies of cultural localism. Rather, Clifford advocates a concern with specific dynamics of dwelling/travelling, particular modalities of inside–outside connection, of passing through-ness, of borders and criss-crossings. This chapter seeks to take up this concern with the ways in which dwelling and travelling are interlinked, and to extend its aims by considering travelling cultures not only in relation to people but also in relation to the very objects that are part of the specific relations of travelling and dwelling.

In many ways, tourism studies have been curiously uninterested in the ways in which the culture of other places has been attributed to objects and is able to travel with those objects, and have tended to take for granted the way in which the culture of others is bound into the physical confines of the object, is inscribed in its very contours, in the practices of acquisition, collection and display (although see Urry 1995: 28–9, for some suggestive comments on objects in tourism). In this respect, it has thus failed to draw upon the longstanding interest in objects in anthropology, including the recent developments in material culture (Appadurai 1986b; Miller 1987; Friedman 1994a, 1994b) and in aesthetics (see Wollheim 1980 for one of the most accessible discussions of art and its objects).

Much of the anthropological literature has focused on the analysis of the exchange of objects as 'tournaments of value' (Appadurai 1986a). This emphasis on the struggles through which value is created will be maintained here, but the specific focus will be on the relations of travelling and dwelling that interlink, but by no means overlap, with the relations involved in the exchange of objects. In this way, it is hoped to highlight the means by which the boundedness of culture in objects is secured by particular modes of travelling and dwelling – the spatially ordered confinement of a culture within the apparent closed opacity or physical integrity of the object. What is being suggested here is that it is as a consequence of the assumption of the object's ontological coherence, in terms of its physical bounded-ness, that the study of tourism has failed to examine the organisation of both the provision of more or less temporary 'homes' for travelling-in-dwelling objects *and* the carriers or movers of objects that dwell-in-travelling. The consequence of this double omission has been that tourism studies have not been able to identify the significance of the travelling/dwelling relations of people and objects for the practices of tourism. Certainly, as noted above, the movement of objects – the souvenir, the postcard, the photograph – has sometimes been recorded as an adjunct of the movement of tourists, but because these movements map more or less directly on to those of the person of the tourist, the objects themselves tend to be seen as little more than the traveller's extended baggage. The suggestion being made here, however, is that objects help to comprise tourism; more than this, it is not simply objects-in-motion but also objects-that-stay-still that help make up tourism. It is further suggested that looking at the career or biography of objects, as they move or stay still, will add to what we can say about the lives of people that travel (and then go home), that is, tourists.

Appadurai provides a rationale for this approach; he writes:

> even though from a *theoretical* point of view human actors encode things with a significance, from a *methodological* point of view it is the things-in-motion that illuminate their human and social context.
>
> (Appadurai 1986a: 5)

Tracing the social and cultural movement of objects, Appadurai claims, helps identify the dynamic, processual aspects of social life, illuminating not simply the small-scale shifts in an object's meaning, but also broader transformations in social organisation itself. What I want to do here is to consider both some of the ways in which the capacity of objects to travel and stay still is constituted in and helps secure particular relations of dwelling-in-travelling and travelling-in-dwelling, and to suggest that these relations are constitutive of both the very object-ness of objects and the organisation of space. In this way, I hope to be able to make some comments about the nature of contemporary tourism, pulling out the interdependence of the travelling and dwelling of both people and objects and the importance of their mutual interrelationship for understandings of culture, place and space.

TRAVELLER-, TOURIST- AND TRIPPER-OBJECTS

Thus, the thesis being proposed here is that objects are an important part of tourism and travelling cultures. But clearly, not all objects have a direct or immediate relationship to tourism, and tourism itself is only one, albeit very powerful, travelling culture. Indeed, as Clifford says, travel is only one mode of displacement; however, like him, I choose to use it here (in conjunction with dwelling) precisely because of its 'historical taintedness, its associations with gendered, racial bodies, class privilege, specific means of conveyance, beaten paths, agents, frontiers, documents and the like' (Clifford 1992: 110). Indeed, it is precisely in order to be able to specify this taintedness in more detail that the study of objects is advocated here. However, before embarking upon this more detailed consideration, it may be helpful to make a few preliminary remarks.

In the relationships between the movements of people and the movements of objects that comprise tourism, the movements of objects are not simply responsive to those of people. Rather, the career or biography of objects – their emergence, movement or salience in relation to other social practices, including but by no means confined to those of economic exchange – also has the capacity to influence not only the preferred destinations of the tourist but also the nature of the tourist practices undertaken once the tourist arrives. For this reason, it may then be helpful to think in terms of the object–people practices of tourism, without automatically privileging either objects or people as the prime 'movers' in such practices, but, rather, to see their travelling–dwelling as mutually implicated.[1]

However, although it is impossible to indicate *a priori* which objects are implicated in tourism in terms of kinds or classes of object, this does not mean that a hierarchy of objects does not emerge in the object–people practices of specific formations of tourism. So, for example, just as tourists themselves have been ranked according to their presumed degrees of knowingness in their journeys as travellers, tourists and trippers (indeed, this hierarchy of respect is, in part, established by reference to the supposed authority of people's use of objects in their travelling and dwelling, including their ability to recognise an object's unique aura), so too can objects be hierarchically ordered in value in relation to how the cultures of which they are held to be the bearers are constituted in specific practices of dwelling and travelling. This hierarchy is, in part, established by reference to the respect that the objects are held to be capable of provoking among the people they encounter in their journeys by nature of their object-ness – that is, it is an ordering of their very integrity. While this hierarchy is obviously simplistic (and one whose value judgements are not to be taken for granted, but are precisely part of the phenomenon to be studied), it provides a useful, if necessarily schematic, way into the investigation of the organisation of the object–people practices that comprise contemporary tourism.

In general terms, then, it is suggested that the integrity of objects is related, in part, to the specific relations of travelling-in-dwelling and dwelling-in-travelling in which they are constituted. Indeed, it is through these relations that the integrity of their object-ness can be seen to be constituted. In sum, travelling-dwelling practices have what might be called object-effects (to adapt the more familiar notion of subject-effects).

I shall now summarise the characteristics of each type of object. First, there are what one might call *traveller-objects*, those that combine the ability to travel well in the sense that they retain their meaning across contexts and retain an authenticated relation to an original dwelling. More precisely, traveller-objects are those objects whose ability to travel well is integrally linked to their ability to signify their meaning immanently, most commonly by an indexical reference to their 'original' dwelling.[2] Examples of this stratum of objects include artworks, handicrafts and items of historical, political or religious significance in relation to national or folk cultures. Significantly, traveller-objects do not necessarily have to move to acquire their status as such – indeed, typically, they stay still, although their images frequently move.[3] Furthermore, there may well be legal restrictions on the movement of traveller-objects across national boundaries; and disputes between countries about the proper location of such objects, such as, for example, the Elgin Marbles, indicate that the ability to enforce dwelling in a specific territory – what Appadurai (1993) calls 'the repatriation of difference' – is an indicator of national cultural integrity.

Traveller-objects are objects whose immanent bounded-ness is secured in relation to an original dwelling by practices of symbolic binding that may occur, paradoxically, in their travel (or, more commonly, the travel of their images); they appear to be full of meaning but are closed or self-contained as objects. They are objects in which meaning is deemed immanent – in which place and culture are bound together in a smooth movement through space as a consequence of practices of symbolic binding or interpretation that make themselves invisible, in part through their consistency. An especially interesting technique in this respect is that which interprets physical markings in such objects as 'traces', and, in so doing, establishes an indexical sign of the immanence of meaning in the physical features of the objects. More generally, the consistency of the practices of symbolic binding or interpretation smoothes the journey of these objects and compacts the meaning it produces into their apparent opacity and plenitude.[4]

In contrast, while *tripper-objects* also travel well, this is in a different sense to the traveller-object, for it is not that their movement (or that of their images) is actively facilitated, merely that it is not restricted, for typically they are not bound by ritual, convention or legal tie to a particular place or dwelling. In addition, their meaning is continually reconstituted by their dwellings as they travel, especially by their final dwelling. More specifically, tripper-objects are those objects whose travelling is teleologically determined by their final resting place, as something to be brought home. Objects directly related to tourism in this stratum include not only mass-produced souvenirs and mementos but also 'found objects' such as pebbles from a beach, 'incidental objects' such as tickets, matchboxes or packaging, and personalised objects such as photographs and postcards. A much larger group of objects might also be included in this category, however, including many consumer goods. In all cases, the ways in which place and culture may be recombined in specific dwellings-in-travelling along the way are rendered incidental to the object – as when a mass-produced souvenir manufactured in one place and purchased in another as a gift for someone who stayed at home is installed on a mantel-piece or added to a collection. Moreover, while the object may have 'personal', 'sentimental' meaning in its final resting place, this is a meaning which is not deemed intrinsic to the object and, thus, is not publicly valued. Tripper-objects are objects whose object-ness is lost in space, as the binding practices in which place and culture are combined in physical characteristics are undone (or rather, never take shape) in the travelling-dwelling practices of tripping.

Tripper-objects, in contrast to traveller-objects, are thus objects whose meaning appears not as immanent but as arbitrary, imposed from outside the object by external context or final dwelling place. This apparent arbitrariness, or perhaps, less pejoratively, openness, indeterminacy or lack of bounded-ness, is neither the inevitable consequence of a specific mode of production nor of specific physical features, their simplicity or complexity, but is rather constituted, at least in part, by practices of travelling/dwelling in which a journey 'home' is retroactively defining but unable to fix meaning physically or objectively. The teleological ordering of these practices, while not necessarily putting a break on the tripper-object's travels, does not sustain its movement for long, and does not enforce the bounded-ness of the object, rendering it vulnerable to damage[5] and destruction, and, at its most extreme, effecting the redundancy of the object as physical thing. The integrity of the tripper-object is further undermined by the relative lack of interest in its images or representations, for such representations are uncommon, and where they exist, are not clearly tied to the objects which they depict by processes of authentication or documentation.

Third, there are *tourist-objects*, which it seems lie somewhere in between these two types. This claim, at least in relation to contemporary tourism, is meant in a more precise sense than may at first be apparent. Tourist-objects are those whose movement in particular relations of travelling/dwelling produces an object-ness which is neither closed nor open, but in-between: in between open and closed in their meaning, and in between there and here in their journeying. They are neither objects whose travelling as objects of integrity is made possible in relation to an original dwelling, nor objects whose travelling is that in which the final resting place erodes the integrity of their object-ness. They are objects for whom (apparent) movement is all; they are objects that are in and of the in-between. Ironically, given that the 'here' and the 'there' are themselves rendered insignificant except in so far as they signal movement, the distance travelled can as well be virtual as real.

Tourist-objects thus currently include a wide range of objects, from forms of clothing (including, I would suggest, Clifford's T Shirts), through television programmes and alternative health products, to types of food. One example is provided by the 'Global collection' of 'colourful products, gifts and accessories' from the British chemist Boots, which asks its customers:

> How often have you longed to fully experience the world; to escape into the exotic East; lose yourself in the vast expanses of the West; or simply be refreshed by the sheer vitality of the North?
>
> Explore these new products and you'll find a unique choice of ingredients from the four corners of the world for you to experience in many exciting new ways. Boots Global Collection: make the discovery.
>
> (Boots promotional leaflet)

The range of products includes some from each of the 'four corners of the world', such as 'On Top of the World' bath foam from the North, 'Desert Rain' shampoo from the West, and 'China Glaze' two-in-one shampoo and conditioner from the East.

Tourist-objects may be identified as such by their (putative) place of origin, by their medium of distribution, or by their marketing – in each case, what is important is their self-conscious location in mobility. Moreover, as this last comment indicates, the mobility of tourist-objects is in part secured through an accompanying (although not always simultaneous) movement of representations or images, including not simply illustrations or documentation of existence of the objects concerned but also instructions for their use. In the mobility of tourist-objects, image and object are mutually authenticating (albeit the authenticity is sometimes achieved through the adoption of a playful style). For example, 'West Coast Surf' bath bubbles is described in the following terms:

> With skin toning minerals found naturally in the Pacific, West Coast Surf revives your skin like a plunge off the Californian coast.
>
> Directions: pour under running water.

In these relations of travelling and dwelling, objects and images are able to stand as warranty for each other.

GLOBAL COSMOPOLITANISM

> The first restaurant to usher in the idea that Japanese food could be friendly and fun as well [as] fashionable, Wagamama launches a cookbook this month, *Wagamama: The Way of the Noodle*...that's part recipe guide and part quasi-philosophical tract ("Food Intelligence = Open Mouth + Open Minds"). In the wake of the restaurant's success, others have followed suit, eschewing the slogans but extending the concept of Japanese as smart fast food.
>
> (Jacques Peretti, *The Face*, December 1994: 153)

Obviously, the account of the hierarchy of objects of travel presented so far – traveller-, tripper- and tourist-objects – is not only tainted in that it describes a movement of objects that is shaped by the practices of Euro-American tourists, but is also overly schematic and simplifies both the complexity of the practices of travelling and dwelling within which objects acquire distinctive biographies and the force of these object-biographies in shaping their travels. Indeed, in relation to the travel of people (as opposed to objects), Clifford advocates the notion of discrepant cosmopolitanisms as a way of avoiding this kind of simplification; as he says, it is a means of avoiding 'the excessive localism of particularist cultural relativism, as well as the overly global vision of a capitalist and technocratic monoculture' (Clifford 1992: 110). What he seeks to identify through the use of these terms are the diverse forms in which relations of travelling and dwelling are combined, all of which are at odds with a fixed opposition between either fixed or mobile cultures.[6] As such, the notion of discrepant cosmopolitanism is clearly also of value in the study of the objects as well as the people of travel, especially in so far as it undercuts the tendency to view some objects – for example, locally produced and exchanged objects – as essentially static, and others – such as commodities – as somehow essentially mobile. Not all locally produced and exchanged objects remain in place and not all objects produced as commodities are mobile: moreover, it is clear from even a cursory consideration of the career of objects that their capacity to travel is never fixed once and for all.[7] So, for example, locally produced and exchanged objects may be drawn into commodity exchange and circulate as tripper-objects, only to be let fall and die as commercially ordered fashions change or may be revived in the diversions of gift-giving, or, through the by-ways of display and collection, acquire the status of traveller-objects (Appadurai 1986a).

It will thus be helpful to consider, in more detail, some of the more specific conditions of objects of travel in terms of particular forms of discrepant cosmopolitanism. The quotation with which this section begins is an example of what seems to be an increasingly influential form: one within which travelling-in-dwelling and dwelling-in-travelling are made more or less indistinguishable – and as such, is a form of cosmopolitanism which provides the conditions of existence for a sub-set of what have so far been called tourist-objects. It can be described as global cosmopolitanism.

The notion of cosmopolitanism is coming under increasing scrutiny; very loosely, it is taken to refer to a capacity in people 'to "open" out to others who are often geographically distant' (Lash and Urry 1994: 255) or 'an orientation, a willingness to engage with the Other' (Hannerz 1990: 239). More specifically, it is taken to presuppose 'extensive patterns of mobility, a stance of openness to other and a willingness to take risks, and an ability to reflect upon and judge aesthetically between different natures, places and societies' (and, they might have added, objects; Lash and Urry 1994: 256). This is the broad sense of the term that will be employed here. However, in line with the approach adopted throughout this chapter, it will not be seen as a capacity of people alone; rather, it will be taken to refer to the outcome of a set of object–people practices in specific relations of travelling/dwelling, in which not only people but also objects are constituted as adopting a stance of 'openness to others'. In short, global cosmopolitanism refers to a mutual capacity between people and objects to be 'open' to each other (and, in this sense, it differs from Lash and

Urry's notion of 'reflexive objects', for they seem to argue, adopting a line from Baudrillard, that reflexivity – or, in my terms, openness – in objects is accompanied by the 'flattening' of subjects[8] (Lash and Urry 1994: 133)).

In the case of the Japanese food concept described in the quotation from the magazine *The Face*, this would suggest that 'food intelligence' should be understood as both people's intelligence about food, and food's intelligence about people. The latter phrase indicates the ways in which assumptions about people's eating practices are built into the food itself, such as, for example, the requirement that food can be produced and consumed in a relatively brief period of time. It thus refers to the ways in which norms and values about eating are, literally, objectified; or, to put this the other way around, it refers to the processes in which objects are given integrity in the way in which they are made to objectify a preferred mode of use, or usability. Significantly, in this and the other cases to be discussed below, this usability is apparently independent of either first or final (or, indeed, intermediate) dwelling. But this context-independence is, paradoxically perhaps, a consequence of the way in which the objects of global cosmopolitanism contain within themselves an awareness or knowledge of a preferred context-of-use; that is, they have, inscribed in their very composition, a technologically interpreted and mediated context-of-use, what I prefer to call an environment.[9] In this way, they carry their own immediate environment with them as part of their very object-ness.

The openness of objects in what I am calling global cosmopolitanism is indicated in descriptions of objects in terms not only of intelligence but also of the character traits of people – noodle bars are not simply selling fast food, they are selling *smart* fast food, and this food is *friendly* and *fun* as well as 'fashionable'. But perhaps the most evocative notion to describe this form of discrepant cosmopolitanism is the idea of the *user-friendliness* of objects; user-friendliness is the quality in objects that reciprocates the *open-mindedness* of people (see Chapter 7 on subject-performances around food).

What is indicated by this vocabulary is that global cosmopolitanism is a cosmopolitanism in which the supposed opportunities and excitements of openness to the other are seen to be in need of tempering as a consequence of an assumption of the potential for discord, or misunderstanding. These are the assumed risks of 'misuse', which stem from a lingering, but nonetheless persistent, perception of the object's assumed ontological hostility to people, a view deriving from the longstanding Western opposition between objects and subjects. In this view, objects are, potentially at least, untrustworthy; they can let you down. Global cosmopolitanism is a cosmopolitanism in which these risks are mediated by relations of friendliness, in which people and objects exist in companionship, a relation in which they challenge but do not confront each other, open up, but do not merge, a calculated mix of immersion and distance, trust and hostility.[10]

This in-between-ness is created in specific relations of travelling-in-dwelling and dwelling-in-travelling, in practices in which objects of dwelling travel and objects of travel dwell. Examples of the former include not simply the motel that Clifford describes, but also the Main Street USA of Disneyland, described by Sharon Zukin as 'an ensemble of archaic commercial facades' that combines 'fantasies of domesticity and illicit mobility' (1991: 222)[11] and the just-this-side-of the wild-side street of the international fashion clothing company Benetton, in which, it seems, life itself, while displayed in its infinite complexity, is nonetheless the same the world over:

A guy sells incense, children beg, a parked car spills over with vegetables for sale, lovers kiss good-bye, a skinny man raves about salvation, a vendor serves steamed tripe to a hurried customer, someone sprawls face down on the sidewalk, a drug dealer chants 'loose joints' quietly to no one in particular, a woman floats by balancing a bag of clothing on her head, people bump, a little girl buys spices for her mother, activists clutching clipboards ask for signatures, a moto-taxi barely misses a distracted delivery boy, five kids play soccer and dodge cars, a wild-eyed girl tap dances for money, an old woman drags a shopping cart, a cat paces in search of something to eat, a baby stroller weaves its way through a crowd, three girls all dressed the same burst out laughing, a junk seller pushes his cart and sings of his wares, the wind lifts a swirl of dust, cigarette butts and newspaper, the smell of exhaust and roasted chestnuts rises with it . . .

(*Colors*, 5, Autumn 1993: 64)

Examples of the latter, that is, objects of travel that dwell, include domestic objects named by reference to an-'other' place, such as many of those illustrated in a recent Habitat catalogue (1994). This brochure, shot 'on location in India, Poland and the UK', begins, by way of introduction, with the claim that:

Experiencing different cultures and ways of life is now an everyday occurrence. In this catalogue we celebrate the skills and visual inspiration of many countries, with simple designs that can reflect how you live.

(Habitat 1994: inside front cover)

Many of the items are named in relation to a place, such as, for example, 'Brighton teaspoon', 'Sienna armchair', 'Mandalay sectional seating', 'Baltimore bedlinen', 'Skye mug' and 'California guntuft wool rug'. In these cases, the meanings conventionally associated with places elsewhere are transferred to the domestic object in question through an act of naming, at the same time that the object is visually located in the illustrations of a Habitat-display-dwelling – travelling is superimposed *within* dwelling to create objects of travel that dwell.

These two sets of examples suggest that objects move in relations of travelling-in-dwelling *and* relations of dwelling-in-travelling in the practices of global cosmopolitanism. However, a further feature of global cosmopolitanism is the reversibility of these relations of travelling-in-dwelling and dwelling-in-travelling. So, for example, other objects in the same Habitat catalogue invert the strategies of naming and illustrating, travelling and dwelling just described. These objects, not immediately recognisable as Western domestic items are *visually*, not nominally, placed elsewhere, typically in their place of production, vaguely located though it is, 'somewhere' in India or Poland.

To take one example, in one double-page spread, the left-hand page is filled by falling sheets of vividly-coloured cotton cloth, hung from what look like wooden slats. On the right-hand side is the image of the entrance to a tent, made out of similarly vivid material, in the dark interior of which it is possible to see the backs of two figures, both wearing turbans. The text on the left-hand page encourages the viewer to see the cloth as an object of dwelling, in that it is depicted as a representative part of the localised culture it is illustrated as coming from, symbolised by the wedding we are told is occurring in the tent on the right-hand side. The text reads: 'The bright intensity of drying cotton lengths is mirrored by the tenting of a Rajasthani wedding celebration' (Habitat 1994: 124).

In buying the cloth, the consumer is, it seems, being encouraged to buy another culture, another, 'authentic', way of life. The placing of the cloth in a setting which foregrounds a threshold – the opening to a tent – places it as a product in-between two cultures; Habitat is represented as the mediator or cosmopolitan intermediary of their differences, the bringer of 'authenticity'. In some ways, then, these objects can be seen to aspire to be traveller-objects (in that they are visually located in relation to an original dwelling), but, significantly, they are simultaneously relocated by the rest of the catalogue which foregrounds the space of final display, the ideal home. In doing so, this representational strategy draws attention to the possibilities of the active re-constitution of the object-from-elsewhere within a dwelling, as the cloth is also shown furnishing the interior of the virtual space of a Habitat home. In the case of this second group of objects in the catalogue, then, dwelling is superimposed within travelling which itself is superimposed within dwelling. However, and this point will be picked up again later, the place of this final dwelling is not clearly identified – it is not seen to be in need of placement – although presumably it is that part of the catalogue which has been shot 'on location' in 'the UK'. As such, it is a space of representation rather than an instance of the representation of space illustrated in the 'on location' (or in place) shots in India (Lefebvre 1991).

In the context of the catalogue as a whole, the very distinction between dwelling-in-travelling and travelling-in-dwelling is called into doubt – indeed, is represented as reversible – as the reader turns the pages of the catalogue, flipping from one mode of representation to another, from objects of travelling-in-dwelling to objects of dwelling-in-travelling to objects of dwelling-in-travelling-in-dwelling. In short, it is not only the re-constitution of the objects in the catalogue through the use of representational strategies in which objects are constituted in relations of travelling-in-dwelling and dwelling-in-travelling, but the presentation of them as if these strategies were interchangeable that underpins the promise that the Habitat individual can acquire the 'simplicity and informality that we seek' (Habitat 1994: 87). It is the interchangeability of travelling-in-dwelling and dwelling-in-travelling, this more-or-less open, more-or-less closed reconstitution of the object, that creates the possibility for the viewer to recognise themselves as part of a global cosmopolitanism. These are the travelling/dwelling relations of objects of the flow.[12]

Moreover, so this example suggests, the flow has the properties of a Möbius strip,[13] in that it not only makes possible a slide from the space of representation to the representation of space, but defines the one as the obverse side of the other. Another example – taken from a magazine called *Chile Pepper*, concerned with 'spicy world cuisine' – illustrates this point in more detail. The cover of the June 1993 edition of this magazine claims that it is going to explore 'Cuisines in Conflict. The Foods of Yugoslavia and Cambodia'. Inside, we find not only documentary features on 'imperilled, but still surviving, dishes', but also advertisements for cook-books from other places, such as The West Indies Cookbook, spicy products such as Panda Brand Hot Chile Sauce, and a summer gift guide, including 'original design chile or kokopelli T-shirts', and a quiz with questions such as:

Question: What is a Churrasco?
Answers:
1. A cross between Cheerios and Tabasco sauce.
2. A small animal indigenous to Ecuador.
3. The center-cut of tenderloin, buttlerflied, with the fat removed.
4. One of the finest restaurants in the Houston area.

(Chile Pepper, June 1993: 44)

The article which begins with this quiz, ends both with an address of where to take 'your culinary adventure to South America' (that is, at answer 4) and a recipe for a dish offered there. In these instances, it seems, the openness of objects – in this case, food, the spiciness of which is such that it can simultaneously be eaten and enjoyed anywhere and be tied to an elsewhere (albeit in some cases a disappearing elsewhere) – is achieved in relations of travelling and dwelling in which the places of the space of representation (South America, the West Indies) are created as the obverse of the places of the space of representation (in which the adventure of travel can be experienced by following a recipe or visiting a restaurant). The flow is thus not only the set of interchangeable relations of travelling-in-dwelling and dwelling-in-travelling in which the objects of global cosmopolitanism move, but also a set of relations within which the representation of space and the space of representation are rendered mutually interdependent, as the relations between them are made explicitly and necessarily *reversible* in the twists and turns of the objects' movement, as in a Möbius strip.[14]

THE FLOWS OF CULTURE AS TECHNOLOGY

It's not just the mechanics of the product. It's also the environment around the product. . . . So if you can surround your product with your own culture – without ever denigrating other cultures or being racist in any way – it can be a powerful advantage.

(Hayek 1994)

The question then arises: what (tainted) conditions make the existence of flows[15] possible? In this section, it will be suggested that the object–people practices of global cosmopolitanism refigure space not in relation to the cultures of 'other' places,[16] but in relation to the places of the culture of technology, or perhaps, more accurately, the places of culture as construct, that have been called environments. (In doing so, it helps make visible that the combination of travelling and dwelling that constitutes space in relation to 'other' places was an ordering that had been taken for granted; see Strathern 1991; Harvey 1996). More specifically, it will be suggested that environments or contexts-of-use are designed into the object-ness of the objects of global cosmopolitanism through techniques in which culture as place is put to work, standardised, operationalised, and redistributed as a construct or property of (some) objects.

Let me give an example of one of these techniques by which the concept of culture as construct is brought into being in the object–people practices of global cosmopolitanism. It concerns the ways in which producers of what have been called tourist-objects seek to control their movement so as to compact user-friendliness into objects, producing their special quality of integrity or trustworthiness. One aspect of this control is the development of the marketing study of product and country images, a specialism which has been described as 'an important subfield of consumer behaviour and marketing management'.[17] Some recent publicity for a book in this field claims:

> Thousands of companies use country identifiers as part of their international marketing strategy, and hundreds of researchers have studied the ways these identifiers influence behavior. As markets become more international, the more prominently the origin of products will figure in sellers' and buyers' decisions. The time is ripe for practitioners and academicians to delve into the insights offered in this seminal volume so as to better prepare for meeting the competitive challenges of the global marketplace.
>
> (Papadopoulus and Heslop 1993)

Chapters include: 'Countries as Corporate Entities in International Markets', 'The Image of Countries as Locations for Investment', 'Images and Events: China Before and After Tiananmen Square' and 'Global Promotion of Country Image: Do the Olympics Count?'.

One approach within this field has developed surveys to measure public perceptions of 'trust' in products according to their perceived 'country of origin'. The development of this approach appears to be motivated by the wish on the part of producers to identify calculable factors which influence public perceptions of 'risk' associated with products identified in relation to their perceived country of origin. These factors, once identified and measured, are held to be open to influence through the association of product brands with selected dimensions of national identity (thereby helping to produce 'smart', 'intelligent' or 'user-friendly' objects).

This concern is, for example, an explicit aspect of the deliberations of the manufacturers of Swatch, the Swiss Corporation for Microelectronics and Watch-making (SMH). Nicolas Hayek, a senior executive (in an interview with William Taylor, 1993) claims that the Swiss production location of Swatch offsets its cost disadvantage. The buyers of Swatch are said to be 'sympathetic' to the Swiss: 'We're nice people from a small country. We have nice mountains and clear water'. He attributes the company's success to the fact that he understood that:

> we were not just selling a consumer product, or even a branded product. We were selling an emotional product. You wear a watch on your wrist, right against your skin. You have it there for 12 hours a day, maybe 24 hours a day. It can be an important part of your self-image. It doesn't have to be a commodity. It shouldn't be a commodity. I knew that if we could add genuine emotion to the product, and attack the low end with a strong message, we could succeed....
>
> We are not just offering people a style. We are offering them a message.... Emotional products are about message – a strong, exciting, distinct, authentic message that tells people who you are and why you do what you do. There are many elements that make up the Swatch message. High quality. Low cost. Provocative. Joy of life. But the most important element of the Swatch message is the hardest for others to copy. Ultimately, we are not just offering watches. We are offering our personal culture.

You mean people can look at a watch from Hong Kong and then look at a Swatch and sense a different culture?

It's not just the mechanics of the product. It's also the environment around the product. One thing we forget when we analyze global competition is that most products are sold to people who share our culture. Europeans and Americans are the biggest groups in the world buying products from Asia. So if you can surround your product with your own culture – without ever denigrating other cultures or being racist in any way – it can be a powerful advantage....

The people who buy Swatches are proud of us. They root for us. They want us to win. Europeans and Americans are damn happy if you can show that their societies are not decadent – that every Japanese and Taiwanese worker is not ten times more productive or more intelligent than they are.

(Taylor 1993)

In this interview, Hayek illustrates the ways in which the culture of a technologically-mediated interpretation of the place-of-origin may be designed into an object such as a Swatch, and helps to create its surrounding ambience, context-of-use or environment. More generally, country-of-origin surveys seek to measure perceptions of 'risk' and 'trustworthiness' associated with the cultural dimensions of national identity, and, in the process, allow the national identity of specific countries to be disembedded from specific places and mobilised as cultural resources, or properties of objects. (It is perhaps not surprising but nonetheless disturbing that such surveys have found that perceptions of a product in terms of its country of origin are related to some rather predictable 'cultural' expectations, those which are euphemistically termed 'patriotism' or 'ethnocentrism', for, as Penelope Harvey suggests, 'stereotyping is . . . a form of decontextualisation in which the specificity of the relationships within and between national units is achieved' (Harvey 1996: 102).) In these scientistic measurements of consumer expectations, culture is simultaneously technologically dis-placed and enhanced. Once so enhanced, culture as construct may then, as apparently in the case of Swatch, be used to re-place objects in a new space – the space of the multiple flows of global cosmopolitanism, bringing with it its own environment of use as one of its object properties.[18]

With this example in mind, let me return to the notion of culture as construct or technology and its relation to the space of flows. Once again, Clifford's investigation of 'travelling cultures' provides a helpful starting place. As noted earlier, he problematises the notion of the field in the techniques of ethnography, pointing to its reliance upon the assumption of a notion of locale as a bounded site for and of study. This presumption of the sanctity and impermeability of the boundaries of places and cultures in space he relates to the privileging of relations of dwelling over relations of travel in the practices of anthropology, claiming that anthropologists have been 'homebodies abroad'. Clifford's concern to identify the significance of the importance of relations of travelling as well as of dwelling is part of his concern to problematise the spatial mapping of the world that enabled an evolutionary, hierarchically ordered, plural placing of cultures. In *The Predicament of Culture*, Clifford develops this critique of anthropology's own spatial binding of cultures further, extending his analysis as he recognises that there has been a move beyond this plural placing of culture.

To develop this argument, he puts forward an interpretation of the reception of Marcel Mauss's documentary approach to the study of cultures. I will briefly outline this here because it provides a way of understanding not only the profound transformations that have occurred in the discipline of anthropology in the second half of the twentieth century but also the processes by which the development of a notion of culture as construct has defined a new space in the global cosmopolitanism of Swatch and other tourist-objects.

Mauss's approach was premised on the belief that the totality of society is implicit in its parts or organising structures, and was methodologically secured in the concept of 'total social facts'. This concept, Clifford implies, holds within it one of the enduring 'predicaments of culture' in the twentieth century. In some respects, its continuity with the plural conception of culture mentioned earlier is apparent, yet, as he writes:

> If every 'fact' is susceptible to multiple encoding, making sense in diverse contexts and implicating in its comprehension the 'total' ensemble of relations that constitutes the society under study, then this assumption can serve as encouragement to grasp the ensemble by focusing on one of its parts.
>
> (Clifford 1988: 63)

Clifford suggests that this encouragement was taken up and has been adopted as an enabling charter for a broad range of synecdochal techniques of studying and appropriating culture. But he also notes another legacy of the idea of social facts: relativism. This is a relativism arising as a result of the increasing significance of relations of travelling and dwelling that disturb the ordered space of plural cultures:

> the idea is ambiguous and finally troubling. If it legitimates partial cultural descriptions, if offers no guidance as to which code, key or luminous example is to be preferred.
>
> (Clifford 1988: 64)

From this point of view, there is no end to the wholes – or places – to which (the objects of) culture may belong. However, as Clifford recognises and this chapter has intended to show, this recognition can be put to work to create an effect not simply of dis-placement but also of re-placement. For, while this reconceptualisation of culture as always open to construction is unsettling, it also provides the basis for an alternative space. Indeed, Clifford notes that, while this relativism calls into doubt the fixed – and cartographically mapped – hierarchies of evolutionary models of culture previously dominant in the discipline, it has also functioned as a precursor of what can be described as a post-plural conception of the relation between culture and space, object and environment.

This is a conception in which culture becomes 'superorganic', as Friedman (1994a) puts it; and, one might also add, super-territorial. It is no longer clearly rooted in a place or a territory, and neither is it the outgrowth of a people. Instead, it is constructed in the strategic, technically mediated couplings of any social fact with (one of) the many possible environments (not places) selected in techniques of interpretation – in the case of Swatch above, this is the environment of 'nice people from a small country... [of] nice mountains and clear water'; thus, culture 'becomes arbitrary with respect to those who possess it' (Friedman 1994a: 67). This understanding of culture as construct is not simply confined to the practices of anthropology but is widespread; indeed, the thesis proposed here has been that it is being extended and refined as it is fixed in objects as the property of user-friendliness through a rapidly growing set of techniques in advertising, marketing, the media and the service professions, including tourism. This is the creation of objects as artefacts,[19] that is, it is the creation of objects in which context-of-use is constructed as an object-ive property. Furthermore, it is suggested that these techniques require and make use of specific relations of travelling and dwelling, those in which travelling-in-dwelling and dwelling-in-travelling are more or less indistinguishable. These are the relations of flows. These flows are the conduits of the new space of global cosmopolitanism produced by an apparatus of object-ivity, and this apparatus is not simply made up of television, video, multimedia, but also of a growing technology of culture.

OBJECT–PEOPLE PRACTICES, THE PROJECT OF GLOBALISATION AND TOURISM

At the beginning of this chapter it was suggested that an understanding of the travels of objects, as well as those of people, needs to be developed to understand specific formations of tourism. What this brief consideration of global cosmopolitanism as a specific set of object–people practices suggests is that a new space is being created for tourism: in this space, tourists travel in a 'world where the only frontiers are in your mind',[20] in which 'being there' is a combination of selective subjects and partial objects. It is a space of the in-between, in which dwelling and travelling are rendered indistinguishable, a space in which the combination of place and culture is a matter of technological know-how or user-friendliness and open-mindedness. It is a space of artefacts and flows.[21]

However, by describing this form of discrepant cosmopolitanism as global I am not implying that these relations of travelling-in-dwelling and dwelling-in-travelling are evenly dispersed across the world. I am not suggesting that 'we' do all seek simplicity and informality; nor do I mean to suggest that the (unevenly distributed) participants – objects and people – are equal partners in this set of practices. Flows do not flow all ways: while they create a 'world where the only frontiers are in your mind', it is also a world in which the very question 'Where do you want to go today?[TM]' has been claimed as a trademark for the computer firm Microsoft Corporation. Moreover, global cosmopolitanism is a form of cosmopolitanism in which the in-between-ness of both people and objects requires the ability and desire to move into and out of relations of open- and closed-ness, and this is not a propensity that is pre-given in either people or objects. Rather, it is a propensity that has to be created.

Indeed, Hannerz says of all cosmopolitanisms that they are:

a matter of competence, and competence of both a generalized and a more specialized kind. There is the aspect of a state of readiness, a personal ability to make one's way into other cultures, through listening, looking, intuiting and reflecting. And there is cultural competence in the stricter sense of the term, a built-up skill in manoeuvring more or less expertly with a particular system of meanings and meaningful forms.

(Hannerz 1990: 239)

Hannerz further suggests cosmopolitans have what he describes as 'decontextualised cultural capital' that can be 'quickly and shiftingly recontextualised in a series of different settings' (1990: 246). More specifically, as a propensity of people, the openness to objects which has been described here as characteristic of global cosmopolitanism has been described by Featherstone (1991) as part of the lifestyle of the new middle classes. As such, it is an individualised capacity for 'calculated decontrol' and 'dedistantiation' in which the (middle-class) person is enabled to move backwards and forwards between immersion in and distance from objects through the acquisition of a specific set of cultural competences. It is a propensity of people that is both selective and exclusionary, ordering distinctions of taste in which other (people's) relations to objects are valued negatively.

In addition, however, what the examples above suggest is that the unevennesses and inequalities of global cosmopolitanism – its discrepancies – are not simply a consequence of the propensity of (some groups of) individuals or people, but simultaneously a capacity produced in (some groups of) objects in specific relations of travelling and dwelling, namely flows. These objects do not require the travelling/dwelling relations of contextualisation (as do both traveller- and tripper-objects) in order to achieve integrity as objects; they move as a consequence of their own effects,[22] carrying within themselves their own contexts of use or environment as user-friendliness. As the outcome of specific technical practices in which culture operates as a construct, this is an enhancement which is accorded to some objects and not to others. In this way, global cosmopolitanism contributes to the formation of new hierarchies, and transforms the terms of object–people practices in tourism.

What both sides of the argument suggest, then, is that the in-between open and closedness of objects and people in global cosmopolitanism should not be equated with disinterestedness; rather, this form of cosmopolitanism represents a specific set of interests and investments: it is a combination of selected subjects and partial objects in a technologically-mediated space of flows.[23] It is tainted. Nevertheless, despite this selectivity (of people) and partiality (of objects), I have chosen to describe this form of cosmopolitanism as global because it helps constitute an *épistème* in which the boundaries between things – between people, places and cultures – are being transgressed and then redrawn. In this way, it can be linked to the wider project of globalisation as a play of forces and forms that Deleuze (1986, quoted in Rabinow, 1992: 234) has called 'fini-illimité', the creation of diversity by the endless combination of bits and pieces. The attention paid to the travelling/dwelling of objects here may help to highlight other aspects of this project. In particular, it suggests that the project of globalisation is one in which the abstract, cartographically ordered space of some other kinds of travelling cultures (including some kinds of tourism) is called into doubt, put into flux, and refigured through the movement of people and objects in flows. It is a shift from a cartographical ordering of space in terms of plural places or contexts of culture to a figuring of space as post-plural environments or constructs of culture (Strathern 1991).

This is a space of flows in which time–space compression occurs,[24] in which objects and people are dissected by the cut'n'mix of boundary crossing and return, in which culture as technology refers back into and outside itself, creating environments by design, and objects come to take on new capacities. It is a space which is not homogeneous, but its heterogeneity is not unplanned; rather it is a space in which subjects and objects do not come face-to-face, but inter-face. The possibilities for tourism of this new space of flows are only just beginning to be explored, but they have the potential both to expand the kind of journeys possible – through the incorporation of time–space compression and the multiplication of perspectives – and to provide the basis for new kinds of hierarchy among both travelling people and objects.

ACKNOWLEDGEMENTS

I would like to thank Jeanette Edwards, Penelope Harvey, Beverley Skeggs and John Urry for their comments on an earlier draft of this chapter.

NOTES

1   An important issue here is the question of whether the distinction between objects and people is itself being broken down in various practices of travelling and dwelling; an obvious point of departure for such a consideration is the literature that considers the significance of the construction of women as sex-objects in specific forms of tourism (Enloe 1989; Truong 1990; Lee 1991; Chapter 2 above).
2   From this point of view, the legitimisation of the relation of distance between people and objects which Bourdieu (1984) identifies as part of middle-class cultural authority is in part established by those practices in which the constitution of object-ness is defined in terms of immanence of meaning.
3   Ben Davis writes:

> In Western culture, museums serve both as our memory and to give value to evidence. Something in a museum is worth more, perhaps, because it is provided with constant care, and as it is researched and written about it accumulates value. An object without an anecdote is impoverished. Circulating images of such objects is a critical acknowledgement that those objects have a significance.
>
> (Davis 1994: 68; and see Chapter 7 below)

4   In his essay in *The Predicament of Culture*, Clifford discusses the workings of the interpretative practices of what he calls the art-culture system – including classifying, cataloguing and displaying – and these clearly function in relation to many traveller-objects as well as the cultural objects that are the focus of Clifford's study.
  A more detailed study of the processes of aestheticisation suggests that the object-ness of art works has long been a key focus for artistic practice and critical debate. So, for example, a number of artistic movements have sought to lower the threshold of aesthetic attention so that it encompasses the mundane objects of everyday life. Other artistic movements have problematised the relation between the physical object and the aesthetic object. So, for example, the Surrealist movement was self-consciously concerned with defamiliarising the object; indeed, in his two *Manifestos of Surrealism*, André Breton described Surrealism in terms of 'the crisis of the object'.
  In an interesting discussion of hand-painted Pop Art, Dick Hebdige suggests that Pop was the 'revenge of the clunky referent on modernism's aspiration to transcend the mere materiality of things' (1995: 107). He quotes some of Pop's exponents, including Rauschenberg and Thiebaud, to support this view:

> I think a picture is more real when it is made out of the real world.
>
> (Rauschenberg)

There is no poor subject. A pair of socks is no less suitable to make a painting than wood, nails, turpentine, oil and fabric.

(Rauschenberg)

I like to see what happens when the relationship between paint and subject-matter comes as close as I can get it – white, gooey, shiny, sticky oil paint [spread] out on top of a painted cake to 'become' frosting. It is playing with reality – making an illusion which grows out of an exploration of the properties of materials.

(Thiebaud)

Hebdige also identifies a number of distinctive strategies which were concerned with an exploration of the object-ness of objects, contributing to what he calls 'the seductive power of the object' in Pop. These include 'moving in microscopically on the familiar to defamiliarise it. The eye is forced to make rapid adjustments of focus as the contours of some object that we feel we should recognise dissolve into patterns of fractal complexity. We are thrown through the object into Chaos' (Hebdige 1995: 116).

He further suggests that Pop was not 'about' appearances – nor was it 'about' consumer culture, painting, serial production, repetition, TV, advertising, the implosion of subject–object distinctions, the disappearance of the depth model – for it was not 'about' anything. Rather, it 'presented, and what it presented, it presented in the face and on the face of what it represented' (Hebdige 1995: 107). As he goes on to show, this re-evaluation of the object in the artistic practices of Pop was intricately combined with discussions on the status of interpretation, with some critics suggesting that the dream of the pure object was fatally flawed. From these examples, it is possible to see the ways in which the (in)visibility of object-ness and practices of interpretation are inter-related in the art-culture system.

5 A label that has often intrigued me is that which informs the user that what might appear to be 'imperfections' in the object – even signs of damage – are, in fact, not to be understood as such, but are rather, a trace of the original dwelling or site of production. So, for example, irregularities in the weave of cloth used in the manufacture of some Western fashion clothing are sometimes so described. Such labels can be seen as explicit attempts to give the item physical integrity, but, in their very visibility as a label, they should perhaps be seen as no more than sticky tape.

6 Hannerz seeks to make a similar point in his discussion of 'cosmopolitanism and varieties of mobility' (1990: 240–5).

7 In this respect, it is important to point out that the practices of symbolic binding by which objects are accorded integrity are various; nevertheless, the processes of branding are an important component of binding in many forms of cosmopolitanism. See Lury (1993, 1996) for further discussion of the significance of branding in contemporary culture.

8 In *Symbolic Exchange and Death* (1993), Baudrillard discusses the adoption of a testing mode by objects; he writes:

We live in a *referendum* mode precisely because there is no longer any *referential*. Every sign and every message (objects of functional utility just as much as fashion features or any televised information, polls or discussions) is presented to us as a question/ answer. . . . Tests and referenda are, as we know, perfect forms of simulation: the question induces the answer, it is *design-ated* in advance. . . . The object today is no longer 'functional' in the traditional sense of the term; it doesn't serve you, it *tests* you.

(Baudrillard 1993: 62, 63)

9 I use this term here following Luhmann's account of the significance of the 'theoretical turn' that began in the nineteenth century when the terms *Umwelt* and environment were first used. He suggests that this turn, which contributed to the current resurgence of ecological thinking, proposes that 'systems define their own boundaries' (Luhmann 1989: 6). In this understanding, systems differentiate themselves and thereby constitute the environment as whatever lies outside the boundary. He writes:

The environment is not a system of its own, not even a unified effect. As the totality of external circumstances, it is whatever restricts the randomness of the morphogenesis of the system and exposes it to evolutionary selection. The 'unity' of the environment is nothing more than a correlate of the unity of the system since everything that is a unity for the system is defined by it as a unity.

(Luhmann 1989: 6)

In my adaptation, the objects of global cosmopolitanism are being created as if they were systems in this sense: the context-of-use or environment is the correlate of the object/system.

10 As Hannerz notes:

The cosmopolitan's surrender to the alien culture implies personal autonomy vis-a-vis the culture where he originated. . . . Yet the surrender is of course only conditional. The cosmopolitan may embrace the alien culture, but he does not become committed to it. All the time he knows where the exit is.

(1990: 240)

11 Zukin continues:

'This is what the real Main Street should have been like,' one of Disneyland's planners or 'imagineers' says. 'What we create,' according to another, 'is a "Disney realism," sort of Utopian in nature, where we carefully program out all the negative, unwanted elements and program in the positive elements.' And Disneyland succeeded on the basis of this totalitarian image-making, projecting the collective desires of the powerless into a corporate landscape of power.

(1991: 222)

12 The object-effects of the flow are such that, as Jameson comments in his discussion of video, to select a single item, text or object from a flow – even as an example, as I have done here – and to discuss it in isolation is 'to reify the experience of the total flow from which it was momentarily extracted' (Jameson 1991: 78).

13 The Möbius strip or band is the one-sided surface with a single edge that is obtained by giving a strip one twist and sticking the edges together. It creates a topological space that is said to have 'unexpected' or 'unfamiliar' properties.

14 The difficulties involved in maintaining the hierarchy between traveller-, tourist- and tripper-objects in the context of the consolidation of the flows of global cosmopolitanism are illustrated by the conundrums that face the archivists of digital museums. Davis summarises some of these:

The three main concerns for digital museums are storage, retrieval and information. *Storage* involves methods of recording images and data, file formats, compression ratios, and annotation fields. What level of detail is held in the fields of information about an object? . . .

Digital archivists must also determine what parameters to place on the *retrieval* of this kind of information. Who can get at information about artworks, for instance, that provide reference for the art market? How is software constructed to allow access to certain information and restrict access that might endanger the security of the work?

And finally, how is *interaction* with the information performed? Can the data and digital information be removed from the collection for any purpose? Can enough bits be accessible for reproduction? . . .

Our relationship to original works of art may also change in the process, along with our ideas of connoisseurship.

(Davis 1994: 68)

15 The notion of 'flows' is addressed in the work of anthropologists such as Appadurai (1993) and Hannerz (1993) and the cultural critic, Jameson (1991).

16 The difficulties involved in the maintenance of the space in which there are fixed 'other' places and cultures is indicated in an editorial for *Colors* magazine, published by the

Benetton clothing company, which, while describing itself as 'a magazine about the rest of the world', is not sure what this means:

> In theory, it means that we're as concerned with your culture as we are with ours. But because this magazine is produced by people from about 30 different countries, published in five bilingual editions and distributed globally, we're not sure anymore which culture is ours. We have cultural vertigo, we feel dizzy.

17 In using this example here, I do not mean to imply that, as a set of techniques, global cosmopolitanism draws only on the social scientific knowledges of marketing and advertising, for it also draws upon techniques developed in the fields of visual arts and design. Indeed, it is possible to see clear lines of influence between the practices developed in the context of Surrealism and those of global cosmopolitanism. So, for example, one of the ways in which the so-called crisis in the object provoked by Surrealism was achieved was by deliberately pluralising the contexts in which the object was perceived, specifically by removing it from the contexts where we conventionally perceive it and placing it in surprising ones. As it appeared simultaneously in multiple contexts, 'the object' was put in crisis because its solid identity could no longer be established through conventional practices of situatedness. Another technique adopted by the Surrealists was to distort the scale of objects *vis-à-vis* one another. Both techniques had the effect of revealing the constructedness of objects, their dependence for meaning on context and conventional norms of perception. These aesthetic techniques are clearly visible in the practices of cultural management which are described here as global cosmopolitanism. Examples include the deliberate defamiliarisation of objects by representing them in surprising situations, and the use of a cut'n'mix combination of objects, in which objects the properties conventionally associated with one object are mixed with those of another. The latter technique results in what might be called hybrid objects. More obvious borrowings from Surrealism include the use of giganticism and miniaturisation.

18 In Baudrillard's terms, reality is tested, and then reality tests you in return 'according to the same score card', and 'you decode it following the same code, inscribed in its every message and object like a miniature genetic code' (1993: 63).

19 In *Symbolic Exchange and Death* (1993), Baudrillard quotes Michel Tort's definition of the artefact:

> The artefact is something other than a controlled transformation of the object for the purposes of knowledge: it is a savage intervention in reality, at the end of which it is impossible to distinguish what in this reality arises out of objective knowledge and what results from the technical intervention (the medium).
>
> (Baudrillard 1993: 64)

Jameson seems to suggest something similar in his description of the videotext as a kind of artefact, and offers the following description of 'the medium' (which can, perhaps, be seen as a specific form of flow):

> Capitalism, and the modern age, is a period in which, with the extinction of the sacred and the 'spiritual', the deep underlying materiality of all things has finally risen dripping and convulsive into the light of day; and it is clear that culture itself is one of those things whose fundamental materiality is now for us not merely evident but inescapable.... We postcontemporary people have a word for that discovery – and this is, of course, the word *medium*, and in particular its plural *media*, a word which now conjoins three relatively distinct signals: that of an artistic mode or specific form of aesthetic production; that of a specific technology, generally organized around a central apparatus or machine; and that, finally, of a social institution.
>
> (Jameson 1991: 67)

As he points out, most aesthetic concepts do not require this simultaneous attention to 'the multiple dimensions of the material, the social and the aesthetic' (1992: 67).

20 This is a slogan adopted by Fujitsu in the promotional material which was part of their display at the 1992 Expo in Seville. Penelope Harvey's discussion of this Expo provides a fascinating interpretation of the *fini-illimitè* (see Note 22) of this enterprise.

21 If the interchangeability of travelling and dwelling is accepted as a defining feature of global cosmopolitanism, an alternative, only apparently divergent, way to describe this space is McLuhan's notion of the global village. However, as Clifford would no doubt point out, to do so would still leave the question of where the prospective ethnographer should pitch his/ her tent.

22 In adopting this formulation, I am indebted to Penelope Harvey's discussion (1996) of different relations between culture and technology adopted in the displays at the Seville Expo.

23 While flows are described here as limited in their accessibility, it is also important to recognise that they are shaped by what Appadurai (1993) calls scapes, that is, 'by the historical, linguistic and political situatedness of different sorts of actors: nation states, multinationals, diasporic communities, as well as sub-national groupings and movements (whether religious, political or economic), and even face-to-face groups, such as villages, neighbourhoods and families' (1993: 275–6).

24 According to Jameson, flows can be seen in terms of a constant stream of 'multiple materials, each of which can be seen as something like a shorthand signal for a distinct type of narrative or a specific narrative process' (1991: 86). This analysis provides a basis from which it is possible to see how a flow may provide the conditions for time–space compression, for it makes possible multiple, cross-cutting narratives and temporalities of objects and images. Jameson further suggests that the flow can be seen as providing the conditions in which there is a 'ceaseless renarrativisation of already existent narrative elements by each other' (1991: 88), and suggests that it will lead to 'the structural exclusion of memory' (1991: 71). Appadurai suggests that it provides the conditions for nostalgia without memory (Appadurai 1993: 272).

5

'McDISNEYIZATION' AND 'POST-TOURISM'

Complementary perspectives on contemporary tourism

George Ritzer and Allan Liska

INTRODUCTION

Tourism, like much else in the social world, is undergoing a dramatic transformation. One way to look at these changes is to argue that they constitute a stage that is continuous with modernity; they are part of advanced modernity. The most obvious problem with such a view is that the new world seems so different that it appears to lack much, if any, immediate connection with its modern ancestor. Hence, a second way of thinking about this change which takes the position that it is both part, and a reflection, of the movement from a modern to a totally new and discontinuous post-modern society. While there is much merit in this mode of thought, one is led to wonder whether the changes are dramatic enough to qualify as an entirely new social form. Furthermore, such a view tends toward the kind of periodization attacked by post-modernists. Worse, it involves the kind of grand narrative that is the *bête noire* of post-modern social theorists, especially Lyotard.

It seems questionable, if not pointless, to pursue the issue of whether or not the social changes associated with tourism (or anything else, for that matter) have been continuous enough to allow us to retain the modern appellation; or dramatically different to require a new post-modern label. Rather than looking at modernity and post-modernity as epochs, it would be far more useful to view them as alternative perspectives to be brought to bear on the analysis of changing social phenomena. It is this course that we will follow in this chapter. Specifically, we will look at tourism as one domain (of many) characterized by substantial social change. We will look at those changes first from a modern point of view and then from a post-modern perspective. Our objective is not to ascertain whether or not we have, within this domain, left the modern age or entered a post-modern world. Nor is it to determine whether one of these perspectives is better than another. Rather, our goal is to use both perspectives in order to see what new light can be cast on the changing nature of tourism and, perhaps, on the social world more generally.

A MODERN APPROACH TO TOURISM

There is no shortage of theories of modernity among the classic sociological theorists (Marx, Weber, Durkheim and Simmel), or among their contemporary offspring such as Giddens (1990, 1991, 1992), Beck (1992), Bauman (1989, 1991) and many others. In this section we will use a modern perspective, 'the McDonaldization of society', developed by one of the authors of this chapter (Ritzer 1996). This perspective, strongly influenced by Weber's theory of rationalization, is a modern grand narrative viewing the world as growing increasingly efficient, calculable, predictable and dominated by controlling non-human technologies. While most grand narratives (such as that of Karl Marx) offer a utopian view of the future, this one, following Weber, has a more dystopian emphasis upon the increasing irrationality of rationality.

The logic of this perspective leads to the view that tourism, like much else in society, is growing increasingly McDonaldized. The highly popular Disney theme parks can be seen as paradigms of this process (Bryman 1995). Indeed, these parks are discussed at various points in *The McDonaldization of Society* in order to illustrate the reach of the process of McDonaldization. Bryman has examined the Disney parks from the point of view of McDonaldization and has found them to be largely congruent.

Disney World (to take a specific Disney park) is efficient in many different ways, especially in the way it processes the large numbers of people that would easily overwhelm a less rationalized theme park. The set prices for a daily or weekly pass, as well as the abundant signs indicating how long a wait one can expect at a given attraction, illustrate calculability (although, as we will see, Disney World is also in a sense a shopping mall oriented to getting people to spend far more than they do on their daily pass). Disney World is highly predictable – there are no midway scam artists to milk the visitor; there are teams of workers who, among their other cleaning chores, follow the nightly parades cleaning up debris, including animal droppings, so that visitors are not unpleasantly surprised when they take an errant step. Indeed Disney theme parks work hard to be sure that the visitor experiences no surprises at all. And Disney World is a triumph of non-human technology over humans. This is not only true of the numerous mechanical and electronic attractions, but even the human employees whose performances (through lip-synching, for example) and work (following scripts) are controlled by non-human technologies. Finally, there is no lack of irrationalities of supposed rationality at Disney World: long lines and long waits make for great inefficiency; costs (for food, the unending hawking of Disney products, both in and out of the parks) mount up, become incalculable, and often make what is supposed to be an inexpensive vacation highly costly. Most importantly, what is supposed to be a human vacation turns, for at least some, into a non-human or even a dehumanizing experience.

Disney's theme parks came of age in the same era as McDonald's. Fascinatingly, the original Disneyland and the first outlet of the McDonald's chain both opened in the same year – 1955. They are based on and manifest many of the same principles. McDonald's has arguably been the more powerful symbol and force in our age, if for no other reason than its 18,000 or so outlets worldwide (with over 3,000 more planned for 1996) are more ubiquitous than the few Disney theme parks. Of course, it could be argued that Disney's movies, television programmes and products make it even more omnipresent than McDonald's. But if McDonald's has been the paradigm of rationality for society as a whole, Disney has certainly been the model for the tourist industry (Bryman 1995: 179). For example, it could easily be argued that, to the chagrin of professional gamblers, Las Vegas hotels, and the city in general, are increasingly coming to exemplify the Disney model. Las Vegas looks increasingly like a huge theme park and many of its large hotels are, at least in part, theme parks. This is a trend that was begun several decades ago by Circus Circus and is epitomized, at least until it too is surpassed, by the MGM Grand. According to one expert on gambling, 'Las Vegas is [already] gambling's Disney World' (Grochowski 1995). While McDonald's itself has not been without influence in the tourist industry, it is Disney and its phenomenal success that has been most responsible for bringing the principles of McDonaldization (or of rationalization) to the tourist industry. Combining the two, perhaps we can talk, if the reader will excuse the creation of another, uglier, neologism – the 'McDisneyization' of the tourist industry.

Whatever its source, it is easy to argue that the tourist industry in general, and virtually every theme and amusement park in particular, has been McDisneyized, at least to some extent. Cruise ships are being McDisneyized, taking on the appearance increasingly of floating theme parks. (And Disney has its own cruise ship, the Big Red boat, to take tourists to Disney World.) Beyond cruise ships, theme parks and casinos, shopping malls have been McDisneyized, coming to look more and more like amusement parks; the largest (Mall of America in Minneapolis and the West Edmonton, Alberta mega-mall) include rides, even roller coasters. One could extend this list much further, but the point is that through the influence of the Disney theme parks, at least in part, many aspects of the tourist world have been McDonaldized. Not only do these tourist attractions look more and more like a Disney theme park, but they come to embrace the four basic principles of McDisneyization and to generate new irrationalities of rationality.

We have not yet mentioned the package tours that receive much attention in *The McDonaldization of Society*. Yet while such tours are undoubtedly highly McDonaldized, we are faced with a problem here, since Urry (1990) argues that such tours, or at least the most standardized of them, have passed their heyday and are in decline. They represent the application of Fordism to the tourist industry, but in Urry's view we have moved into a post-Fordist era in tourism (and elsewhere; see Chapter 7 below). However, the McDonaldization thesis builds upon and has much in common with Fordism; indeed Ritzer argues that McDonaldization runs counter to the view that we have moved from a Fordist to a post-Fordist society. Urry's argument on the decline of standardized tours appears to stand in direct contradiction to the McDonaldization thesis, at least in that sector of society.

Although Urry is undoubtedly right in arguing that the rigidly standardized tours he describes have been in decline for some time, the package tour remains alive and well and highly McDonaldized. Today's tours may be more flexible than their forerunners described by Urry, but they are still highly McDonaldized. But the more important argument to be made here is that today's tours are less McDonaldized than their predecessors precisely because, at least in part, of the very success of McDonaldization. That is, it is because so much of the larger society has been McDonaldized that there is less need to McDonaldize the package tour itself. Take standardized meals, for example. In the past, one of the reasons that tour operators had to offer standardized meals was that the food available at a given tourist site would likely prove too unusual and unpredictable and therefore unpalatable for many tourists. However, now tourists can generally be safely left on their own at most locales since those who want standardized meals will almost undoubtedly find them readily available at a local McDonald's, or an outlet of some other international chain of fast-food restaurants. Failing that, the modern tourist is even likely to feel comfortable at indigenous fast-food chains, like Nirula's in India which specializes in Mutton burgers. Similar chains, or indigenous spin-offs, in many other sectors (such as Benetton in clothing, Body Shops in cosmetics; see Chapter 4 on 'tourist-objects') make most tourist sites quite familiar and comfortable for the majority of tourists. As a general rule, as society itself grows more and more McDonaldized, there is less and less need rigidly to standardize the package tour.

More generally, in *The Tourist Gaze* (1990) Urry argues that there are nine social practices associated with what we normally call tourism. In the case of the package tour, Urry was implicitly questioning the McDonaldization thesis, while in this case that thesis casts doubt on his iteration of touristic practices. Among other things, Urry argues that tourism is the 'opposite' of 'regular and organised work', that tourism often involves movement of people to a 'new place or places', that tourist sites are 'outside the normal places of residence and work' and there is 'a clear intention to return "home"', that tourist sites are of 'a different scale or involving different sense', and that they are separate from everyday experience and 'out of the ordinary'. In all of this there is the sense that tourism is different from, separate from, our day-to-day lives; we tour in order to see and experience something different (Urry 1990: 2–3). In fact, Urry later argues that tourists do not want to 'gaze' on and frequent that which is ordinary; that which is not visually distinct (1992a; and see Chapter 1 above on visuality).

While all of this is certainly true to some extent, and more true of some people than others, the McDonaldization thesis leads to the view that people increasingly travel to other locales in order to experience much of what they experience in their day-to-day lives. That is, they want their tourist experiences to be about as McDonaldized as their day-to-day lives. (They may even delight in finding and frequenting a McDonald's in some far-off locale such as Moscow or Beijing.) Accustomed to a McDonaldized lifeworld, many people appear to want:

1 Highly predictable vacations. They may not want to be in lock step with fellow tourists, but many want few, if any, surprises. One could argue that as our everyday life grows more and more predictable, we have less and less tolerance for, and ability to handle, unpredictable events. The last thing most of today's tourists want to experience is an unpalatable meal, a wild animal, or a rat-infested hotel room. Said a Hawaiian hotel official, 'The kids are safe here; there's low crime, you can drink the water and you can speak the language' (quoted in *Travel Weekly*, 16 March 1995). In addition to avoiding the unfamiliar associated with a different culture, many tourists want the things they are familiar with on a day-to-day basis. Thus, for example, the cruise ship *Norway* features a television in each cabin offering, among many other things, another key element of McDonaldization – CNN (Carpenter 1994).

2 Highly efficient vacations. The same point applies here: accustomed to efficiency in their everyday lives, many people tend to have little tolerance for inefficient vacations. They tend to want the most vacation for the money (hence the popularity of cruises and package tours), to see and do as much as possible in the time allotted, and so on. Maiden voyages on cruise ships are often avoided by knowledgeable tourists because the inefficiencies have yet to be eliminated.

3 Highly calculable vacations. Many people want to know in advance how much a vacation is going to cost and they abhor cost overruns. They also want to have

itineraries that define precisely where they will be at a given time and for how long. Cruises, for one, typically have all of these characteristics and it is this that goes a long way toward explaining their booming popularity.

4 Highly controlled vacations. This can take various forms. For example, there is a preference for dealing with people whose behaviour is tightly controlled by scripts (just as with McDonald's employees; Leidner 1993, and Chapter 8 below) rather than with those who are free to behave as they wish. Disney parks are infamous for the tight control they exercise over not only how their employees behave, but how they dress, how long their hair and nails can be, what kinds of jewellery they may wear. Then there are the routines on cruises (bingo and Dicey Horse Racing to line-dance lessons and napkin folding to pool olympics and aerobics classes) that tend to give order to many vacationers' days. For another, sites which house advanced technologies (modern aeroplanes, cruise ships, hotels, amusement parks) are preferred both in their own right as well as for the control they exercise over both employees and other tourists.

Of course, this all brings with it the same kinds of irrationalities that come with the McDonaldization of all other sectors of our lives. In addition to its dehumanizing character, tourism often does grave danger to the eco-system, hence the growth in interest in 'sustainable tourism'. However, we often will accept the irrationalities, just as we accept them in our daily lives, as a modest cost to pay for the gains from McDonaldization. The central point in this context is that McDonaldized tourism stands in opposition to all of the points made above by Urry about tourism; it is less and less likely to offer the kinds of differences outlined by him. Increasingly, our vacations are more and more like the rest of our lives.

To put this in its most extreme form, it could be argued that McDonaldization is undermining the fundamental reason for tourism. That is, if people have in the past toured to experience something new and different, and if tourism itself, as well as the locales to which one journeys, are McDonaldized, then there is little or no reason to tour. Could it be that the McDonaldization of tourism will eventually mean its own demise? Probably not. Tourism will continue to flourish. Increasing affluence, at least of some segments of society, will continue to fuel tourism. Culturally, tourism offers people a number of hard-to-resist symbols of success and sophistication. Those who rebel against McDonaldized tourism will unquestionably force some tour operators and tourist sites to de-McDonaldize. Most importantly, there will continue to be a market for McDonaldized vacations. Raised in McDonaldized systems, accustomed to a daily life in those systems, most people not only accept, but embrace, those systems. Thus, instead of being put off by McDonaldized vacations, many will gravitate toward them. We could even envision a world tour of McDonald's restaurants (or Disney theme parks). In addition to mandatory visits to McDonald's in Moscow and Beijing, who wouldn't want to visit Norway and eat McLaks (grilled salmon sandwich with dill sauce on whole-grain bread); the Netherlands and devour a groenteburger (a vegetable burger); Uruguay and feast on McHuevos (hamburgers with poached egg) and McQuesos (toasted cheese sandwiches); and Japan where one can find a Chicken Tatsuta sandwich, fried chicken spiced with soy sauce and ginger, with cabbage and mustard mayonnaise? This itinerary is presented with a sense of irony, but on second thoughts our guess is that some clever tour operator could earn much income from such a tour.

While many welcome highly McDonaldized tours, there are certainly others who are willing, even eager, to take risks when they tour. However, for many of those who desire to see the extraordinary, there is also a desire to have McDonaldized stops along the way, and to retreat to at the end of the day. The ideal in this case is the right combination of non-McDonaldized and McDonaldized elements.

Then there are those tourists who appear to want nothing to do with anything McDonaldized. But while it is still possible to experience something approaching totally non-McDonaldized travel, it is growing increasingly difficult to find. The main reason is that those who profit from such activities rapidly McDonaldize any escape route from rationalization discovered by a significant number of people. This has been underscored once again recently by Heywood in his work on mountain climbing (1994). He sees the latter, and recreation in general, as an effort to escape the increasingly rationalized lifeworld. He contrasts sport climbing, which has already been rationalized to some degree, with adventure climbing which is more of a pure sport. However, even in the latter Heywood sees signs of increasing rationalization. He concludes that 'attempts to evade or resist rationalization are becoming increasingly rationalized from within' (Heywood 1994: 179). The same point can be applied to tourism in general and development constitutes a grave threat to those who want to avoid completely rationalized settings when they travel.

All this rationalization flies in the face of the idea that tourism is growing increasingly diverse; 'tourism is growing into a series of "tourisms" ' (Parrinello 1993: 239). McDonaldization clearly implies homogenization, not diversity. Surely, however, 'lethal' tours (of the world's nuclear waste dumps) or 'deviant' tours (pornographic film-making around the world; Rojek 1995) would be able to evade McDonaldization? We think not. There are already tours of this sort and there will be more of them as soon as enterprising agents find that there are enough people involved to make the effort profitable. Thus, the growing diversity of travel represents only a momentary barrier to McDonaldization. More generally, the future of McDonaldization lies in being able to apply its principles to smaller and smaller market niches.

Whatever happens, tourism will continue to flourish, but the McDonaldization thesis leads us to believe that, at least for some, anticipatory technologies (Parrinello 1993) such as videos, the Internet and especially virtual (or techno-) touring will not only prepare people to travel, but replace journeys to far off locales (Faiola 1996; Loving 1996). Faiola argues that it is extremely unlikely that people will travel via the Internet rather than in person. But he is discussing the Internet and not virtual touring. In any case, he may be a bit too optimistic for our McDonaldized age. As the technology of virtual reality improves, some people will find that it is far more efficient to 'visit' Thailand in the comfort of their living rooms than actually to journey there. They will also find a virtual visit more predictable than a 'real' one; there are no surprises on a virtual tour. Virtual tours will be highly calculable; one will know precisely how long one's 'trip' will take and what it will cost. Non-human technology reigns supreme in virtual touring and it exerts great control over the tourist while it controls others completely out of existence. Of course, there are those irritating irrationalities. A virtual tour can hardly promise the same kind of human experience afforded by a 'real' tour. The issue of reality, or rather its absence, brings us directly on to a discussion of post-modernism and tourism.

POST-MODERNISM AND TOURISM

Post-modernism is a popular theoretical perspective and it is often and easily applied to tourism. The problem with most such analyses, indeed with most applications of post-modern social theory, is their reliance on a general characterization of that theory. The fact is that there are profound differences among the major practitioners of post-modern social theory, Baudrillard, Foucault, Lyotard, Jameson, Virilio and so on (Ritzer, forthcoming a). There are even important differences within the bodies of works of many of these thinkers. Thus, one must always be wary of general statements about post-modern social theory.

The place to begin this discussion is with the more specific and concrete idea of the 'post-tourist'. Feifer is most often linked to this idea and its major elements (1985). First, the post-tourist finds it less and less necessary to leave home; the technologies discussed previously – television, videos, CD-ROM, the Internet and virtual reality – allow people to 'gaze' on tourist sites without leaving home. Second, tourism has become highly eclectic; a pastiche of different interests – visits to sacred, informative, broadening, beautiful, uplifting, or simply different sites. The post-modern tourist simply has a lot more choices; for example, one can take a pleasure voyage on one of the huge cruise ships or choose a much smaller, but still comfortable, ship and take an expedition cruise to more remote locales (Houser 1994). Then, there is the growth of eco-tourism (Hill 1995) as well as lifestyle cruises (and other kinds of vacations) such as those for seniors, as well as for gays and lesbians (Tazzioli 1995). Third, post-tourists are seen as realistically simply playing a series of games; they play at and with touring; they recognize that there is no 'authentic' tourist experience (MacCannell 1989).

Rojek has also analyzed post-tourism in terms of three basic, albeit different, characteristics (1993). First, the post-tourist accepts the commodification of tourism; it and the products hawked along the way are all manifestations of consumerism (see Chapter 4). Second, tourism is seen as an end in itself, and not a means to some loftier goal. Third, post-tourists are drawn to the signs, especially the more spectacular signs, associated with tourism. Munt (1994) discusses 'other', middle-class, post-tourists who seek to distance themselves from crasser post-tourists.

Bryman sees Disney as fitting reasonably well with the idea of the post-tourist, indeed Disney 'may well have played a prominent role in stimulating the attitude of the post-tourist' (Bryman 1995: 177). In fact, Bryman adds additional weight to the idea of post-tourism by, for example, discussing the simulacra, the fakes that are more real than real, associated with post-tourism in general, and more specifically with Disney.

The obvious questions seem to be: Are we in fact in the age of the post-tourist? Have we left the era of the modern tourist? These may be the obvious questions, but once again they are really the wrong questions. As before, they imply the kind of periodization and grand narrative rejected by most post-modernists. The real question is: Do these post-modern ideas cast new and interesting light on tourism? Bryman makes the point that what Disney has to offer in this realm is not so new; its precursors had characteristics that could be described as post-modern.

The idea that there is a close linkage between commodification, consumerism and tourism is worthwhile and worth exploring. Post-modernism has long been linked with the consumer society (Featherstone 1991; Baudrillard 1993). Clearly, tourism has become a commodity to be advertised, marketed and sold much like every other commodity (Urry 1990). However, what is not emphasized enough is the degree to which tourism can become little more than a means to sell lots of other commodities (see again Chapter 4 above on tourist-objects). Again, Disney offers a wonderful example of this. A trip to Disney World is a desirable goal in itself as far as the Disney corporation is concerned, but perhaps more importantly it is the gateway to the sale of lots of other Disney products. The process begins on entering the theme park, which can be viewed as a thinly disguised shopping mall set up to sell primarily a wide array of Disney products. It ends with the Disney Village Marketplace which is open late for those who want to shop after they have visited the park. Indeed, it is increasingly difficult to differentiate between shopping malls like Mall of America and theme parks such as Disney World (Barber 1995). The former is a mall with an amusement park, the latter an amusement park with a mall. We will have more to say about this kind of 'implosion' later in the chapter, but other examples are the way that Las Vegas is currently being transformed into 'the world's largest theme park' (Grochowski 1995), and the coming of Segaworld, the world's first interactive entertainment theme park, to London, combining the theme park with virtual reality (May 1995). The only real difference between contemporary mega-malls and amusement parks is in the relative mix of shops and amusements.

There is a broader kind of implosion taking place involving various corporate purchases and mergers (such as Disney and broadcasting giant Capital Cities/ABC). These are designed to increase the horizontal and vertical integration of organizations involved in consumption in general, as well as in tourism in particular. Barber describes not only malls, but commercial strips and chain eateries, as theme parks (1995: 128). More specifically, there is a sense in which McDonald's is a theme park: a food chain featuring its own Mickey Mouse (Ronald McDonald), its miniature non-mechanical rides in the 'playlands' outside, its commercial tie-ins with celebrities and with hit films, and its pervasive claim on American lifestyle. While McDonald's might not be the kind of tourist destination that malls have become, they are an integral part of such malls and many other tourist sites.

The growing popularity of outlet malls, often adjacent to resorts, also reflects this kind of implosion of shopping and amusement. According to one industry insider: 'Shopping has more and more become recreation. . . . You can combine your vacation or weekend away with outlet shopping' (McEnery 1995). And some outlet malls, like Potomac Mills outside Washington D.C., have become tourist destinations in their own right. Similarly, more Canadian package tours now go to the West Edmonton Mall than to Niagara Falls (Davidson 1995). Timothy and Butler examined cross-border shopping between the United States and Canada, and concluded: 'There are strong indications that under some conditions shopping is the primary motive, if not the only significant one, in the decision to make such a trip' (1994: 17).

A woman who plans travel programs for shopping malls states: 'Tourism is California's No. 1 business and shopping is the No. 1 thing tourists want to do' (*Seattle Times*, 1994). A large proportion of the time and money devoted to vacations is spent on shopping while on vacation. And some, as we have seen, have taken this to its logical extreme – shopping has become the vacation.

Returning to our main example, Disney World is selling Disney products and visitors may easily spend far more on over-priced Disney goods (leading to incalculability) than on the visit to the park itself. But that is just the beginning. Visits to the parks help to fuel interest in shopping at the Disney store in the local mall (which, in turn, had probably played a role in creating an interest in visiting the park). Visits to the parks and mall shops stoke up interest in Disney movies, the Disney channel (both of which, of course, helped create the interest in visiting the theme park and the shops), Disney books, Disney recordings, and so on. The point here is that we have a well-integrated, synergistic system to sell and keep selling Disney products. Yes, Disney World is itself a commodity and part of the consumer society, but it also plays its designated role in a highly integrated system oriented to selling the wide array of Disney commodities.

Barber has recently summed up (and extended) much of what is being said above with his concept of 'McWorld':

> McWorld is an entertainment shopping experience that brings together malls, multiplex movie theaters, theme parks, spectator sports arenas, fast-food chains (with their endless movie tie-ins), and television (with its burgeoning shopping networks) into a single vast enterprise that, on the way to maximizing its profits, transforms human beings.
>
> (Barber 1995: 97)

The various components of McWorld give us, as tourists (and more generally), a choice of goods and services to consume (although they are goods and services of a very limited type), but what they seek to limit, if not eliminate, is our ability not to consume.

It is also the case, as the post-modernists suggest, that signs are central to contemporary tourism; in touring, people are certainly consuming a wide array of signs. It is important that we understand the nature and significance of those signs and the ways in which they relate to other signs. McDonald's and Disney are important signs in themselves and within each is a wide array of key signifiers. Much the same could be said for all of the major icons of tourism – Las Vegas in general, as well as each of its major hotels; the major cruise lines; Paris and the Eiffel Tower; India and the Taj Mahal, and on and on.

However, while signs are critically important, an undue emphasis on them leads one to ignore the more material aspects of tourism. Bauman is one who makes this argument in a more general critique of post-modern social theory:

> To many people ... reality remains what it always used to be: tough, solid, resistant and harsh. They need to sink their teeth into some quite real bread before they abandon themselves to munching images [on a visit to Disney World or in front of the TV].
>
> (Bauman 1992: 1550)

The analysis of the new 'means of tourism' allows us to get at the more material aspects of tourism, without losing sight of the significance of signs. This idea is obviously derived from Marx's ideas on the means of production. It is a specific aspect of a wide range of new 'means of consumption' (Baudrillard 1988) being created today, to a large extent in the US (Ritzer forthcoming b). For example, the fast-food restaurant is one of the new means of consumption (see discussion in Chapter 8 below). It is a structure that has revolutionized the way people consume their food. Further, as the model has been extended to many other domains, it has revolutionized the way people consume virtually everything. The shopping mall, and its more recent extension into mega-malls, is another revolutionary new means of consumption. But, perhaps the most important of such new means is the credit card (Ritzer 1995). Like the fast-food restaurant and Disneyland, a product of the United States in the 1950s, the credit card is clearly a revolutionary new means of consumption that has, in turn, revolutionized consumption in general.

The new means of consumption are not unrelated to tourism. Obviously, fast-food restaurants and other chains have, as pointed out earlier, permitted package tours to become less standardized. Malls, especially the mega-malls, have, as we have seen, become tourist attractions in their own right. Furthermore, since much of tourism is about selling things, it has been profoundly affected by the coming of age of the mall. Disney World, as we have seen, is in a sense a mall; Las Vegas hotels, cruise ships and many tourist destinations have taken on some of the characteristics of a mall. And the tourist ships turn at least some of their destinations into shopping malls:

> While shopping is good on either side, cruise ships usually dock off Philipsburg [St. Martin], the capital on the Dutch side, and its Front Street is very popular. With as many as eight cruise ships and with pedestrian and motor traffic competing for the same street space. . . .
>
> (Newbern and Fletcher 1995)

Above all, modern tourism would simply be impossible without the credit card. The credit card can be seen as a meta-means of tourism (and consumption). That is, it is a general means that permits one to make full use of all the new means of tourism. A trip to Euro Disney, or a world cruise, among many others, would be virtually unthinkable without a credit card. Returning to the theme of implosion in this context, many cruise ships issue passengers their own cruise card to make shopping and gambling easier while at sea.

Beyond all of this, it is important that we consider the new means of tourism themselves. The Disney theme park, the cruise ship and the modern Las Vegas hotel, among many others, are all such means. They are of great symbolic importance, but they are also carefully designed structures that lead people not only to come, but also to behave the way the designers want them to. In the case of the Disney theme park people are forced to make at least two treks through Main Street and to distribute themselves in a certain way throughout the park. The Las Vegas hotel makes it easy for visitors to get in, but harder to get out and visit other hotels. In any case, the hotels and casinos are so vast ('hyperspace' in Baudrillard's terms) that one has little need or desire to go anywhere else. The hotels are structured to lead people to spend money and, most importantly, to lose money at the gaming tables and slot machines (it is hard to avoid the casinos, even if one wanted to). And, perhaps nothing is more structured than the modern cruise ship.

Thus, we are in the midst of the development of revolutionary new means of tourism. We will undoubtedly see the increasing spread and utilization of techniques being pioneered in places like Disney World, the MGM Grand, and the Princess Cruise Line. These developments have clearly given far more people the opportunity to do far more things; large numbers of tourists are able to do things today that would have been unimaginable not too long ago. While this constitutes greater freedom in one sense, in another sense these new means of tourism are highly constraining.

In fact, the major examples used here – Disney World, the Las Vegas hotel, and the cruise ship – have many of the characteristics of Erving Goffman's 'total institution'. Recall his definition of total institutions as places 'of residence and work where a large number of like situated individuals, cut off from the wider society for an appreciable period of time, together lead an enclosed, formally administered round of life' (Goffman 1961: xiii). A Disney theme park, a Las Vegas hotel and a cruise ship fit perfectly under this definition; they are total institutions. However, there are differences compared with Goffman's prisons or mental hospitals. Stays are much shorter and, more importantly, the control that is exerted is not nearly as blatant and brutal. It is the more post-modern, gentle, subtle, 'soft', rather than the modern, 'hard', form of control. No one accompanies the visitors to Disney World and insists that they go through Main Street at least twice, or that they disperse themselves throughout the park. They do so because the park is structured to lead them to do so. But, as Foucault showed in his work on the Panopticon, gentle and subtle forms of control can be far more troubling than the blatant and brutal forms (Foucault 1979). People do not know how they are being controlled, or even that they are being constrained. Without such knowledge, it is difficult, if not impossible, to question and rebel against the control. Not all of the new means of tourism exert such a high level of control, but the above are models that many in the tourist industry will seek to emulate in the future.

Perhaps the ultimate in a tourist site as a total institution, as well as illustrating the fact that virtually anything can be turned into such a site, is the planned 'Ossi Park' ('Ossi' was the Easterners slang term for the Cold War) in what was East Germany (the German Democratic Republic).

> One-day visitors will be required to leave by midnight, as they were in the GDR; guards will patrol the border; attempts to escape will lead to hour(s)-long imprisonment. All visitors will be required to exchange a minimum of hard currency for easternmarks.... [The whole park will be surrounded by barbed wire and a wall and will] include badly stocked stores, snooping state secret police...and scratchy toilet paper known as 'Stalin's Revenge' whose texture, according to an old GDR joke, ensured that 'every last ass is red'.
>
> (cited in Barber 1995: 133)

How do we account for the new means of tourism? Obviously, many factors are involved. Ultimately, however, they are being created and pushed by material interests. There are vast sums of money to be made by creating these new tourist 'machines' designed to ensnare tourists and wring every possible dollar from them. That these are figuratively and sometimes even literally machines makes it clear that they are quite material forms. Post-modernists must not lose sight of this in their rush to focus on the signs associated with them. People are consuming signs, but at least in part that is a result of the fact that they are being coerced into doing so by these new structures. We need to understand the intimate relationship between signs and structures in the contemporary world of tourism (and many other contexts as well).

The issue of authenticity is central to the literature on tourism (MacCannell 1989). Authenticity is also of concern to post-modernism in general, and post-tourism in particular, specifically under the heading of simulacra. A post-modernist such as Baudrillard would argue that we live in a simulated world and that is nowhere more true than in the realm of tourism (Baudrillard 1983). MacCannell (1989) argues that tourists are searching, not always successfully, for authentic experiences. The logic of post-modernism, with a society increasingly dominated by simulations, would lead us to believe, if we assume that MacCannell is correct, that tourists are increasingly doomed to failure in their search for authenticity.

We have already offered an overview of Ossi Park, the planned simulation of life in the old German Democratic Republic. Among the other examples are 'Fort Clatsop', in Astoria, Oregon, where tourists can find a 'full-scale replica of Lewis and Clark's winter camp' (Houser 1994). There is also an example used by Baudrillard, the caves of Lescaux in France. A tourist who journeys to the authentic site will find that the caves have been closed and an exact replica, a simulation, of the caves has been opened to the public. While these are extreme cases, most 'authentic' tourist destinations have been turned into at least partial simulations. Not all such efforts are successful. A notable failed attempt was Disney's plan for a Civil War theme park outside Washington D.C. 'with fake Indian villages, a replica farm, mock Civil War battles and a faux fair'. As with the caves of Lescaux, this simulation was to be constructed 'within hailing distance of real Indian trails, actual farms, a county fairground and a town that was sacked and burned by Union troops' (cited in Barber 1995: 135). Incidentally, the coming of virtual reality will mean a vast increase in the scope of such simulations. There is already, for example, a virtual tour of the tomb of the Egyptian queen Nefertari (Stille 1995). And this says nothing about the increasingly popular, totally simulated, tourist destinations such as Disney World.

But we will develop a different argument here, one anticipated in the previous section. That is, rather than seeking authenticity as MacCannell suggests, it could be argued that people raised and living in a post-modern world dominated by simulations increasingly come to want, nay to insist on, simulations when they tour. For one thing, it is increasingly difficult to differentiate between the simulated and the real; indeed Baudrillard argues that the real has disappeared, imploding into the world of simulations. In such a world, the tourist would not know an 'authentic' experience even if one could be found. For another, living on a day-to-day basis with simulations leads to a desire for them when one becomes a tourist. Accustomed to the simulated dining experience at McDonald's, the tourist is generally not apt to want to scrabble for food at the campfire, or to survive on nuts and berries picked on a walk through the woods. The latter may be 'authentic', but they are awfully difficult, uncomfortable, and unpredictable in comparison to a meal at a local fast-food restaurant or in the dining room of a hotel that is part of an international chain. Most products of a post-modern world might be willing to eat at the campfire, as long as it is a simulated one on the lawn of the hotel.

Thus, we would argue, in contrast to MacCannell, that many tourists today are in search of inauthenticity. The enormous popularity of the tourist destinations focused on in this essay – Disney World, Las Vegas, cruises, shopping malls and fast-food restaurants – all speak to the relentless search for inauthenticity. Blissfully content with our simulated lives, why should we search for anything but inauthenticity in our leisure-time activities?

Baudrillard makes this point about Disneyland, 'a perfect model of all the entangled orders of simulation' (1983: 23). Take, for example, the simulated submarine ride to which people flock in order to see simulated undersea life. Strikingly, many go there rather than the more 'genuine' aquarium (itself, however, a simulation of the sea) just down the road. How many actually go to the sea to view (say, by snorkeling) undersea life? And for those few who do, has not the sea itself been altered (simulated) to accommodate the tourist? In fact, it has, at least in one setting:

> For the snorkeling enthusiast, the place to head is Folkestone National Marine Reserve, Park and Marine Museum at Holetown [Barbados]. A taxi there costs about $12 from the ship. The government has built an area where the novice can swim and follow a series of underwater markers that picture what fish are likely to be seen.
>
> (Newbern and Fletcher 1995)

But all is not entirely lost, since the McDonald's built on Barbados was forced to close after only six months!

Certainly, there are those tourists who continue to search out authentic settings and they can, at least to some degree, still find them. However, visits to them tend to be more expensive than to inauthentic locales. More importantly, it is likely to grow increasingly difficult to find the authentic. Authentic tourist sites are likely to go the way of the caves at Lescaux. That is, they are apt to be shut down and to have exact replicas built nearby. Failing that, they are likely to be so altered by the demands of catering to large numbers of tourists that they are apt to become simulated versions of their original pristine forms.

Let us use another example from Baudrillard's work. Suppose we wanted to spend our vacation among the people of a primitive tribe, the Tasaday. This sounds like an authentic experience. However, Baudrillard regards the Tasaday, at least as it exists today, as a simulation, since the tribe has been 'frozen, cryogenized, sterilized, protected to death' (Baudrillard 1983: 15). It may at one time have been a 'real' primitive tribe, but today what exists is nothing more than a simulation of what the tribe once was. And now we are beginning to see simulations of simulations. For example, the new Sega theme park in London will offer simulated (via virtual reality) rides of an already simulated ride in, say, Disney World (May 1995). We move ever more deeply in Baudrillardian 'hyperreality'. Even if we accepted the idea that people know the difference between a simulacra and the authentic, and we assume that at least some people set out in search of the authentic, Baudrillard would argue that their efforts will be thwarted by the fact that these are all simulacra.

This section has been devoted to post-modern ideas that have previously been applied to tourism. We close with the mention of a concept, 'ecstasy', that as far as we can tell has yet to be applied to tourism. By ecstasy, Baudrillard means unconditional metamorphosis, escalation for escalation's sake, a continuing process of spinning off out of control until all senses are lost (Baudrillard 1990). Ultimately, this out-of-control system reveals its emptiness and meaninglessness; it 'shines forth in its pure and empty form' (Baudrillard 1990: 9).

It could be argued that tourism is becoming such an ecstatic form. Given the implosion discussed above, the de-differentiation that is affecting tourism in many different ways (Urry 1994a), anything and everything is coming to be defined as tourism. This is well illustrated by bus tours to shopping centres and even better by the proposed Ossi Park in Germany. With everything defined as tourism, it becomes a meaningless form. Yet, it is escalating dramatically. Baudrillard uses fashion to illustrate the ecstasy of the (post-)modern world, but increasingly tourism is just as good an illustration. It is increasingly obese and cancerous, that is, it is increasingly hypertelic. There is no end to tourism other than limitless increase. There is no end for the tourist than to visit as many sites as possible, if only on the Internet. This is obviously not intended as an exhaustive application of the idea of ecstasy, but to illustrate that there are many more conceptual resources within post-modern social theory that the student of tourism might find useful.

CONCLUSION

There are no grand conclusions to be made here. Indeed, if the post-modern perspective has done nothing else, it has alerted us to the dangers, even the terrorism, associated with grand narratives offering grand conclusions about the past, present and future. What we can say is that social theory, in its modern and post-modern forms, has much to offer the analysts of the changing world of tourism. There is no 'truth' to be uncovered about the contemporary world of tourism. Both the McDisneyized tourist and the post-tourist can be said to exist, but neither thesis gets at the truth of tourism. What there is are concepts that allow us to understand things about tourism that we might not have understood before. That is a modest conclusion, but as post-modernists have shown, social theorists have good reason to be modest about their conclusions about tourism, or anything else for that matter.

Part II

CONTEXTS

6

THE CULTURE OF TOURISM

Jennifer Craik

INTRODUCTION

Since the mid-1980s, another phase of tourism has emerged, namely, one which highlights the cultural component of tourist experiences. This focus has entailed rethinking the nature both of tourism and of its impacts. Specifically, the culture of tourism includes: maximising the culture of tourism products, re-defining tourist experiences, addressing the cultural impacts of tourism, and dealing with the changing culture of the industry itself. A niche form of tourism that emphasises the cultural dimension of tourism above all is cultural tourism (where cultural sites, events attractions, and/or experiences are marketed as primary tourist experiences); the creation of purpose-built cultural attractions for tourists; and the modification of, or access to, everyday leisure attractions for tourists (Britton 1991: 464). Thus the culture of tourism encompasses a range of phenomena from targeted tourism based on culture to the unintended cultural components of mass tourism. The question posed by this chapter is: Has culture become merely a convenient marketing ploy or has a fundamental change to the nature of tourism occurred? In other words, is the culture of tourism a fad or a new social form?

Many of the changes occurring in the culture of tourism have been explained in terms of notions of post-modernism, post-Fordism, flexible accumulation and consumerism. Tourism, it is argued, fits in with trends in economic development towards service-based, consumer-oriented industries associated with the production of symbolic or cultural capital rather than material goods. The role of culture in this process is multi-faceted: culture is simultaneously a resource, a product, an experience and an outcome. This chapter explores the cultural transformation of tourism in terms of four key aspects: the growth of cultural tourism; the manufacture of tourism for tourists; the feminisation of the tourist gaze; and the implications of tourism trends for the management of culture.

The central argument of the chapter is that the culture of tourism has been modified in response to a range of contradictory developments occurring in the field of culture. These include the commercialisation of culture and cultural products; the restructuring of cultural production into the cultural industries; greater government investment in culture accompanied by increasing demands for accountability and demonstrations of value for money; increasing cultural consumption by a wider range of people; and expanding opportunities for training in cultural production.

These trends have – to some degree – converged in the development of cultural tourism, but this convergence is more a convenience than a genuine conversion to the benefits of culture and cultural capital. Yet, the unevenness of those respective developments has been elided in the enthusiasm for the potential benefits of what has been regarded as a more sustainable, benign and community-generated form of tourism. This chapter argues that the culture of tourism has not fundamentally changed, and that the emphasis on culture is short-term. Moreover, even niche developments like cultural tourism will incur significant disbenefits and will undermine rather than enhance the recent commitment to cultural development.

THE GROWTH OF CULTURAL TOURISM

Has tourism come full circle?

During the past decade, types of tourism have diversified as the industry matured and tourists became more demanding. Examples of new 'products', as the marketers like to call them, include special interest tourism, adventure tourism, ecotourism and cultural tourism. Generally, a trend towards more engaged or experiential forms of tourist experience has been a feature of this diversification. Tourism is increasingly evaluated in terms of being rewarding, enriching, adventuresome, and/or a learning experience (Zeppel and Hall 1992). In other words, the cultural component of a tourism experience has become a key feature in its own right.

Some commentators argue that tourism has become the indicative industry of post-modern lifestyles and post-capitalist economies (Zukin 1990; Britton 1991), thus extending the argument that tourism has replaced religion as the source and quest for meaning (Turner and Ash 1976; Schudson 1979). Tourists seek transcendence from everyday life through engagement with Otherness or escape from the familiar: tourism offers a trance-like suspension from the everyday. Yet although the tourist is an outsider, s/he is not completely estranged: 'the tourist *looks* as a stranger but lives somewhere else' (Schudson 1979: 1251; Chapter 2 above).

Tourists revel in the otherness of destinations, peoples and activities because they offer the illusion or fantasy of otherness, of difference and counterpoint to the everyday. At the same time the advantages, comforts and benefits of home are reinforced through the exposure to difference. This is a different argument from that which proposes that tourism is a quest for authenticity, or the search for deep and meaningful cross-cultural communication, self-discovery, origins, cultural forms 'untainted' by 'civilisation', and so on. Rather, it is an ego-centric pursuit, involving a fascination with self-indulgence and self-delusion through simulacra: approximations and analogues of 'the real'.

Cohen (1989) has argued that tourism involves 'communicative staging', or persuading tourists that they are having an 'authentic' experience. Moreover, the components of the experience change over time as the tourist resource, host communities, and preferences of tourists change. Hence, tourism offers 'emergent authenticities' which are dynamic and negotiable, rather than a fixed notion of the experience on offer (Cohen 1988; Dearden and Harron 1994: 89, 95). In the case of trekking in Northern Thailand, the original kernel of the experience – intercultural contact with the hill tribes – became secondary to general recreational activities available on the trek, such as rafting, interacting with the guides, the scenery, and interactions with other trekkers (Dearden and Harron 1992). Undertaking a trek did change attitudes: pre- and post-trek interviews showed that initial concerns about the erosion of trails, garbage, and the ambivalent impacts of tourism, shifted to more prosaic concerns about the lack of toilet facilities and environmental degradation (Dearden and Harron 1994: 96–7). There was a shift from romantic to pragmatic issues.

On the other hand, tourists continue to indulge in the myth of the Other offered by tourism – and signalled in terms such as primitive, native, exotic and different. This is most apparent where the hosts are changed by contact with Western cultures and, for example, exchange traditional dress for Western clothes, a transformation which tourists dislike (see Silver 1993: 310; Dearden and Harron 1994: 88). In other words, there is a good deal of self-delusion involved in the pursuit of tourist pleasure. Although tourists think that they want authenticity, most want some degree of negotiated experiences which provide a tourist 'bubble' (a safe, controlled environment) out of which they can selectively step to 'sample' predictable forms of experiences.

An extreme form of the tourist bubble can be found at totally artificial theme parks which have enjoyed phenomenal success (see Chapter 5). These deliberately created themed spaces (such as Disneyland, Spaceport USA, Sea World, MGM Studios, Many Worlds on Sentosa Island, Singapore, Miccosukee Indian Village in Florida, Jorvik Viking Centre in York, Head-Smashed-In Buffalo Jump Interpretive Centre in Alberta, Aussie World in Queensland, Sovereign Hill gold mining settlement in Victoria, Australia and so on) offer a controlled and controllable environment with predictable kinds of diversity of themed attractions, and above all are safe (Fodness and Milner 1992; Boniface and Fowler 1993; Cohen 1995: 16, 23; Blundell 1996). Even though visitors know that they are not 'real' in any sense, the guaranteed bubble ensures and perhaps promotes enjoyment.

The success of theme parks depends on their ability to tap into a theme that has wide appeal. Although the translation of Disneyland to France has not been a success, the equally unlikely Popeye theme park in Malta has become popular. Similarly, Dreamworld, Sea World and Movie World on Queensland's Gold Coast have been hugely popular, but Koala Land (located directly opposite Dreamworld) has failed and been subdivided into a housing estate. Predicting fickle tourist taste is a challenge.

Interestingly, these artificial theme parks have been far more successful than most preserved 'themed' sites. Even the best require considerable infrastructure to explain them and make them work as tourist attractions – for example, the interpretive centres constructed at points along Hadrian's Wall in England; signage, guides and the interpretive centre at Nederlands Openluchtmuseum in Arnhem; and nature, heritage and city site trails which have developed at many sites.

Moreover, compare the product on offer at theme parks with that offered by local history museums: certainly the former recreates impressions of the real while the latter preserves the authentic, but often the latter are immensely disappointing – under-resourced, lacking appeal or diversity, having poor facilities, staffed by enthusiastic but unprofessional volunteers, and so on. As a general rule, such museums are disappointing – and often meaningless – to the tourist. They are often more relevant for local consumption to reinforce a sense of local identity and history (see Chapter 8 on a Gaelic heritage centre).

A study of the success of marketing Beatrix Potter as a tourist industry in the Lake District in the UK demonstrates the manufacture of simulacra (or 'as if' experience) as the basis of the contemporary tourist experience (see Squire 1994; Cohen 1995: 22). The Lake District has long been a holiday and tourist destination with visitors attracted by the scenery, nature-based activities (walking and water-based) and the 'olde worlde' character of the villages in the area (see Chapter 9 for studies of photography and tourism). Over the past decade, the attractiveness of the area as a tourist destination has been boosted by the emergence of niche tourism based on the success of the fictional character, Peter Rabbit. Thus, nature tourism has been complemented – if not supplanted – by what one might term cultural tourism.

Peter Rabbit's creator, author Beatrix Potter (1866–1943), lived at Hill Top Farm in the village of Near Sawrey; the farm and the village provided the inspiration for her still-popular stories. Perhaps less well known was the fact that Potter amassed considerable land holdings in the area which were, on her death, left to the National Trust, which still manages the properties and the farm. While this latter fact is presented as evidence of Potter as a philanthropist and proto-environmentalist, the bequest also had a more pragmatic function of avoiding the payment of death duties. Touristic accounts of Potter, however, emphasise the more romantic image of the author as benefactor.

The Beatrix Potter tourist experience is centred on Hill Top Farm and its environs, and is packaged in terms of the preservation of her source of literary inspiration in a house that has been maintained as she left it. But the farm and its environs have also been packaged in more general ways as an example of English domestic and natural heritage, while the surrounding villages, scenery and landscape offer a glimpse of a rural lifestyle lost in many other places. Beatrix Potter tourism has also incorporated a range of other attractions: self-guided walks, an art gallery, a multi-dimensional exhibition, and 'Potter inspired excursions and theme holidays' (Squire 1994: 108).

The diversity of the Potter industry has added to, rather than detracted from, the success of this niche form of tourism. As Squire's interviews with visitors showed, the Potter attractions – both authentic and constructed – were simply the backdrop or catalyst for the pleasures, connections and projections that individual tourists derived from their visit. For example, most of the attractions and activities appealed to adult preferences and drew on memories of childhood rather than engaging contemporary children in the story-telling of Potter. This takes up the theme of reminiscence discussed in Chapter 1.

Visitors compared the Beatrix Potter tableaux with their own experiences of childhood and nostalgic images of simple living in a rural setting. In other words, 'both the books and the touristic experience were a means for individuals to identify a lost and hence progressively idealised rural past' (Squire 1994: 111). Rather than seeking more knowledge about Potter, or more engagement with her writings, 'Potter was frequently a *starting* point for other kinds of introspection', especially those associated with nostalgia for Old England, English country life, and preserved heritage.

Ironically, however, success may bring its own downfall. As the Potter industry expands, it encroaches on the apparent authenticity and quaintness of the attractions and experiences of the Lakes District by bringing parking problems, traffic congestion, overcrowding and a lack of facilities. Not only do these affect visitors; resentment of visitors by the locals has become vocal and public. Pubs in local towns feature signs warning: 'Stag parties and tourists not welcome', despite the proliferation of Potter merchandising and other souvenir businesses with which they are cheek by jowl. Ambivalence has also been recorded in towns in the nearby North Pennines where the hyped-up promotion of the touted benefits of tourism are rarely realised or evident to locals (Prentice 1993).

The weather also creates problems: on fine days, the countryside is quaint and suitable for aimless touring and walking; on wet days, driving is difficult and dangerous. A major beneficiary of bad weather is the Peter Rabbit multi-dimensional exhibition which features animated recreations of scenes from the books and a large Potter-inspired souvenir shop. On wet days, the exhibition attracts four times the usual number of visitors (pers. comm.). Normally it is mainly the preserve of Japanese tourists on scheduled tour bus visits. Incidentally, the Peter Rabbit phenomenon defies theories of authenticity and nostalgia in that the Japanese have taken to Peter Rabbit with enormous enthusiasm due not to a shared cultural heritage (as for North Americans and Canadians) but to 'widespread fascination for rural England' (Squire 1994: 112) and a penchant for fluffy animals and toys (such as their apparent obsession with koalas, kangaroos and frilled-neck lizards in Australia; see also Graburn 1995: 64–5).

This example shows how a 'cultural' phenomenon such as a literary figure and her/his products can become the linchpin of a tourist industry, in this case, complementing and revitalising an older nature-based form of tourism. The 'authentic' cultural linchpin becomes a pawn in a game of producing, packaging and consuming a range of sites and activities under that mantle, at the same time providing a rationale and unity to diverse attractions while also encouraging the proliferation of a range of attractions – first to attract tourists and then to keep them occupied.

But while the cultural phenomenon is the excuse for the industry, and the prompt for the development of a range of staged performances (MacCannell 1973; Britton 1991: 455), visitors themselves generate a myriad of cultural meanings about the attractions and activities as the destination gains popularity. Tourists also require – and impact management dictates – more sophisticated and diverse support attractions, services and facilities. Consequently, Squire suggests that more attention should also be paid to the diverse role of producers of cultural tourism, 'how tourism meanings and values change over time ... and how such changes may be expressed and reflected in the built environment' (Squire 1994: 117).

The case of Lancaster County in Pennsylvania provides a contrasting example. This is also a mature tourist destination where 'the distinctive Amish community [is] the principal tourist attraction in a diversified tourist base' (Hovinen 1995: 381). For over a decade, private sector marketing has attracted an increasing number of visitors and transformed numerous aspects of Amish heritage into a range of tourist experiences:

> One can arrange a visit with an Amish family, see windmills and waterwheels, talk with Amish children at a roadside stand, buy craft items from an Amish

woman, visit an Amish bookstore, see traditional multiple-generation farm-houses as well as modern-style Amish houses, and even view Amish-occupied parts of the country where few tourists intrude and agriculture remains the predominant occupation.

(Hovinen 1995: 383)

These experiences, 'from the garish to the offensive, through the more or less carefully staged, to the unstaged and authentic', offer tourists a variety of activities but, according to Hovinen, pose a threat to the maintenance of Amish heritage. Without appropriate public sector involvement and community incorporation, he argues that Lancaster County tourism may have sown the seeds of its own destruction and, more critically, of its distinctive character (see Chapter 8 below).

In sum, in contrast to what is commonly assumed, the cultural experiences offered by tourism are consumed in terms of prior knowledge, expectations, fantasies and mythologies *generated in the tourist's origin culture* rather than *by the cultural offerings of the destination*. Moreover, while cultural tourism and cultural components of tourism may revitalise an existing tourism industry and cultural production, such developments can also threaten the culture of the destination and longer term cultural integrity (see Craik 1995a). In this sense, tourism has come full circle, revitalising the educative and enlightenment role of early tourism as a training – or finishing school – for travellers.

The Grand Tour revisited?

As argued above, tourism is increasingly packaged in terms of cultural values and experiences, usually alongside notions of escape, hedonism and exploration. The culture of tourism is changing as cultural dimensions are incorporated into its very terms. The degree to which culture is part of tourism and, conversely, to which tourism is a source of cultural knowledge, trainings and experiences (what Bourdieu calls the acquisition of cultural capital) is the issue which frames this section.

The term 'cultural tourism' has become an umbrella term both to identify specially organised culture-based tourism experiences and to provide unity and add depth to a diverse range of culturally-related aspects of tourism more generally. The former concept can be conveniently divided into cultural tourism as 'experiential tourism based on being involved in and stimulated by the performing arts, visual arts and festivals'; and heritage tourism which includes 'visiting preferred landscapes, historic sites, buildings or monuments' and seeking 'an encounter with nature or feeling part of the history of a place' (Hall and Zeppel 1990: 87). The latter concept can include a multitude of special interest tourist preferences: 'anthropology, antiques, archaeology, art, architecture, biblical history, castles, cave art, crafts, festivals, gardens, historic houses, history, literature, military events, museums, music, dance, opera, painting, pilgrimages, pottery, mythology, religion, spirituality, and textile arts' (Hall and Zeppel 1990: 87).

This cultural mantle provides a way to reconsider the motivations of tourists, the range of tourist experiences, and the ways in which destinations can be packaged. It seems to have developed as a response to a number of conditions: greater sophistication and travel experience among tourists; international competitiveness between broadly similar destinations; the 'exhaustion' or declining popularity of previous or traditional tourist attractions; international growth and diversification of markets and sites; globalisation of culture and international dissemination of cultural knowledge and development of international patterns of cultural taste; and the recent emphasis on new approaches to cultural development internationally.

These new approaches to tourism revisit some of the features of Grand Tour tourism which, during the sixteenth and seventeenth centuries, saw groups of England's social elite travel to demarcated cultural sites in Europe to witness classical antiquities and the legacy of Renaissance culture (see Towner 1985). The original aim of the Grand Tour was 'to prepare young gentlemen for diplomatic careers, for which...depth of acquaintance [with European people and sites] was a prerequisite' (Hibbert 1969; Harkin 1995: 655). Two stages have been identified: first, the age of reading and speaking, when tourists actively engaged with guides, locals, and each other; followed by the age of observation, in which people learned by looking or visually taking in the vistas and splendour of continental culture (Adler 1989; and see Chapter 9 below). Travel:

> served as a means to facilitate national and international relations by making contacts, learning foreign languages, and engaging in debate with others. During this period, travel was dominated by the aristocracy rather than the wide cross-section who had undertaken pilgrimages....Gradually...the eye became as important as the ear as the source of knowledge and as the object of social trainings. Knowledge was acquired through seeing, verifying and ordering the world. Observation, witness and hearsay were techniques of the eye and became the new form of travel – sightseeing.
>
> (Craik 1991: 27–8)

With the growth of scientific approaches to knowledge, recording and under-standing, travellers became increasingly preoccupied with gaining historical insights, acquiring aesthetic tastes, displaying connoisseurship, and generally demonstrating visionary ways of looking. These pleasures and educational mandates were strictly for men. As Richter has noted, travel was 'seen as compromising the reputation of young women' (1995: 73). The nineteenth-century expansion of the tourist trade and non-elite groups of tourists saw a generalisation of these preoccupations into more organised, predictable and marketable forms. Women's involvement in European tours began with the organised tours of Thomas Cook and the like which provided a respectable context for 'well-bred ladies' to travel. Gradually the educational and cultivating aspects of tourism were diluted in more prosaic quests for exploration, escape and pleasure. The twentieth-century popularity of sun and sea tourism epitomised this new tendency.

This short account suggests that the Grand Tour was a highly developed and purposeful act of educational travel by an elite social group organised around the quest for knowledge, culture and cross-cultural intermingling. Often, such lofty motivations were not fully realised and contemporary accounts record less serious motivations and indecorous behaviour on the part of some of these travellers. Nonetheless, a broad comparison between the self-improving aim of the Grand Tour and the educational experiential motivations of at least some forms of cultural tourism are undoubtedly valid. For example, as with the Grand Tour travellers, evidence suggests that the truly self-improving cultural tourist is in the minority, emanating from relatively privileged social classes (Hughes 1987; Bywater 1993). The majority of tourists are primarily interested in 'historic monuments and sites, followed by museums and then by art and music' (Bywater 1993: 32). In other words, there is a hierarchy of preferences for different types of cultural tourism attractions that reflect majority cultural tastes. These do not conform to the hierarchy of cultural forms proposed by the gatekeepers of culture. In fact, it is the reverse.

Such a pattern of preferences has implications for developing a profile of the typical cultural tourist. From her study of cultural tourism in Europe, Bywater, for example, has identified three types of cultural tourist. The genuine cultural tourist (the 'culturally motivated' tourist) who chooses a holiday because of its cultural opportunities constitutes only 5 per cent of the market (Bywater 1993: 42); a larger minority (perhaps a third) of tourists are 'culturally inspired' to make a once-in-a-lifetime visit to a special site or attraction; while up to two-thirds of all tourists ('culturally attracted' tourists) would like some cultural attractions at destinations they choose for other reasons.

Another attempt to characterise cultural tourists has been proposed by Silberberg (1995: 362–3). He distinguishes four degrees of consumer motivation for cultural tourism which he breaks down by resident and tourist status: only 5 per cent of residents and 15 per cent of tourists are greatly motivated (specifically attracted) by cultural tourism; 15 per cent of residents and 30 per cent of tourists are partly motivated (prompted by cultural and other reasons); 20 per cent of residents and 20 per cent of tourists have adjunct motivations (may include cultural activities at a destination chosen for other reasons); and 20 per cent of residents and 20 per cent of tourists are accidentally motivated (any cultural visits are an unplanned, contingent activity). The remaining 40 per cent of residents and 15 per cent of tourists are not interested in cultural tourism 'under any circumstances'.

These figures suggest that only a minority of tourists are truly cultural tourists (of the Grand Tour type) while a significant number are 'culture-proof'. Of those in the middle, many tourists may be motivated to take advantage of cultural attractions once other primary motivations to travel have been met. Snaring the cultural tourist and packaging cultural resources for mainstream tourists is not as easy as is often assumed. Advocates of cultural tourism too often hope to attract the 'ideal' cultural tourist who is highly motivated to consume culture and possesses a high level of cultural capital; yet most cultural tourism consumers are adjunct, accidental or reluctant visitors.

The consequence is that cultural tourism (or the cultural component of tourism) is not as lofty or self-improving as its advocates would have us believe. Nonetheless, shifting preferences to include a cultural component of a visit indicate a restructuring of the orientations and motivations of an increasing number of tourists. But while much of the marketing strategy has been primarily geared towards the greatly motivated group, and is driven by the hope to expand this group through attractive activities and packages, these profiles suggest that the majority of visitors (both resident and tourist) are relatively reluctant cultural consumers for whom culture takes second or third place to other motivations and activities.

As Silberberg has argued, the 1990s tourist has different priorities from the 1980s counterpart (1995: 364). Whereas spending money (88 per cent), seeing natural beauty (60 per cent), understanding culture (48 per cent), and visiting a new place (44 per cent) topped the list of preferences of American travellers in the 1980s, understanding culture (88 per cent), seeing natural beauty (73 per cent), gaining a new perspective on life (72 per cent), and visiting a new place (57 per cent) were the 1990s priorities. Accordingly, opportunities for promoting tourism around cultural attractions has expanded enormously, and partnerships between the unlikely bedfellows of tourism operators and cultural producers have been encouraged (see Hughes 1989; Moulin 1990; Zukin 1990; Britton 1991; Zeppel and Hall 1991, 1992; Boniface and Fowler 1993; Bywater 1993; Silberberg 1995; and Chapter 8 below).

As to whether the recent growth of cultural tourism and cultural attractions as tourist attractions constitute a return to the Grand Tour type of tourism, the evidence is thin. Visitor profiles suggest that cultural tourists are a distinct minority despite increased opportunities to include cultural components in tourism packages. They are drawn from the genre of 'chic travellers' who are wealthy, '*avant garde*, culturally sensitive, and ecologically responsible' (Silver 1993: 314–15). Cultural attractions that appeal to a wide cross-section (exemplified by Disney-type attractions or simulacra exhibitions, but including accessible cultural forms such as rock musicals and 'tourist' art and craft), are more likely to be longer term successes than tasteful packaging of 'elite' cultural forms (such as opera or theatre; see Gauntlett 1993). Even so, some opera has been successfully marketed – such as the annual Glyndebourne opera festival in England; the summer season of La Scala opera house in Milan; and the Opera in the Outback touring programme in South Australia. Generally, however, the appeal of culture to tourists takes second place to other motivations, experiences and appeals.

Defining the culture of tourism

This chapter has developed the theme that the culture of tourism has been influenced or modified by the growth of cultural tourism with the intention of providing new opportunities to develop attractions and experiences, and to attract new groups of tourists. The following definition of cultural tourism reflects that shift:

> [Cultural tourism consists of] customised excursions into other cultures and places to learn about their people, lifestyle, heritage and arts in an informed way that genuinely represents those cultures and their historical contexts.
>
> (Craik 1995b: 6)

This definition embodies an educational and experiential component as well as a romanticised idea of culture and cultural intercommunication. It is also consistent with expanded ideas about leisure activities and cultural consumption. Indeed, tourism has somewhat *converged* with leisure and cultural consumption to the point where sites and activities are shared (or contested between different user groups). Very often, sites justified as tourist attractions (such as open air cultural configurations and cultural centres, e.g. London's Southbank, New York's Madison Square Gardens and the Sydney Opera House) attract higher local use (frequently by non-paying users) while primarily local facilities (shopping complexes, cultural centres, restaurants) attract a tourist clientele (e.g. the Edmonton Mall, Sydney's Darling Harbour, Vancouver's Gas Town, Chinatowns in many cities; Getz *et al.* 1994; Finn and Erdem 1995).

The implications of such changes are complex. The cultures of tourism and leisure become intertwined sometimes in complementary ways (e.g. stimulating the quantity and quality of local craft production) but sometimes in contradictory ways (e.g. the accompanying provision of sexual services). Thus, while culturally-sensitive tourism is frequently promoted as sustainable and compatible with local values and habits, there is growing evidence that cultural destinations may become 'victims of their own success' (Bywater 1993: 31). Visitor management strategies such as daily quotas, steep entry fees and time/activity restrictions, are examples of techniques employed to satisfy the desire of visitors to see and experience sites while limiting their impacts on locals and on the sites themselves (Hall and McArthur 1993).

Two other strategies have also been adopted: *moulding culture for tourism and tourists*, and *moulding tourism and tourists for culture*. The former entails developing specialist products such as tourist arts by, for example, reorienting the displays, services and products of museums and art galleries; or mounting tourist-oriented festivals, such as a Shakespeare festival, film festival, or indigenous cultural festival (see Cohen 1992, 1993). In contrast, the latter entails modifying tourist attractions and potential destinations to incorporate or highlight cultural features.

The growth of heritage tourism in Britain is a good example of injecting a tourism focus to existing sites, activities and attractions (Millar 1989, and Chapters 1 and 8 in this book). All kinds of sites with an historical association (be that a person, event, or activity) can be re-worked through – at a minimum – commemorative plaques and informative materials; at a maximum, the 'heritage' is celebrated in a dedicated museum or display; and most commonly, the theme is complemented in the focus of pub or tea-room decor, souvenirs and tourist mechanising. The availability of merchandising in the form of souvenirs is particularly important since such purchases 'validate the acquisition of learning and cultural experiences' (Zeppel and Hall 1991: 32; Harkin 1995: 657–8). Most important is the ability to translate the site, historical figure, remembered activity, or experience into physical, durable and portable mementos which can serve as tangible reminders of the visit, through T Shirts, key rings, fridge magnets, posters, figurines, reproductions or art/ craftwork.

One particular challenge for heritage sites is to maintain distinctiveness while developing a commercially viable enterprise. Millar cites the example of three attractions which all offered steam roundabouts as an incentive activity, thereby running the risk of losing their specific attractiveness for visitors; similarly, the economies of scale that have prompted the National Trust to make commissioned products available nationally 'detract from the visitors' experience of the special qualities of a particular heritage site' (Millar 1989: 11–12).

Across the board, it is possible to trace the emergence of specific genres of tourist art. Cohen's analysis has entailed distinguishing specific types and relating them to types of commercialisation (1992: 13, 1993: 3). Tourist art, he argues, is a 'fuzzy field' incorporating elements of ethnological arts, commercial arts, souvenirs and fine art. These various types and hybrid forms are the object of four distinct types of commercialisation: complementary commercialisation or the production of art/craft that remains popular with locals; substitutive commercialisation, where a declining craft is spontaneously reoriented to a tourist market; encroaching commercialisation, where external forces sponsor the reorientation of a still-viable craft for tourism; and rehabilitative commercialisation, or the sponsored reorientation of a declining craft for an external market.

This typology suggests that combining culture and tourism is a complex and strategic activity which involves reconciling local cultural producers to niche marketing possibilities and modifying cultural production accordingly. Cohen argues that tourist art is dynamic and adaptive: this may involve modifying motifs and designs to better suit tourists' tastes or expectations, standardising products, simplifying detailed art work, developing miniature or gigantic versions of objects, replacing traditional materials with industrial ones, and turning functional objects into decorative ones. Klemm (1989) has argued that the consequence is that traditional arts (such as Shakespeare and classical music) are bolstered at the expense of new artists and performers and new and innovative arts forms (including youth culture). Thus the culture of the tourist can have a significant influence in modifying local cultural production.

Cohen has also distinguished tourist art in terms of its sources: local or ethnic; novel or synthetic; and national or international genres (1992: 6). Local and ethnic art ranges from functional traditional art to commercial traditional art; novel or synthetic art ranges from reintegrated art to souvenir novelties; and national and international genres range from popular arts to assimilated fine arts. Cohen argues that two contradictory developments in tourist art can be detected:

> On the one hand, popular souvenirs, as they become standardised, tend to be industrially produced by people often unrelated to their original produ-cers...though touristic, they are thus neither *ethnic* nor *art* any more, even if they have preserved their character as (external) ethnic markers. On the other hand, some assimilated ethnic fine artists tend eventually to lose the ethnic label as they integrate into a national art world, and their art thereby ceases to be an ethnic marker.
>
> (Cohen 1992: 6)

Plastic tikis, totem poles, cuckoo clocks, Dutch clogs and boomerangs are examples of the former, while Aboriginal or Inuit art, 'Persian' carpets, Benin sculptures, soapstone carvings and Aztec jewellery are examples of the latter development. Cohen's analysis demonstrates that cultural production, distribution and consumption involve a dynamic set of processes that defy any simple translation into tourism product. Cultural products for tourism have significant ramifications for cultural producers, for commercialisation and marketing practices, consumers and tourists, and on tourism itself (for an overview, see Cohen 1992: 9–24). Many analysts have concluded that, although cultural tourism has often been seized upon as offering a bonanza for indigenous, ethnic and cultural producer groups, the actual benefits of entering cultural tourism are very mixed, including the vexed issue of copyright (see Blundell 1993; Anderson 1996). Equally, the diverse forms of commercialisation of tourist art have different implications for practices of cultural production in destination communities, and are further complicated by systems of distribution and marketing which tend to favour external operators at the expense of locals.

Despite the growth of cultural tourism, there is still scant information about the consumers of tourist art especially that accounts for historical, cultural and demographic differences among those visitors. One detailed study shows that, while authenticity and strangeness are important factors in the motivations of tourists to buy tourist art, the shopping experience, personal meanings, and relationship with the intended recipient are equally important. Thus, the perceptions of available tourist art and purchasing decisions were made on the basis of a range of factors emanating from the tourist's destination culture, knowledges, intentions, and outcomes: 'tourism experiences and authentic crafts hold the potential for creating uniqueness and feelings of specialness in what may otherwise be a life impoverished of meaning' (Littrell *et al*.1993: 211). In other words, the culture of tourism and tourism culture relate more to the original culture of tourists than that of the destination (the culture of the producers).

THE MANUFACTURE OF TOURISM FOR TOURISTS

Sights and sites

While sights/sites have been the mainstay of tourism, the combined pressures of visitation rates and heightened expectations of visitors have resulted in more elaborate forms of preservation and presentation. Many localities are attracted to develop tourism because they believe that simply having an attraction is sufficient to attract tourists; it is assumed that tourists will flock there irrespective of marketing (the lack of) and infrastructure development. As they discover to their surprise and cost, tourism is a demanding industry, in terms of the cost of infrastructure, maintenance and the need to regularly upgrade facilities and tourist packages.

For example, a plan to develop tourism opportunities in towns in far western Queensland found considerable naivety about what was needed to develop a tourism industry. There was a lack of suitable infrastructure and there was considerable competition and jealousy between different towns (Arts Queensland 1995). It was found that tour buses would only stop in a town with at least six attractions and facilities that catered for diverse tourist needs – namely, one or more attractions (such as museums, galleries, historic sites, lookouts, or parks), adequate eating and drinking facilities, accessible and well maintained toilet facilities, souvenir and shopping outlets, and choice of accommodation. As well as providing this diversity of facilities, a town had to upgrade the standard of presentation of its key attractions and services. In terms of selecting suitable attractions to develop, it was often difficult to decide which town should be earmarked for development as, say, a 'typical' outback town, a sheepshearing town or a mining town. Thus, the micro-politics within and between communities became a significant factor in proposing appropriate forms and levels of tourist development.

Moreover, tourist development depends on a high level of cooperation between private and public agencies – underpinned by community goodwill – in order to coordinate such facilities and promotional activity associated with a tourism push. The role of different levels of government is crucial in facilitating development: local government is characteristically dominated by developer interests; regional government by parochial boosterism and regional economic development; while national government can afford to take a broader view and a strategic approach (though this may not trickle down effectively to the level of tourist sites).

Such trends and tensions can be observed internationally, as many (perhaps too many) destinations have looked to tourism to revive flagging economic fortunes and secure political incumbency (see Ashworth and Tunbridge 1990; Urry 1990; Boniface and Fowler 1993; Hall and McArthur 1993). According to Britton, there are three ways by which this can be done: transforming 'existing cultural attractions or "curiosities" ' into tourism products (historic sights or cultural spectacles); creating attractions (such as resorts or theme parks); and injecting a tourist component into existing commercial leisure ventures (such as shopping centres, historic town centres; Britton 1991: 464). Crucial to success is the ability to package and promote the integrated tourism product in a way that is sufficiently attractive to potential visitors, usually not just by promoting a single tourist experience but through a range of potential experiences for different fractions of the market. This is less a quest for authenticity than the presentation of a 'vehicle for experiences which are to be collected, consumed and compared' (Britton 1991: 465). Both Britton and Zukin (1990) have called this the development of symbolic transactions as the basis of capital accumulation.

The proliferation of culture-based services and products is part of the shift towards 'the emerging sociospatial organisation of consumption (pivoting around a production nexus of entertainment industries, producer services, aesthetic production, and commercial property) which is sustaining a rapidly expanding service economy that generates consumption-biased (rather than demand-led) development' (Britton 1991: 469). Consumption-based cultural industries are especially attractive because they are deemed to be 'somewhat immune, or countercyclical, to the usual property and business cycles' (Britton 1991: 470).

Britton argues that there are four main forms of cultural capital: built environments (amusement and theme parks; cultural centres, casinos, shopping centres); spectacles (events and festivals); property markets (internationalisation of real-estate speculation and development); and festival markets (dock redevelopments; tourist-oriented malls and entertainment centres; Britton 1991: 470–3). Not only do these forms share a trend towards large-scale developments, multiple facilities and attractions, and complex management processes, they entail a convergence or blurring between tourist and everyday leisure activities. Moreover, the spaces and places in which consumption occurs are as important as the products and services consumed. This theme of 'spatial embeddedness' is developed by Zukin (1990). Consumption occurs within, and is regulated by, purpose-built spaces for consumption characterised by the provision of consumption-related services, visual consumption, and cultural products. Circuits of cultural capital operate within broader financial parameters.

In other words, cultural capital is not just of symbolic importance; it 'plays a *real*, i.e. material, role in moving financial capital through both economic and cultural circuits. It is integrally involved in real investment and production. It creates real economic value' (Zukin 1990: 53). In addition, it influences trends in physical infrastructure, as well as shaping new demands for labour. Thus, the continued growth of the tourism industry must be placed in the context of new forms of consumer development and in particular the convergence between patterns of consumption, leisure and tourism.

Sites and sights are increasingly used – if not planned – for mixed purposes and diverse groups of users. While this is attractive from a 'democratic' and economic point of view, it often entails vexed management decisions and impact mitigation practices. There is also a risk of creating a diffuse image of a site that fails to capture the interest of intended target groups. For sites such as cultural centres, galleries and museums, the trend creates mixed pressures which make it difficult to determine the appropriate product mix and marketing strategy. In the case of museums, for example, it has been argued that the shifting focus has eroded amounts spent on conservation to the point where the integrity of collections has been threatened. In other words, short-term marketing strategies (creating a 'tourist' appeal) may have the effect of undermining long-term policies and the value of collections.

Experiential tourism and cultural improvement

As tourism becomes merged with cultural development, tourist experiences embody aspects of self-improvement, education, discovery and individualism (see Chapter 1). These cannot, however, be reduced purely to forms of 'cultural' improvement. As Silberberg (1995: 364) has stressed, tourists usually want more than just culturally-related experiences, and hence tourism packages must integrate cultural products and activities with other kinds of products and experiences. Thus, a weekend travel and accommodation package might include a set of admission tickets to a variety of cultural and non-cultural activities (theme park, museum, theatre, gallery, heritage site or musical). This strategy is more successful than just a cultural attraction 'passport' or similar scheme.

Nevertheless, there is an interesting relationship between 'true' cultural tourists and 'casual' cultural tourists: while the former tend to be better educated, earn more and possess more cultural capital (Hall and Zeppel 1990: 89–91), they seek out new forms of cultural tourism experiences and hence spearhead new forms of tourist development (Cohen 1972: 175). And while some specialist forms of cultural tourism and specific ventures are successful purely catering for niche markets, they benefit from other ventures which package modified cultural experiences in forms that are more attractive to larger, accidental cultural tourists. Merchandising (through posters, caps or T Shirts) is an especially effective way to create synergies between 'elite' cultural tourism and 'casual' cultural tourism.

Greater understanding of the diversity of the demographic profile of the distinct market shares of cultural tourists is essential if more effective development and marketing of cultural tourism is to be achieved. Too often attention is focused on the 'high yield', 'elite' cultural tourist – a rare and fickle beast – at the expense of more broadly based strategies and appeals. As one commentator noted, research on leisure patterns by Australians suggested that 'a visit to a cultural institution is as popular to the average Australian as attending a football game', indicating 'a new found awareness and public interest in cultural matters' (Hall and Zeppel 1990: 91).

The consumption of tourism is also a class-related phenomenon. For a start, the proportion of the population which constitutes tourists (i.e. which takes a break away from home for more than one night) varies significantly between countries and is related to the economic well-being of nationals. For example, an estimated 44 per cent of EC residents did not take a holiday in 1985 (Leontidou 1994: 78); compared with about 40 per cent of Americans and 20 per cent of Australians. In other words, tourism is dependent on national habits and is a 'class pursuit' (Hughes 1987: 209–

10; Craik 1991: 44). Cultural tourists are a subset of these: for example, tourists at arts festivals 'tend to be "up scale" – they are mature aged, high income earning professionals who are willing to travel to attend major events' (Hall and Zeppel 1990: 89). The characteristics of the dedicated cultural tourist are quite specific:

> Exclusiveness will need to be an evident part of the product. 'Cheap' opera holidays in popular seaside resorts may not have as much appeal as rather more expensive holidays in 'quality' locations. It is interesting to speculate how successful opera holidays aimed at mass markets would be. They may be unappealing to those who do not already go to the opera. The barriers to opera going may already be so great that to risk 'wasting' a holiday on it seems an unlikely option. Those who are regular opera-goers may be alienated by the obviously 'popular' nature of the product.
>
> (Hughes 1987: 214)

The cultural tourist thus trades off various factors and probably balances the desire to attend opera with the exclusiveness and special features of the proffered opera holiday – e.g. opera in the outback; an innovative production; a star-studded cast; or a rarely-performed opera. For the non-opera-goer, placed in 'casual' contact with opera at a chosen destination, the availability of the opera – and time to kill – may persuade the tourist to sample something they never would at home. Thus, while opera holidays may primarily attract the cognoscenti, there are some prospects for enticing new audiences to experience this particular cultural form.

Nonetheless, cultural tourists display predictable demographic characteristics; like the consumers of art and culture *per se*, cultural and heritage attractions appeal to what might be termed 'a better class of person'. Higher socioeconomic groups are over-represented (Hughes 1987: 207–8). These people have a higher income, higher education (tertiary or professional) and higher 'cultural capital'. Participation in the arts and culture correlates with the desire of 'achievers' and the 'societally conscious' to engage in 'ego-enhancing' and 'status conferring' cultural activities (Hughes 1987: 215). Moreover, culture holds a greater appeal to women and young people than to men or older people, something that is curiously understated in the literature.

An international comparison of studies of visitors to art galleries found that the 'public of art galleries is somewhat more female than male, and is exceptionally young, exceptionally well educated, and exceptionally high in the social order' (Australia Council 1991: 51). In attempting to explain this pattern, the Australia Council study distinguished different kinds of 'cultural capital' (competence in and knowledge of the 'high' arts; 1991: 55). They concluded that among the high cultural users, there were two distinct groups: *progressives* who liked modern art, educational and informative media and classical music, and who strongly endorsed the culture of women, indigenous and ethnic groups. *Conservatives*, on the other hand, were high cultural consumers who preferred traditional art, consumed publicly funded media, and were older and possessed lower educational qualifications than the progressives. The implications for cultural tourism development are that products must be able to target appeals to these different segments of the market, or offer a range of products and appeals that can selectively or simultaneously capture both groups.

A much larger group of conservatives, however, is totally uninterested in culture. This group:

which is relatively poor in cultural capital is similarly conservative in its tastes. It visits [galleries] irregularly, perhaps as a tourist, and it is likely to have lower income and educational levels. It watches commercial television and listens to 'light' music on commercial radio. It does not support greater contextualisation of art works, nor does it support greater display of work by socially or culturally marginal groups.

(Australia Council 1991: 55)

This group – predominantly male, of lower socioeconomic status and with lower educational qualifications – lacks or refuses cultural capital; its members are unlikely to consume cultural tourism, although some may become casual or accidental cultural tourists. As the Australia Council concluded: 'it would clearly take long-term advertising campaigns to convince many non-goers that galleries might be places they could appropriately and pleasurably visit' (1991: 59).

What do tourists want to consume? As noted before, there is a hierarchy of preferences of cultural tourism, with the majority preferring historic and heritage attractions or museums, with fewer attracted to art exhibitions and galleries, or the performing arts (see Bywater 1993: 33, Table 1). For example, in 1991, the preferences of American tourists to Europe were as follows: ancient castles and forts (86 per cent), museums (80 per cent), old churches (65 per cent), Roman ruins (64 per cent), parks/gardens (63 per cent), theatre/drama (63 per cent), art galleries (62 per cent), city walking tours (61 per cent), folk dances/customs (44 per cent), local factories (42 per cent), symphonies/opera (37 per cent), jazz festivals (17 per cent), and church organ or choral concerts (16 per cent).

Of those visitors attracted to museums and galleries, the preference is for populist rather than specialist venues. For example, while 6.3 million visited the British Museum in 1992, and 4.3m the National Gallery, other venues drew significantly smaller attendances: Natural History Museum (1.7m); Tate Gallery (1.5m); Victoria and Albert Museum (1.2m); Science Museum (1.2m); and Royal Academy (1.0m) (Bywater 1993: 34). Of visitors to particular art exhibitions, most prefer more popular and accessible works. For example, the most popular exhibitions (in 1,000s) at the Grand Palais in Paris between 1988 and 1992 were 'Toulouse Lautrec' (696), 'Gaugin' (661), 'Degas' (477), 'Seurat' (421) and 'the Etruscans and Europe' (324) (Bywater 1993: 33).

Similar patterns can be seen elsewhere. In Holland, for example, van Gogh and Rembrandt have proved to be significantly more attractive to visitors than Mondrian (Bywater 1993: 34, 36). Yet sometimes visitors can surprise curators. In Australia, an exhibition in 1993 of Surrealism at the Queensland Art Gallery attracted over 110,000 visitors which, given the esoteric content, far exceeded the expectations of curators. Compare this with 138,000 visitors to the 1994 exhibition of van Gogh, an artist with whom the general community was very familiar (Queensland Art Gallery 1994: 15–16). None of its subsequent 'blockbuster' exhibitions – Renoir, Matisse, Post Impressionism and Toulouse Lautrec – have equalled this. It would appear that Surrealism had been popularised through populist artists such as Salvador Dali, Andy Warhol and Roy Lichtenstein in forms that have percolated through popular music, graphics and design, film and television.

In line with the distinction between progressive and conservative cultural consumers discussed above, the more traditional and accessible work of Renoir attracted a larger audience (102,000) than the more stylised – albeit more 'commercial' – work of the lesser known Matisse exhibition (87,780) ('Tourists following their art', *Courier-Mail*, 20 January 1996: 6). The challenge for curators is to balance popular – as opposed to aesthetic – knowledges and interpretations of art work and cultural forms with particular potential groups of cultural consumers.

There is also a need to understand better how visitors use museums and galleries. Although such venues are established on the premise that they are primarily educational opportunities for visitors to inform themselves, a survey of studies of visitor behaviour concluded that: visitors pay very little attention or none at all to exhibits; interactive exhibits are successful in attracting and holding visitor attention; and visitors do not appear to learn or remember a great deal from their visits (Pearce 1988: 108). Average looking time at an exhibit is eight seconds, and visitors only pay attention to a few exhibits that they first encounter. So-called 'museum fatigue' seems to refer to physical tiredness and mental overload; and sets in soon after entering an exhibition space. Accordingly, motivations for visiting museums are various, including status-seeking, sacred and spiritual veneration, and (especially for women) communication with female companions. Adverse weather also boosts attendance figures.

This brief survey of visitation patterns and trends demonstrates that there are close links between the production and consumption of cultural products, the acquisition of cultural knowledge, and the attributes of cultural capital. Cultural tourism and cultural components of tourism must juggle the promotion of particular cultural resources with the understanding of visitor groups. As Hughes demonstrates in the case of opera:

> It seems likely, however, that a performing-arts event such as opera could act as a tourist attraction in its own right. It is to be expected that certain tourists will be present in the opera audience as non-holiday makers, as an 'extension' of the 'normal' journey to attend an opera production (route 2).... [O]ther tourists will be present in the opera audience as holiday makers (routes 1 and 3). The relative importance of each of the three routes to opera remains to be determined. The motivation of the holiday maker and the non-holiday maker will need to be directed at each segment in order to stimulate the tourism flow.
>
> (Hughes 1987: 216)

This example shows the potential as well as the limitations of marketing culture for tourism and using tourism to advance cultural development. Cultural tourism proper remains a minority niche form of tourism; while the cultural transformation of tourism in general has distinct costs and benefits.

THE FEMINISATION OF THE TOURIST GAZE

The issue of the relationship between gender and tourism has, to date, received little overt attention. But implicit in discussions of tourism and in how the history of tourism has been written is a 'masculinist' perspective (Kinnaird and Hall 1994; Richter 1995). That is to say, tourism has been rather uncritically treated in the context of the development of industrial society and forms of exploration and knowledge associated with that. Tourism is regarded as an industry emanating from industrialisation and has been transformed by post-industrialisation. Many feminist critics would argue that this view of history is a particularly male-oriented one, in which masculine pleasures, priorities and outcomes are emphasised at the expense of other dimensions.

Swain cites Richter's observation that gender can be treated 'as an independent variable influencing tourism and as a dependent variable responding to tourism activity' (Swain 1995: 260). Viewed in this light, four gender issues have been identified as needing research: *gendered tourists* (work/leisure, motivations, gendered-related behaviour, and marketing); *gendered hosts* (who does what, differential power relations); *gendered tourism marketing* (sexuality and gender relations); and *gendered tourism objects* as activities and landscapes (Swain 1995: 251). These issues should be considered in the context of the changing role of gender in tourism, namely, an apparent 'softening' of tourism in terms of attractions, activities, tastes and experiences.

To date, however, 'the tourist gaze', as Urry has called it, has been normatively male, that is to say, it is conceived as being structured by voyeurism (Urry 1990). Strictly speaking, voyeurism is defined as gaining sexual pleasure (jouissance) by looking at the sexual attributes or actions of others; voyeurism is a specific form of scopophilia, the pleasure of looking. These terms have been applied to the analysis of film, media and art to capture the normative gaze that operates between spectator and the spectacle. Theorists have argued that the satisfying manipulation of visual pleasure is at the heart of practices of spectatorship. Drawing on psychoanalytic concepts, Mulvey has argued:

> The scopophilic instinct (pleasure in looking at another person as an erotic object), and, in contradistinction, ego libido (forming identification processes) act as formations, mechanisms, which this cinema has played on.
>
> (Mulvey 1981: 213)

The consequence of this is that images of women, in particular, but not exclusively, function as the passive object of the gaze from a masculine point of view. The dominant position of spectatorship is thus *as if* through male eyes, irrespective of the actual gender of the spectator. Any cursory analysis of tourist brochures, advertisements and travelogues finds plenty of examples of these values and attributes used to characterise the special features of particular tourist experiences. As Swain notes:

> predominant tourism brochure representations of men [are] associated with action, power, and ownership, while women are associated with passivity, availability, and being owned. From this perspective, uses of women, sexual imagery, and exotic markers in the tourism industry to market destinations are seen to often reinforce stereotypes and hierarchical divisions of labour. Host societies differentiated by race/ethnicity, colonial past, or social position from the consumer societies are sold with feminised images.
>
> (Swain 1995: 249)

The implications of this approach for some analysts of tourism is that the tourist gaze can be seen as structured in analogous ways, namely, as the objectification of the sight, site or experience for the gratification and pleasure of the normatively male tourist. In this sense, the aim of tourism, as evidenced by the Grand Tour, is seeing, talking about and learning about great sites and sights (historic, cultural and environmental): knowledge and self formation are products of these sensory processes. Ways of looking are interconnected with the developmental logic of industrialisation, through a fascination with invention, newness, technical achievements, heroism and spectacle. Inter-cultural communication and interaction with locals are secondary aims. Hence, the traditional tourist can be said to be normatively male, seeking pleasures associated with aggrandisement, greatness, uniqueness, exploration and intrepidness. Edensor and Kothari show how this has occurred in the packaging of the heritage attractions of Stirling in Scotland – namely Bannockburn Heritage Centre, the Wallace Monument, and the Regimental Museum of the Argyll and Sutherland Highlanders at Stirling Castle. As tourist sites, these 'articulate masculinised notions of place and identity, and male dominated versions of the past which privilege white, male, heterosexual experience and activity' (Edensor and Kothari 1994: 65).

A particular version of this is sextourism, where men travel to destinations with the specific or secondary aim of having sexual encounters with prostitutes and local women (Craik 1991: 104–5). Indeed, prostitution has been described as a 'common by-product of mass tourism' (Crick 1989: 323; Craig-Smith and French 1994: 43). Most attention has been paid to third world sextourism where it has been related to an historical tradition of exploitation and colonisation by first world nationals; but, as Hall has pointed out, sextourism has been part and parcel of tourism everywhere, although it is arguably more exploitative in non-Western cultures (Hall 1994: 144–5). Encounters between locals and visitors are both exciting and profitable, exposing locals to untold riches, different value systems and very different ways of life. While some sex workers are duped into an industry from which they cannot escape, for many, sextourism begins as an adventure or as a passport out of poverty. In Thailand, for instance, it has been estimated that a prostitute can earn between eight and 30 times as much as from a secretarial job (Craig-Smith and French 1994: 141). Perhaps not surprisingly, there are an estimated half a million prostitutes in Bangkok alone, up to a million in South Korea, and 100,000 'hospitality girls' in Manila (Ryan 1991: 161).

Hall has identified four phases of sextourism in South East Asia: indigenous prostitution (local cultural practices); economic colonisation and militarisation (e.g. American troops on leave in Thailand); international tourist substitution as clients; and institutionalisation of sextourism as a profitable and resilient industry which resists governmental and NGO intervention (Hall 1994: 150–1). In recent times, considerable concern has been generated about the implications of this form of tourism on the women concerned, on the escalating incidence of sexually transmitted diseases, and on disruptive consequences for family structures and economies (see Cohen 1982, 1988; Thanh-Dam 1983; Chesney-Lind and Lind 1986; Crush and Wellings 1987; Rajotte 1987). The spread of AIDS has prompted international campaigns about the effects of sextourism. Up to half the sex workers in Thailand are believed to be infected with the HIV virus, of whom about a third have developed AIDS; 70 per cent also have super gonorrhoea (Craig-Smith and French 1994: 141; McCarthy 1994: 19; Hall 1995: 99). The public health implications of such statistics, alone, are cause for alarm. Sextourism – especially in developing societies – also replicates in extreme ways the exploitative basis of the colonial origins of travel and tourism by one group of people seeking to discover, dominate and subjugate others. But even in destinations such as Amsterdam, Hamburg, Berlin, Las Vegas, Nevada, Moscow and Cyprus, sextourism has a dark side despite relatively better conditions and/or its legalisation. Hall suggests that sextourism is unlikely to disappear; rather, '(mass) tourism is sex tourism' (1994: 159).

The connection between tourism and sexual desire has not, however, been the sole province of males seeking females. Wagner studied Swedish female tourists in Gambia who sought out young males for short-term dalliances (1977). Young males frequently regarded such encounters as a source of unimagined wealth, and sometimes as a passport to the West; those who eventually followed their tourist partners home found a very different welcome awaiting them; often they were disowned (Cohen 1971; Craik 1991: 95; Ryan 1991: 163). Once back home, most Swedish women abandoned the tourist's desire to escape the usual disciplines and norms of everyday life by indulging in hedonism, fantasy and unrestrained sexual encounters during the course of a holiday. Not only did this changed persona puzzle the Gambian partners, this normlessness while on holiday was often inexplicable and/or offensive to locals, especially those in non-Western societies, who regarded such behaviour as typical of Western tourists in general.

A slightly different phenomenon has been described in Bali where men act as guides for female tourists as well as offering themselves as 'Kuta Casanovas' (McCarthy 1994: 19–20). They are also known as 'bad boys', 'Kuta cowboys' and 'gigolos'. While the tourists like the exoticness of their obliging guides, the men earn easy money and gain status among their peers. Most encounters are brief flings, but some guides seek to follow their 'girlfriends' to the West, and others have regular girlfriends who return each year. Like other forms of sextourism, a drug culture and the prevalence of sexually transmitted diseases accompanies this custom. Other tourism destinations have also generated groups of young men seeking dalliances with female tourists: 'Latin lovers' in the Mediterranean, professional playboys ('kamakia' or harpoons) in Athens (Boissevain 1989: 154–5; Ryan 1991: 163–4), Rasta men in the Caribbean, West Indian 'beach boys' (Henshall Momsen 1994: 107), and Otavalenos in Ecuador (Swain 1995: 263). Another form of sextourism to have received scant attention is homosexual tourism, which has developed as a niche market. Sydney's annual Gay and Lesbian Mardi Gras is one example of a specialist festivity which began as a local alternative event but has become a key attraction for international tourists.

Whether all such relationships should be condemned is a vexed question. While extreme forms of exploitation and harm undoubtedly occur, much sextourism is merely a short-term escape, or, as one analyst has suggested, 'the brave new world of cross-gender-culture intimate tourism relations' (Meisch, quoted by Swain 1995: 263).

Alongside these traditional patterns of the tourist gaze and sextourism, cultural tourism has engendered a more benign way of looking and other forms of gendered pleasures associated with tourism. Research shows that cultural facilities and events attract more female than male visitors, participants and users, and this pattern is also evident among tourists. Moreover, the pleasures and knowledges derived from cultural tourism entail more 'feminised' qualities than usual encounters with sites and sights. Thus, it is possible to argue that tourism, and especially cultural tourism, has been 'feminised', that is, reoriented towards more experiential, reflective and self-improving characteristics. This is consistent with the results of Smith which suggested that women are the primary taste makers in terms of choosing holiday destinations and activities (Smith 1979). As the number of women travellers increases – especially those travelling alone – the consequences of their preferences and patterns of behaviour will undoubtedly accelerate this apparent 'feminisation' process.

More generally, tourism – and its close relative, hospitality – has become an area of growth for the employment of women (Kinnaird and Hall 1994; Chapter 7 below). While this is to be welcomed in part, many of the available jobs are unskilled, part time, casual, poorly paid, and involve long or unsociable working hours. Jobs servicing tourist facilities, working in hotels and shops, restaurants, craft production and retailing, entertainment venues, and allied services (such as 'masseuses') constitute the majority of available forms of employment. A small number of jobs are available in personnel relations, training and management. While defenders of tourism employment argue that women want 'flexible' jobs, and that tourism does contain a career development track, the facts suggest that the bulk of employment reproduces the low status of women as cheap and expendable labour (see Craik 1991: 66–7).

Two exceptions may be in the areas of employment relating to art and craft production, and farm tourism, where women seem to have more control over their labour (Ireland 1993). Indeed, Swain (1993) and Fairbairn-Dunlop (1994) argue that women derive an income which provides independence, status, and a sense of worth; even if this does not translate to changing general policies on female employment. Moreover, distinctions need to be made between employment opportunities and consequences in developed, as opposed to developing, countries (Cukier-Snow and Wall 1993). Swain concludes that women's production of ethnic arts for tourism is 'a survival strategy of indigenous peoples … in the reproduction of links with the past and the reinvention of future identity' (1993: 50).

MANAGING CULTURE IN THE CONTEXT OF TOURISM TRENDS

Two of the consequences of the preceding discussion of the culture of tourism are that the growth of tourism as an industry has been accompanied by growing governmental interest in its fortunes, and that links are being created between the cultural and tourism industries. At all levels of government, from developed to undeveloped nations, countless policy pronouncements continue to endorse the potential of tourism for economic development and cultural enhancement.

Despite the enthusiasm, there is less certainty as to what role government can most effectively play in tourism. Generally, governments have adopted a hands-off role, as facilitator, in the sense of not wishing to become operators and direct investors (as developer); yet considerable government monies continue to underwrite the provision of infrastructure for tourism (e.g. airports, convention centres, casinos, dock redevelopments, expositions, events) and governments are frequently obliged to underwrite the operation and maintenance of such sites and facilities. During boom times, when tourism development is occurring and visitation levels increasing, governments use tourism as proof of the success of their political management (boosterism).

Governments increasingly direct their energies – at least at the level of rhetoric – towards creating an environment which facilitates private sector investment and activity. The preoccupation in the 1990s has been the development of partnerships between the public and private sector, whether in relation to regulatory conditions (e.g. concerning employment, foreign investment, tax incentives, visas), promotion and marketing, or regional development schemes. Increasingly, there is evidence of policies of consultative clientelism by governments whereby governments accept the mutual desire by the public and private sectors for enhancing tourism investment, support various forms of government investment, and attempt to co-opt diverse interest groups within the tourism community to endorse this approach (see Craik 1992). The risk is that governments become enticed into clientelist relations with major tourism operators, agencies and advocates, and for reasons of political expediency and economic desperation, governments cannot easily extract themselves from continued support for tourism, especially when there is a cyclical downturn in fortunes.

Yet such approaches are very uneven in their outcomes: governments feel that they cannot steer development as they would like because of the arm's-length approach; interest groups frequently feel that their involvement is tokenistic and that their concerns are overridden by industry agendas; while industry sectors are ambivalent – wanting government incentives but abhorring government 'interference'. This tension is especially pronounced where cultural tourism is concerned. As Silberberg has noted:

> But why should tourism operators, most of whom are private sector, for-profit, hard-nosed bottomline types, be interested in packaging and partnership opportunities with cultural facilities and organisations, most of which are not-for-profit?
>
> (Silberberg 1995: 363)

This raises several issues. Is culture inevitably there to be exploited for tourism? Does the cultural or tourism agenda take priority? Should the government underwrite cultural forms from which the private sector is the primary beneficiary? Should non-marketable cultural forms continue to be subsidised by government when tourist demand for cultural products indicates that other cultural forms are much more popular? These issues have been debated with some energy in recent years, as governments simultaneously attempt to reduce public sector funding, enhance cultural industry development, and seek greater accountability for the expenditure of public monies.

There is also the issue of who should pay for what. While the private sector has short-term goals and thus primarily will only commit itself to increasing visitation and promotional activities (the bums on seats mentality), other costs associated with tourism (infrastructure provision, curatorial costs, generic promotional costs, etc.) are usually borne directly or indirectly by the public sector. Governments are caught between the devil and the deep blue sea. On the one hand, they want to incorporate tourism as part of their strategies of boosterism. The glamour and apparent sustainability of tourism are regarded as reflecting positively on political fortunes, and as standing as evidence for governmental action. But on the other hand, governments are also wary of committing public money to expensive and/or unprofitable ventures.

The result has been that governments increasingly have redefined arts and cultural production in industry terms, as sizeable economic sectors, training grounds, and with value-added export potential. While this has been resisted by many sections of the arts community, some defining it as 'the "open pit approach to arts funding" – investment as opposed to sustainable development', the terms under which funding is provided have obliged the cultural industries to accommodate new government strategies (Miller 1996: 3). The result has been that most cultural institutions and organisations – even the biggest and most prestigious – have been obliged to seek out commercial opportunities and to attract new audiences. This has been done with varying degrees of success, but some critics have argued that a major risk of the strategy is that the primary function of a cultural organisation can be abandoned or overwhelmed by this reorientation (di Maggio 1983a, 1983b). The implications for organisations such as museums might be that the traditionally basic function of developing collections may be marginalised by the focus on changing, interactive, popular exhibitions, services and merchandising. In the longer term, this neglect of collections may undermine the credibility of the museum. In this sense, the tourist function of the museum can threaten the cultural integrity of such an organisation.

CONCLUSION

The conclusion of this chapter is that the culture of tourism has shifted to reflect changing priorities and orientations within national and international spheres. Contemporary tourism oscillates between the diverse motivations of escape and exploration; reaffirmation of identity; and the development of a service industry for the future. Tourism has been promoted as the answer to economic decline, providing cultural industries with the opportunity to develop as industries with export potential, as well as a vehicle to cultivate the cultural life of visitors, locals and the public sphere. These are lofty ideals and, from the point of view of government, highly attractive: the crass overtones of tourism can be reframed; economic ills addressed; training schemes in creative and service jobs promoted; and cultural identity fostered. The tourism industry, itself, after some initial hesitation, has pounced on the cultivation of tourism as a cultural commodity and phenomenon with considerable enthusiasm, prompted by new opportunities to package and market its product and to entice new markets. There remains, however, considerable ambivalence among the arts and cultural communities, partly reflected in tensions with the tourism industry. Partnerships work better in theory than in practice.

What is clear is that tourism is a constantly evolving culture and that tourism development changes the dynamics of the cultures in which it is embedded. There is no single cultural form or consequence of the contemporary set of changes that are occurring. Nevertheless, since the dynamics of cultural production are about cultural differentiation and elitism, while tourism is about cultural identification and access, the gulf between the two threatens to increase, not decrease. The acculturation of tourism may not therefore bring the mooted synergies and benefits; rather, it may well exacerbate long-standing hostilities and demarcation disputes between rather odd bedfellows.

ACKNOWLEDGEMENTS

Thanks to Robyn Trotter for research assistance, and to Chris Rojek for comments on an earlier draft.

7

PERFORMING THE TOURIST PRODUCT

Philip Crang

INTRODUCTION: THEORISING TOURISM EMPLOYMENT

It has become something of a statistical mantra that tourist activity will become the largest source of global employment by the year 2000 (see Shaw and Williams 1994). However, this prediction is plagued not only by the murkiness of its measurements but also by a theoretical doubt over just what is the social and cultural character of tourist related employment. This chapter considers how to theorise the nature of tourism employment and, more specifically, what relationship that theorisation might have to sociological and cultural understandings of employment more generally.

With regard to the latter, much tourist-related employment – concerned with the provision and delivery of holidays, accommodation, travel, tourist attractions, experiences of eating out and so on – has traditionally been studied and analysed through conceptual concerns that have sat somewhat outside the mainstream preoccupations of the sociology of work. For example, emphasis has often been placed on both the interpersonal relations between employees and tourists and the cultural character of the tourist institutions in which these occur. One particularly striking case of this is hotel and catering labour (see Wood 1992a, 1992b). Here, drawing on the seminal work of Whyte (1948, 1949), attention has been devoted to the temporal and spatial co-presence of production and consumption in hotels and restaurants and the organisation of the interpersonal service encounters between employees and customers. There has also been a dominant concern with the illicit and marginal character of hotels and restaurants. This has emphasised the sometimes criminal underlife of these institutions (Hayner 1936; Mars 1973; Prus and Vasilokopoulos 1979); the various informal reward systems that employees participate in within them (Mars and Nicod 1984); and the associated psychological and sociological deviances of workers attracted to such occupational cultures (Mars *et al.* 1979). For some, these traditional concerns are problematic because they over-emphasise differences with work in other areas of the economy, and because they separate studies of tourism employment from the wider debates coursing through the sociology of work. Examples of the latter include the debates on labour process deskilling (although see Chivers 1973; Humphreys 1985; Transnationals Information Centre 1987), and on flexible work organisation (although see Gabriel 1988; Kelliher 1989; Bagguley 1991). There is a concern, then, that an unhealthy 'myth of uniqueness' has grown up around much tourism-related employment (Wood 1992b:

60), a myth which obscures 'the extent to which [this] work ... differs little in kind and quality from similar work in manufacturing' (Wood 1992b: 16).

Notwithstanding the evident importance of questions of deskilling and flexibility to tourism, I will critique the claim that there is nothing distinctive about tourism-related employment. In order to do that I begin by drawing on some managerial theories in the tourism and hospitality industries. These theories have often very starkly set out tourism employment's supposed differences to its constructed 'others' of manufacturing and back-office work. I then briefly outline the justifiable criticisms levelled at these accounts. However, the conclusion I draw from these debates is not an adjudication over the difference or similarity of the rhetorical construction called 'Tourism Employment' to other constructed sub-sectors of paid work. Instead, my concern is with retrieving and reworking some of the conceptual concerns developed in accounts that emphasise tourism employment's distinctiveness. I do that not so much to reinforce that emphasis on empirical difference, but rather to open up neglected conceptual spaces for the theorisation of all employments. To re-phrase the point, my concern is with how accounts of a representational entity called tourism employment and its differences might provoke us to theorise all employment in ways we currently neglect, and how these theorisations might then help to explain the differences and similarities of jobs within and especially beyond tourism-related industries.

More specifically, this difference is to be understood as a shift in the kinds of organisational and workplace geographies to which we should pay attention. The first half of this chapter examines how managerial accounts of tourism employment shift attention away from the usually dominant concerns of management–labour relations and their organisational geographies of surveillance (Dandeker 1990) towards the socio-spatial relationships between producers and consumers and their organisational geographies of display (see Crang, P. 1994, forthcoming). This shift is explicit in the established concern in tourism studies with the co-presence of employees and their customers in the so-called 'service encounters' of tourism-related industries (see Czepiel *et al.* 1985). It is implicit in the discursive association of tourism employment with moral dilemmas of honesty–dishonesty, trust–distrust, and the seen–unseen. But above all it is reflected in the dramaturgical or performative metaphors used to represent much tourism-related employment, where workers are said to take on roles, workplaces become stages, managers become directors, and so on.

I suggest that this turn to the performative geographies of display, and their role in constituting the character of jobs, opens up a conceptual agenda still underexplored in the sociology of work more generally. In part this is an acutely social agenda, perhaps most famously illuminated by Goffman's work on the social performances within the 'interaction order' (see Goffman 1956, 1967, 1983; Drew and Wootton 1988). But it is also a fundamentally cultural agenda, as attention is paid to the construction of meaningful products and the representational labour involved in their production. So while theories of deskilling or flexibility can and should 'travel' to studies of tourism production, and the extent to which they 'travel well' should be opened up for critical analysis, the potential theoretical significance of the constructed entity called tourism employment goes beyond the extension and re-working of conceptual agendas established elsewhere. In the second half of the chapter I try to elaborate on this assertion by investigating the 'geographies of display' in tourism work. I do this by drawing out a number of dimensions of the 'socio-spatial relations of provision' of tourism products, or the social and spatial connections between tourism producers and consumers. These connections, I argue, help to determine the precise character of a tourism product, the labour involved in its production and the relationships between employment and employee. Investigating their character in a particular employment situation allows an analysis that goes beyond generalised assertions of the dramaturgical character of tourism work into the specific constructions and contestations of tourism sites and their performed personae.

CONSTRUCTING AND CONTESTING THE DIFFERENCE OF TOURISM EMPLOYMENT

However, I begin this analysis with some more generalised assertions concerning the supposed distinctiveness of tourism-related employment proposed within much management writing. At the heart of arguments for tourism employment's distinctiveness is a particular set of claims about the generic qualities of tourism products *per se* (see Smith 1994). These draw on a number of common and interconnected claims for the character of tourism as a distinct complex of services. These characteristics include:

1 intangibility, an inability to be 'sensed as goods can' (Berry *et al.* 1988: 223);
2 the experiential character of tourism products, such that tourism work is 'creat[ing] the right kind of experience for consumers' (Schneider 1988: 353), through an 'expressive performance' (Saleh and Ryan 1991: 325);
3 the doubly indeterminate quality of tourism products; whereby an excellent product, while not being threatening, is surprising, possessing that 'something extra' (Mars and Nicod 1984: 28), 'some aggregated net value of benefits perceived in the service encounter over what had been expected' (Klaus 1985: 18); and whereby service encounters, as social interactions, are likely to involve the unpredictable and the contingent for those working at producing them (Weitz 1981);
4 the interactional constitution of tourism services, such that production processes are part of the product (Lehtinen and Lehtinen 1991), consuming tourists are also producers, and tourism products are a process in which the quality of social interaction with both employees and other consumers is vital;
5 behind all of this, a particular workplace geography involving the spatial and temporal co-presence of producers and consumers in tourism production processes (see also Urry 1990).

These familiar understandings of service products are productive for managerial writers because they allow and legitimate debates over the appropriate character of managerial surveillance in tourism-related industries. In particular, they are often used to throw into question the precepts of scientific management and its logics of work task pre-determination and worker deskilling (Braverman 1974). This questioning is not just a matter of doubting the political efficacy of the oppositional management–labour relations thereby fashioned, i.e. the character of the social relations that surround deskilled labour processes. Rather it involves suggesting that tourism products are largely made up of indeterminate social encounters which actually constitute their labour processes. In this account, then, the tourism labour process cannot be pre-determined by management, and there is an inherent requirement for the 'indeterminate skills' possessed by the employees working in it (Crompton and Jones 1984). Hence, emphasis is laid on the fundamental difference between the labour processes of service-composed products and those in manufacturing.

Bell (1973: 163) argued that 'the fact that individuals now talk to other individuals, rather than interact with a machine, is the fundamental fact about work in a post-industrial society'. And this is echoed in both the tourism management literature, such as Sheldon's claim that '[t]he tourism/hospitality industry is essentially a people industry' (Sheldon 1989: 496), and in studies of particular tourism-related occupations. Hochschild, for example, contextualises her fascinating account of American flight attendants with the claim that:

> the modern assembly-line worker has for some time been an outmoded symbol of modern industrial labor; fewer than 6% of workers now work on assembly lines. Another kind of labor has now come into symbolic prominence – the voice-to-voice or face-to-face delivery of service....
>
> (Hochschild 1983: 8)

One response to such distinctions is to reiterate the importance of managerial strategies of deskilling and routinisation, and to advocate their extension into these new work situations. This can be pursued through the minimisation of employee–customer interactions and hence of direct labour involvement in indeterminate encounters; for example by combining technology with self-provisioning by tourists to shift more of the production process 'backstage' where routinisation is more easily accomplished (Gershuny 1978; Chase 1981; Jones 1988). Alternatively the 'frontstage' tourist contact work itself can be routinised, through the sort of pre-determinations of the encounter structure, pioneered and most famously associated with fast-food retailers, but much more generally actioned through set service routines that aim to minimise or indeed exclude the improvisational practices of employees (Leidner 1993). In either case the claimed benefits are heightened control of both staff and product quality, and hence the ability to market a guaranteed experience to consumers across a geographically dispersed set of production/consumption sites.

But more frequently the discursive construction of 'service' or 'tourism employ-ment' is used to legitimate forms of managerial surveillance that set themselves up in opposition to those of routinisation and tight monitoring. Pre-eminent here are a range of Human Resource Management strategies which emphasise control over more autonomous jobs and workers through the latter's adherence to organisational values and 'culture' (Mill 1989). Emphasis is particularly placed upon how the value-adding intangibles and indeterminates of the generic tourism product, that something extra, require resources that management cannot conceptualise and deliver in detail. As Jan Carlzon, the former Chairman of SAS airlines, puts it: 'Giving someone the freedom to take responsibility releases resources that would otherwise remain concealed' (Carlzon 1987: xv; see also Schlentrich 1992).

Indeed, on occasions a stronger claim is made: that attempts to routinise and closely monitor service delivery are liable actively to devalue the product, as tourists discount what service providers do for them by feeling it to be compulsory, not meant for them, and hence stripping it of cultural meanings of concern, care and attention. In this vein, the management consultant Gerry Egan talks about the MALPU syndrome of McDonald's, where the scripted greeting of 'May I help you?', delivered at speed hundreds of times a shift, becomes only a signal of counter staff's availability rather than any profession of hospitality (Egan, pers. comm.). A claim is made, then, for a need to manage autonomy in inter-personal work if value-adding elements of the product are to be maintained and developed. In turn this is seen as giving such work a particular character. Here, for example, is populist management guru Tom Peters eulogising generally about customer contact work under the heading 'Theatre on the retail stage':

> Retail, whether in the classroom or the showroom, is a performing art.... That's why I love retail. Sure, I have to count on the organiser of the seminar to bring in a good crowd, to select an adequate conference facility and to get a hundred logistical details just so.... But after that, it's my show or your show. The conference hall opens, the body shop's door clanks upward, the school bell rings and we are absolutely, positively in charge. It's our stage.... Retailing also allows you – no, it requires you – to reinvent.... For a great actor or actress, each day is a golden opportunity to experiment with a new approach – in fact, with nothing less than a new persona. What are you going to be today?...what's your new twist?
>
> (Peters 1994: not paginated)

But what particularly interests me here is the re-imagining of the workplace that is associated with such claims. For the figures of the factory and the line are largely replaced with a cultural reconstruction of the workplace as stage, and of '[t]he service encounter...as theatre' (Sparks and Callan 1992: 219). Debates over strategies of surveillance are developed through a concern with processes of display, as a dramaturgical discourse becomes pre-eminent. This general construction of work as performance, and product as impression management and persona creation, is then worked through in a number of more specific managerial understandings. In recruitment the emphasis is placed upon 'personality' and 'talents', rather than on supposedly impersonal technical skills, as managements search for the 'right kind' of 'service-oriented people' (Schneider 1988: 354; see also Jones and Decotiis 1988; Townley 1989). Once recruited, workers have to be 'directed' into their 'roles'. This may be through workplace environments or 'sets' – '[m]anaging the elements of the physical environment of the service organisation is one means to characterise services and, in addition, to affect the way in which they are delivered and perceived' (Upah and Fulton 1985: 255). It may involve the 'costumes' worn by employees – '[a] person who is not dressed for the part will not be able to play that part effectively' argues Solomon in discussing the 'packaging of the service provider' (Solomon 1985: 69). Emphasis is also placed on the coaching of staff in the surface acting skills of communicational interaction (Sparks and Callan 1992). And some managements even train their staff in a 'deeper' Stanislavskian level of performance in which these surface managements of the body – eye contact, smiling, open gestures, etc. – are established through forms of 'emotional management' such that they stem from states of feeling. 'I smile because I really am pleased to see you' (Hochschild 1983).

These performative understandings of tourism practices are not just limited to management writers. For example, Mike Crang's review of the critical stances taken towards heritage tourism in the United Kingdom argues for the need to move away from viewing heritage as a static object, to be evaluated as either real/authentic or ideological, and towards seeing it as an (inter)active process, a 'spinning of experiences from the past' as tourists engage in dialogues with the resources as heritage sites (including employees). As he puts it, 'it is performance that creates heritage', and these performances are undertaken by both consumers and producers (Crang, M. 1994: 341–2; and see Chapter 9 below).

Paying conceptual attention to these performative metaphors has its dangers of course. They can be associated with a romanticisation of tourism employment, 'obscuring the very real drudgery faced every day by many of the industry's employees' (Wood 1992b: 10). Moreover, they are often worked through a number of conceptually confused distinctions: such as the opposition between services and manufacturing (see Walker 1985); or that between industrial and post-industrial society (see Kumar 1978); or the opposition between tangible goods and intangible services (which ignores the tangible transformations and embodiments of services and the culturally meaningful and malleable character of goods; see Lovelock 1988) . They are beset by empirical difficulties: in particular, through concentrating on tourist-contact staff, they do not include all those employed in the tourism industry (Lennon and Wood 1989). And as legitimations of particular managerial theories and practices, especially those associated with Human Resource Management, they are based on a neglect of other managerial strategies which are being pursued (such as the routinisation of tourism encounters), and offer a far from convincing account of how managerial strategies are developed and deployed. These notions downplay both external competitive environments and internal managerial class fraction formation and competition (see Armstrong 1989; Legge 1989; Guest 1992). In sum, these dramaturgical accounts of tourism work are partial, associated with confused conceptual distinctions, and are often used to legitimate managerial strategies that require a more complex and critical analysis.

However, it would be a pity to respond to these criticisms with a simple dismissal of such dramaturgical understandings of tourism employment. For a start, as an explicit manifestation of a more implicit and complex set of ordering discourses that construct just what social practices it is that managers, consumers and employees expect to constitute tourism work, these understandings matter despite their conceptual and empirical confusions. They constitute a way into discursive formations that have shaped the cultural understandings of what tourism as a matter of fact involves. More specifically, through the application of managerial theories, they are a powerful tool in managerial constructions of tourism-related jobs and workplaces. Second, and in terms of the theorisation of tourism employment, they also provide a complementary route to the application and critique of theories established through research on other work situations, such as those of deskilling and flexibility. They offer an alternative to shoe-horning tourism employment into conceptual moulds cast elsewhere, and raise the possibility of re-focusing theoretical understandings of paid work more generally. Far from marginalising studies of tourism employment, some of the peculiar concerns reviewed above may actually destabilise the dominant sense of what is theoretically central and marginal about paid work in contemporary capitalist societies in the first place.

Unsurprisingly, then, I will pursue these dramaturgical understandings further. But in doing so I do not want to make appeals to some supposedly homogeneous entity called tourism employment. Rather, I will establish some of the dimensions of difference along which we might plot the variable social and cultural characters of performances and employments within and beyond tourism-related employment. What this involves is unpacking the much emphasised co-presence of production and consumption in tourism, to think out exactly how that co-presence is defined, organised, mediated and politicised. For whereas the connections between processes of commodity consumption and the sociologies and geographies of provision have been highlighted by a number of writers (see, for example, Fine and Leopold 1993; Sack 1993; Crang, P. 1996), the connections between processes of production and these 'socio-spatial relations of provision' are less well documented. Here I begin the process of documentation through identifying four interrelated dimensions that constitute producer–consumer interactions. These are: the socially constructed definitions of the settings in which tourism product provision takes place; the spatial and temporal structurings and uses of those settings; the media or materials through which product provision is organised; and the identity politics which are played out through the interactions between employees and tourists.

SOCIO-SPATIAL RELATIONS OF PROVISION

Definitions of the setting

The production and consumption of tourism are fundamentally 'geographical' processes. At their heart are constructions of and relationships with places and spaces. These places include destinations, which are differentiated through processes of social and spatial distinction and symbolically and materially restructured through their incorporation within economies of taste (Connell 1993). They also include the spaces of mobility that construct travel to these destinations, which are likewise resources for both self-formation and economic valuation (Curtis and Pajaczkowska 1994). In turn, these places and spaces operate as settings for the performances of both producers and consumers, helping to establish the precise character of a tourism product and its performance. The first set of socio-spatial relations of provision to address are therefore the culturally constructed characters of the settings within which tourism employees and tourists encounter each other.

These cultural constructions impact on product performances through providing pre-established, if rarely tightly fixed, social definitions of the settings being produced and consumed. These definitions are partly bound up with specifying the formations of leisure associated with tourism products – as spectacle, entertainment, convenience, hospitality, professionalism, education, and so on. They also involve placing products through a number of dualistic understandings of home and away – of inauthenticity and authenticity (MacCannell 1989; Silver 1993); of familiarity and alterity (Goss 1993); of the modern and the primitive (MacCannell 1992); of work and leisure; of present and past; of urban and rural; of private and public; and so on. In a process of social-spatialisation they establish the meaningful settings that tourists consume and that tourism employees help produce (Shields 1991).

In analysing these definitional processes with regard to tourism employment, two issues are of particular importance: first, to examine the ways in which these definitions provide constructions of the set upon which tourism employees work and hence of the roles that they are expected to play; and second, to determine how tourism employees actually are involved in these definitional processes. An initial example here is Bouquet's study of the provision of Bed and Breakfast accommodation by farming families in south-west England (Bouquet 1987). This involves accommodating guests in the farmhouse in which the family lives, and is largely a task overseen and undertaken by women members of the household. Bouquet considers how this work was caught up in and in turn recast two sets of cultural meanings about the farmhouse setting in which it takes place. First, it was set within, and involved the reproduction of, discourses of the rural and the urban. Here it 'act[ed] as a mediator between urban and rural values' (Bouquet 1987: 99), with an urban culture being brought into the household through the guests and the changes necessary to accommodate them, and rural culture being represented to guests by their hosts and the farmhouse. Second, it intervened in debates over the domesticity of this space. Bouquet argues that constructions of the domestic are central to notions of hospitality, because hospitality is 'the domestication of persons brought into the household for one reason or another...' (Bouquet 1987: 103). The character and organisation of domestic space is therefore crucial in determining the kind of hospitality being produced. In this case, of particular importance were the forms of integration and segregation of guests from permanent members of the household and their spaces, forms that helped to define the kinds of hospitality on offer and to re-work more traditional discourses of hospitality within the farming households concerning the provision of food and accommodation for farm workers (see also Ireland 1993). In addition, the provision of Bed and Breakfast accommodation played a crucial role in re-working the internal household understandings of domesticity, both in terms of their content and in terms of the household politics of their formation.

The construction of hospitable spaces is also the concern of Hochschild (1983) when she examines the aeroplane workplace of flight attendants. This place of travel is likewise constructed through engagements with understandings of domestic space and domesticity. In this case, this involves achieving friendly service through combining the commercialised provision of air travel and mobility with notions of the private, non-commercialised welcoming of guests into a home. Hochschild notes, for example, how attendants with Delta Airlines were encouraged in their training to think of passengers as if they were 'personal guest[s] in your living room' (1983: 105), with the hope that this would facilitate care in the air. Moreover, these definitions of the passenger cabin both guided and were embodied in the stage personae held by the attendants. Here, for example, is Hochschild on the constructions of femininity that women flight attendants in the United States have to deal with:

> [Women flight attendants] ... are also a highly visible distillation of middle-class American notions of femininity. They symbolize Woman...female flight attendants mingle with people who expect them to enact two leading roles of Womanhood: the loving wife and mother (serving food, tending the needs of others) and the glamorous career woman (dressed to be seen, in contact with strange men, professional and controlled in manner, and literally very far from

home). They do the job of symbolizing the transfer of homespun femininity into the impersonal marketplace, announcing in effect 'I work in the public eye, but I am still a woman at heart'.

(Hochschild 1983: 175)

These attendants worked in a setting that attempted a co-option of private space and its sanctioned forms of behaviour into the public, commercial realm. And they were required to embody that displacement in their portrayals of femininity.

A rather different example of the meaningful character of tourism-related work is Jacobs's recent study of the production of an Aboriginal heritage and art trail at J. C. Slaughter Falls near Brisbane (Jacobs 1995). Commissioned by Brisbane City Council in part as 'a tourist place which self-consciously serves the insatiable appetite of the cultural tourist for the "authentic" Australia in which "the Aboriginal" has become a key ingredient' (Jacobs 1995: 213), and produced by Aboriginal art production company 'Campfire Consultancy', this 1.5km walking trail runs past a number of newly produced artworks including paintings on rock surfaces, tree carvings, rock arrangements and a ceremonial dance pit. For Jacobs, fundamental to the site are various competing constructions of authenticity. At times, for example in much of the City Council promotional literature for the trail, this authenticity is understood in heritage terms as tradition – manifested by traditional techniques and styles within the art – thus facilitating primitivist locations of aboriginal culture and creativity in a long (and nearly lost) past. But in fact there is much more than tradition at J. C. Slaughter Falls: it is not a 'traditional' Aboriginal place; all the artworks were newly produced; many are designed to weather, hence requiring continual re-production; and much of the site's 'authenticity' is drawn from the contemporary authorisation of the art works by the Brisbane Aboriginal Council of Elders, rather than just through their traditional designs. In this small tourist site, then, authenticity is not simply an uncontested late-colonial imposition by tourism promoters that taps into more widely spread primitivist discourses; it is also actively used by the Aboriginal trail producers to legitimate contemporary artistic labour and political structures (see the parallel analysis of the Gaelic heritage centre in Skye in Chapter 8). The definition of this tourism setting is contested; and that contestation of the setting is part of what the production of this site allows.

These diverse examples raise a number of issues. For a start, they illustrate how tourism employees work in settings whose characters are constructed and contested within cultural discourses that imagine the kinds of places and spaces that they are. In tourism settings, discourses concerning formations of leisure and the imaginative geographies of home and away are particularly important. The studies reviewed earlier illustrate this with reference to product qualities of rurality, domesticity, hospitality and authenticity. These definitional processes also clearly need to be recognised as bound up in, and deploying resources from, much broader cultural circuits that construct the 'imaginative geographies' held by tourism producers and consumers (Said 1978). The construction of these geographical understandings is most simply but least fruitfully accessed through analyses of how tourism advertising invents places to be consumed (see Goss 1993 on the constructions of the Hawaiian Islands as a place of alterity; and see Reimer 1990).

However, more subtly, we can analyse how employees participate in much more complex cultural circuits, including:

1 tourism producers (themselves made up of many different factions, each potentially possessing very different kinds of understandings, and including employees themselves as one of these);
2 promotionalists;
3 commentators (including a variety of tourism journalists and also academics);
4 agencies of state regulation;
5 tourists who assign varying meanings to products and position them socially through their very presence or absence;
6 geographical knowledge producers beyond the field of tourism (including academic geographers but also more 'popular' providers of geographical understandings);
7 participants in the cultural circuits of other commodities which possess a touristic quality, such as food and drink (see Chapter 4 on tourist-objects).

In turn, the cultural understandings of settings constructed within these complex cultural circuits impact on work situations not so much through their projection on to workplaces, workers and work tasks, but more because the performance of those cultural understandings is part of what these employments actively involve. So, in Bouquet's account, the women working in farmhouse Bed and Breakfast accommodation had actively to mediate understandings of the urban and rural and the public and the private, and not just passively receive them. And in Hochschild's analysis, flight attendants did not simply work in an airline cabin that merged domesticity and commercial exchange, but had actively to work at producing such a setting. Tourist places are not just imagined places, they are also performed places; and tourism employees are not just actors on a stage, they have to act out that stage.

Moreover, given the complexity of the cultural circuits within which the imaginative geographies of tourism are constructed, these performed definitions of work settings are unlikely to be fixed or uncontested. This has two further implications. First, it means that all tourism employees have the potential to be involved in contestations over the very meanings of such settings. And second, it suggests that definitions of these settings are unlikely to provide tightly specified roles and scripts for those producers and consumers interacting within them. Instead, as symbolic interactionists have long stressed, they are more likely to act as a set of orientating presuppositions which initiate a process of setting and role definition which sits at the heart of the interactional process itself (see Turner 1962). So, settings and the roles within them are not determined in a once-and-for-all way prior to the interactions between tourists and tourism employees. Instead they are a matter of negotiation and contestation within those interactions, as tourists attempt to establish what product is actually being offered, and as employees investigate what tourists think the product being offered is, what they would like it to be, and so on.

The spatial and temporal structuring of settings

This brings us on directly to the interactional encounters between tourism employees and tourists. Here it is important to recognise that tourism settings are more than meaningful representations requiring performance, they are also, to use de Certeau's language, structuring spatial strategies that are tactically inhabited and used (de Certeau 1984). Places of accommodation illustrate this particularly clearly. Bouquet's study of the spatial structuring of Bed and Breakfast provision in farmhouses has already been noted, but the theme has been more recently developed in Wood's (1994) study of social control in hotels. His concern is how the provision of a product called 'hospitality', including notions of personal attention, has to be actively managed and produced through mechanisms of social and spatial ordering. More particularly, he is interested in the trend towards 'domestication' in hotels, such that hotel facilities attempt to replicate the well-equipped home as leisure space, and guests are increasingly confined to their rooms. He regards this as a growing way of structuring guests' interactions and experiences of the performed hotel product.

More generally, we can view tourism products as made up of a variety of institutional settings, each of which possess certain structuring strategies aimed at guiding tourists' interactions with each other and with employees. There is, then, a temporal and spatial structuring of the performances put on by tourism producers. Temporally, of particular importance are: the ordering of the service encounter 'chain' (Ventola 1987: 1); the detailed organisation of the activities that make up the encounter; and the extent of pre-determination of the encounter by management. With regard to the first of these, at their simplest level service encounters involve interactional processes of employee and tourist allocation, tourists' want definition, provision definition, delivery, and payment. Clearly, the character of a job is greatly influenced by the ordering of these. If, for example, payment is negotiated subsequent to service delivery, as is the case with jobs heavily reliant on tipping, then particular dilemmas are posed for staff (about predicting and ensuring payment). If customers pay in advance with clear expectations but little guarantee of what will be delivered, as with much package holiday booking, then the politics of the encounter are rather different. At a more detailed level, the temporal organisation of the encounter involves complex negotiations over the beginning and end of interaction, breaks within it, and switches from focused to unfocused interaction (that is, from the pursuit of a joint project to a co-presence in which participants gaze on the activities of each other but carry out separate projects; see Kendon 1988 on Goffman's distinction of focused and unfocused interaction). In both cases, though, the temporal structuring of encounters raises questions of social contracts (legal and moral), tact, trust and risk.

This risk can be minimised through a tight managerial scripting of the encounter. The most obvious example of this is the standardisation of service products, as well as foods, across fast-food chains. As Ray Kroc, founder of McDonald's, argued: 'Our aim, of course, was to insure repeat business based on the system's reputation rather than on the quality of a single store or operator...' (Kroc and Anderson 1977: 86; cited Leidner 1993: 48). But, as noted earlier, such tight regulation just shifts concerns with risk and trust from the temporal organisation of the encounter to its spatiality. These circle around just what is being displayed, where it comes from, and how it got there. Let us reconsider routinised service delivery. In the case of Hochschild's flight attendants, they not only perform the setting or place in which they work (the hospitable passenger cabin, merging public and private space) but also their own geographies as part of the product. For example, when they produce and sell a smile, they have to sell a sense of where that smile comes from. As I have said, Hochschild views this in terms of a pressure to perform not only the surface acting of impression management, but also the deep acting of emotional labour, such that a smile is not just painted on, but rather comes from the heart (and is seen as coming from the heart; see also Wouters 1989). Only if the latter can be effectively conveyed is the friendly smile valued as 'authentic', i.e. assessed as really meant, as more than an enforced commercial exchange. Authenticity in emotional exchange, then, is associated with particular spatialities of display. It makes claims for going beyond surface appearances to something deeper (from the smile to the heart). And it is associated with products that are seen as having been diverted to the consumer from another realm – that of non-commercialised emotional work – rather than purely constructed for them (on the spatialities of authenticity, see Appadurai 1986b).

These issues of the spatial structuring of product display and performance are mirrored on a larger scale within tourism sites/workplaces, as MacCannell classically showed over two decades ago (1973). In thinking about what is displayed to tourists, MacCannell began with Goffman's distinction of front and back regions. For Goffman a front region is where 'that part of an individual's performance which regularly functions in a general and fixed fashion to define the situation for those who observe the situation' occurs (hence this is on-stage with regard to tourist consumers). A back region is 'defined as a place, relative to a given performance, where the impression fostered by the performance is contradicted as a matter of course' (and is hence hidden from tourists; Goffman 1956: 13, 69). One of the most common exemplifications of this spatiality of performance is the formal restaurant, with its clear demarcation of dining room and preparation areas. Here, for example, is George Orwell recounting his own experiences:

> It was amusing to look around the filthy little scullery and think that only a double door was between us and the dining room. There sat the customers in all their splendour – spotless table-cloths, bowls of flowers, mirrors and gilt cornices and painted cherubim – and here, just a few feet away, we in our disgusting filth. . . . A dozen waiters with their coats off, showing their sweaty armpits, sat at the table mixing salads and sticking their thumbs into cream pots. . . . But the customers saw nothing of this. There was a coco-nut mat and mirror outside the dining-room door and the waiters used to preen themselves up and go in looking the picture of cleanliness.
>
> (Orwell 1933: 60–1)

But MacCannell's concern is both wider than restaurants, concerning all tourism settings, and more specific, in that his interest is how the performed settings of tourism production and consumption, or front regions, increasingly expand to incorporate back regions. This results in tourism experiences valued as authentic. This stems from the aura of artificiality associated with signalled performances, and results in a breakdown of any simple on-stage and off-stage distinction, as 'staged back regions' of varying kinds proliferate (MacCannell 1973: 596).

MacCannell's underlying assumption that a search for authenticity underlies all modern tourisms is of course questionable. Certainly, contemporary spatial restructurings of tourism-related interactional settings do not all follow the trend of staged back regions; for instance, the developments towards domestication in hotels noted by Wood increase the rigidity of front and back region boundaries. But his account nonetheless highlights three crucial issues about the spatial structuring of tourism employment. First, it stresses how the character of tourism products, and their associated labour processes, are dependent on the extent and kinds of display to tourists. At its simplest, we can think about how working in front and back regions will be very different. More subtly, we can conceptualise how varying degrees of frontness and backness constitute the very characters of settings.

Second, the emphasis on Goffman's analysis of the presentation of the self shows the ways in which many tourism-related employments, because of their socially constructed performative character, involve practices which both deploy and rework dichotomies of honesty and dishonesty, the seen and unseen, the real and false.

Third, however, MacCannell's analysis begins to suggest that, while tourism employees are likely to get caught up in and use debates over the authenticity–inauthenticity or truth–falsity of what they are producing, these oppositions cannot simply be mapped on to and grounded in the spatial structures of front and back regions. This is not only because empirically front and back regions are often blurred into more complex combinations of frontness and backness. It is also because simple associations of front-stage with a 'put on' performance, and back-stage with 'natural' behaviour, are stultifying to critical analysis. They lead to a replication of the 'tragic' narrative of lost authenticity, in which the real is destroyed by whoever seeks it at the moment of its discovery. This a common refrain in commentaries on tourism products. Accounts of tourism's social implications have a long connection with what Renato Rosaldo calls 'imperialist nostalgia', an innocent longing for that which one has destroyed (Rosaldo 1993). But this narrative is not limited to a concern with 'other' cultures. Here, for example, is an airline passenger, quoted by Hochschild talking about the authenticity of flight attendants:

> When you see them receiving passengers with that big smile, I don't think it means anything. They have to do that. It's part of their job. But now if you get into a conversation with a flight attendant...well...no...I guess they have to do that too.
>
> (Hochschild 1983: 89)

To escape this nostalgic logic, what is needed is an examination of how the spatial structuring of display to tourists helps to shape different kinds, but not extents, of performance. In this light, front and back regions are to be understood as workplace areas designated for performances to different audiences (customers and fellow workers). And frontness and backness are to be seen as product qualities that involve different sorts of acting. To use Falk's distinction (1994), we might think about how frontness requires a 'representational' performance which can deploy both surface appearances and emotional depths in ways that signal their mediated character; and how backness requires a more evidential or 'presentational' performance, i.e. a construction of product and self as outside representational codes. In this analysis, then, tourism products and their performance are to be understood less in terms of the real and the false, and more in terms of how differing sorts of performance are combined. In turn we need to pay particular attention to how these combinations are structured through the spaces of the interactional setting and their positionings of producers and consumers.

There is, however, one further complication to the spatial and temporal structuring of tourism encounters. These positionings of producers and consumers are not necessarily static; rather, employees and tourists enact forms of mobility and immobility. Display to tourists is not just spatially structured in terms of frontness and backness, and temporally structured through the organisation of service routines, it is also chracterised by varying forms of bodily praxis, differently 'moving performances'. Whether, and exactly how, employees and tourists move helps to establish the character of the interaction and the work it involves. It does so through a dialectical relationship with the forms of managerial surveillance that workers need to respond to (both determining and determined by surveillance practices). It does so through the micro-politics of the interaction with tourists that these movements play out. And it does so because movement opens up spaces through which employees can actively use the settings in which they work.

As an illustration of all these points, take the example of waiting as a spatial and temporal practice. As Schwartz has argued, the product quality of having someone waiting to do something for you can be used as an embodiment of the organised dependency of the server on the served, and of the temporarily sanctioned power and status of the consuming tourist (Schwartz 1973). As such it is often an advertised feature of the hospitality sold, being established through service routines and the time–space paths they specify for jobs (though these specifications always have to balance service quality with quantitative efficiency). The prompt timing of interactional initiation, the alert bearing and quick movements of employees, are all features of one sort of quality service. But making someone wait on a service is also a (sometimes) subtle tactic of resistance for employees. As Schwartz puts it:

> The deliberately sluggish movements of many store clerks, telephone operators, cashiers, toll collectors and the like, testify to the ability of the lowly as well as the lofty to dramatize their autonomy.
>
> (1973: 864)

Being just that few seconds later than demanded, taking one's time to appear, moving off that fraction too early, are all ways of signalling momentary escapes from enforced service routines. So, what employees do with their bodies – where they put them, how they pose them – is part of the job they perform; but it also allows ways of actively inhabiting that job (see Chapter 2 on how this embodiment is necessarily gendered).

The mediation of co-presence

We can develop this further by turning directly to the communicational 'materials' through which the interactions between employees and tourists are organised. Studies of the consumption of tourism have emphasised three sorts of consuming practices: gazing at landscapes and people; experiencing bodily sociality and sensory pleasure; and, to a lesser extent, talking. Tourism employees have to work within and at each of these sets of practices.

Let me begin with gazing. Urry has shown us how different sorts of tourist gazes are associated with different formations of leisure (1990, 1992b). Tourism employees are caught up with these gazes in two ways: they work at producing them, coaching tourists into the right sort of gazing through both tuition and exemplification; and they work under these gazes, becoming part of their domains. So, and staying with ideal types rather than real settings, employees working under what Urry calls the collective gaze (a communal gaze, based in shared encounters, seeking the familiar) would have to work at becoming familiar with and to tourists. Those in the spectatorial gaze (communal, but based in brief encounters in which different signs are glanced at and collected) would have to work at providing brief encounters that are memorable enough to be collectable. And so on. In so doing, tourism workers have to inhabit visual practices that are power-laden, in terms of class relations, histories of ethnic power, and sexuality. But as I have already argued they are not just passive recipients of tourist gazes. They actively respond to them. They may hide from them (finding or constructing places shielded from the gazes); they may masquerade within them (using gazes to facilitate the development of one or more personae); and they may pose through them (using the gaze to send a message).

Of course, workers' performances are not confined to the purely visual. Part of what they display are their bodies; produced bodies appropriate for the setting in which they appear. They thus embody the culturally meaningful tourism product, and can act as exemplars of the bodily habitus expected of and desired by tourists. And in turn an intrinsic part of their job can be to practise the bodily pleasures and forms of sociality appropriate to the setting in which they work (see Game 1991; Veijola and Jokinen 1994 and Chapter 2 above), whether that be sun-bathing, swimming, dancing, drinking, flirting, hill-walking, or whatever.

This also reinforces the implosion of the very dichotomy of work and leisure in tourism settings (see also Bowen and Schneider 1985). In this implosion, not only does work involve being surrounded by other people consuming and having fun, but having fun can also become the work itself (see, for example, Marshall 1986). An extreme example would be the 'PRs' hired by bars in many Mediterranean resorts to attract customers. Usually foreign nationals receiving limited pay but free accommodation and drinks, PRs are responsible for recruiting people into the bar and drinking, chatting and flirting with them once they are there. They have to stimulate and perform a particular sort of tourist behaviour, working at getting drunk and having a good time. Advertised informal rewards include the opportunity to use the work position of being a centre of attention, and the labour of making people feel good, to seduce tourists (unsurprisingly, understandings of these opportunities and the ways they are acted on are highly gendered) (see Anon. 1995). Play is rationalised to a work ethic; but, in the same entanglement, commodified labour is also made playful.

Talking is a far less examined aspect of both tourism consumption and production (though for a general account of talk at and as work, see Drew and Heritage 1992). Nevertheless, we can see that varying forms of talk will have to be performed as part of any tourist-related setting. This may involve the construction of quite distinct genres of speech acts. Ventola (1987) examines service encounters generally in this light, and Leidner (1993) explores the standardised conversational exchanges in routinised product deliveries. But it is likely to result in the commodification of many other forms of talk: friendly chat (Leidner stresses how even staff at McDonald's work at customising and ad libbing around the standardised scripts); the welcoming of visitors and guests; flirting; even the geographical lecture (see Munt 1994, on how post-modern travellers are often subjected to these as part of their holiday experiences); and so on. Again, tourism products and their labour processes do not occupy some sealed-off realm of commercial exchange and economic rationality; they entangle an instrumental rationality with a desire for communicative understandings as reached through a number of power-laden media.

Identity politics

A recurring theme of the discussion above has been the role of tourism employees, not just as producers of a product but as part of that very product, producing themselves as part of their jobs. This entails producing their bodies (both through working on them and with them); their expressions; their feelings; in sum their 'performed selves' (Featherstone 1983: 29). Identity politics are at the heart of tourism labour processes.

This can be seen in a number of ways. To begin with, the ascribed characteristics of employees – in terms of gender, ethnicity, cultural capitals, age, bodily abilities, and so on – become an important part of the role-playing process (Adkins 1992; Filby 1992; see also MacCannell 1984 on tourism and the selling of ethnicity). They are part of what is required from an employee. One example of this is how workers' consumption tastes and embodied cultural capitals become important elements of what they bring to a job. That is clearly the case with the PRs discussed above, but is also true of employees in rather different sectors of the market. Here, for example, is travel company Explore's brochure description of one of their employees, Suzi Poole: '... travelled extensively in Europe, the Middle East, Asia and Central America... [her] linguistic abilities helped her obtain a Master's degree in French... [her interests include] photography, scuba diving and art history' (cited by Munt 1994: 112). So here we have an employee representing the product not only face-to-face but also in promotional materials; and doing so through a description that demonstrates professional status and appropriate consumer tastes and expertise, both within and beyond tourism. Within face-to-face interaction itself, employees' ascribed characteristics also act as markers of status that can be used within encounters. This may be defensive – as a 'shield' against incivilities from tourists (Hochschild 1983: 174) – but status can also be deployed aggressively by both employees and tourists to rupture the relations of tact established within the encounter.

However, identities are not just brought to work by employees; they are forged through it. These jobs are spaces in which employees' identities are constituted and policed, not just displayed. This means that there is a complex entangling of employee and employment in performative labour. On the one hand, the character of a job is in part dependent on who is doing it. Employees with different ascribed identities may have radically different experiences of what is apparently the same job. As Hochschild puts it in terms of flight attendants:

> The job of flight attendant... is not the same job for a woman as it is for a man. A day's accumulation of passenger abuse for a woman differs from a day's accumulation of it for a man.... Because her gender is accorded lower status, a woman's shield against abuse is weaker.... Thus the job for a man differs in essential ways from the same job for a woman.
>
> (Hochschild 1983: 174–5)

This means that workplace social relations go beyond the struggles of abstract categories such as labour, management and capital, and instead involve many kinds of more embodied politics (in terms of gender relations, sexuality, ethnicity, age, cultural capital, constructions of self, as well as class). This also means that employees' selves become part of the product being worked at and sold. Products may be personalised, and personhood is commodified. This process can be highly problematic for employees, in that their senses of self have to deal with the constructed identities being sold and produced by tourism institutions. Certainly, that is very much Hochschild's emphasis. She explores (1983) how those who have to work at producing feelings – who she terms emotional labourers – find their performances and their emotions being devalued by consumers increasingly aware of the performative character of their jobs, and indeed devalued by themselves, as feelings produced on order for money seem estranged from any autonomous sense of self. But this is not necessarily the case. Performative work may be experienced more positively. Workers may be able to isolate their paid performances within the realms of the false, distancing themselves from their roles, and playing with them as well as at them. Or they may deconstruct these dichotomies of real and false: individually by enjoying the opportunity to play out multiple personae, seeing none as more false or real than any other; or at the larger scale of a host community, by taking the opportunities for cultural invention through performances. Quite how the identity politics of tourism performance work out are therefore not pre-determined, depending on the power relations within the broader cultural circuits of setting definition and between participants in the production process itself.

In all cases, though, organisations are looking to produce and sell employees' selves as part of tourism products, and employees are working on their selves as part of their labour. More specifically, organisations and employees are involved in a particular discourse of the self – that of the performed self – though the precise persona sought, the understanding of what kind of performance it entails, and the personal resources used to achieve it, vary according to the definitions, spatial structurings and materials of the tourism setting (see also Rose 1989; Casey 1995).

CONCLUSIONS

This chapter has argued that performative metaphors are productive in theorising tourism employment. In part this is simply because these metaphors are in themselves powerful influences on that employment, forming as they do part of broader discourses about contemporary consumptions and productions of peoples and places. They are powerful constructions of the relations between work and self, constructions deployed by both managers and employees. They are not simply descriptive epiphenomena. But these performative metaphors are also worth paying attention to because they are theoretically useful, highlighting conceptual agendas that are underplayed within the more traditional themes of the sociology of work. I have dealt with three such agendas in particular here. First, I have tried to demonstrate how dramaturgical understandings foreground an analysis of employments that pays attention to their constitutive geographies. Goffman's work was characterised by its radical contextualisation of social life and social selves, and while he neglected the broader social and cultural processes through which contexts are forged, his 'geographical imagination' still leaves a powerful and vital imprint on accounts of tourism work performance (Gregory 1994).

Second, and more specifically, performative metaphors emphasise a set of rather neglected constitutive geographies of employment, in that they supplement a concern with the practices of managerial surveillance with an interest in the geographies of display to consumers (Knights and Willmott 1990). Of course, for each employment situation the precise geographies of display and forms of performance cannot be assumed. Here I have argued that they need to be analysed according to the complex socio-spatial relations of provision between the employees and the consumers of what they produce.

Finally, an attention to the performative quality of employments also makes explicit how the labour being undertaken is not only economic but also cultural. It provides an analytical framework that can explore the 'de-differentiation' of economy and culture to be found in contemporary worlds of work in which the products of labour are cultural representations and that labour itself involves the mobilisation of culturally meaningful selves (Du Gay 1993; Crang forthcoming; see also Lash 1990; Lash and Urry 1994; and other chapters in this book). Indeed, it expresses that de-differentiation in ways that go beyond the fusions of reality and representation to be found in the more common accounts of an image-dominated post-modern society. In thinking about tourism and tourism-related employment as performances of commodified products, we can escape the logic of the advertisement to analyse how these commodity-signs are not simply imagined constructions but are temporally and spatially constituted constellations of embodied social practices.

8

A PEOPLE'S STORY

Heritage, identity and authenticity

Sharon Macdonald

INTRODUCTION

There is a story which I have heard, in various versions, many times in Skye. It goes like this:

> There was an old woman [or man] living in township X. One day a couple of tourists come by and start asking her questions. 'Have you ever been outside this village?' they ask. 'Well, yes. I was at my sisters in [neighbouring township] not so long ago.' 'But you've never been off the island?' 'Well, I have, though not often I suppose.' 'So, you've been to the mainland?' She nods. 'So you found Inverness a big city then?' 'Well, not so big as Paris, New York or Sydney, of course . . .' she explains, going on to reveal that she has travelled to numerous parts of the globe.

This is one of a large repertoire of jokes which highlight local people's awareness of touristic images of themselves, their ability to play along with those images, and their enjoyment of subtly disposing of them. It also highlights the conceit of tourists who assign local people only the role of object of the tourist 'gaze' (Urry 1990).

An abiding concern in tourism research has been with the implications of being an object of the tourist gaze, and, in particular, its implications for identity and authenticity. This chapter takes up this concern by exploring a heritage centre – *Aros: The Skye Story* – which opened on the Isle of Skye, in the Scottish Hebrides, in 1993. Through an analysis of *Aros* – especially its exhibition – and its makers' claims about it, my aim is to examine how far the centre can be seen to involve a commodification of culture and history. My information is drawn primarily from interviews with various individuals involved in tourism and heritage on Skye, and unless otherwise specified all quotations are taken from interviews in October 1994 with Donald, one of the centre's creators. I also draw on documentary sources, observations of the centre, and my earlier and ongoing ethnographic research on identity in Skye (Macdonald 1997).

A heritage centre is, I suggest, a useful site in which to explore questions about local identity and the performance of culture for tourism. It is a purpose-built representation of what is considered an appropriate depiction of the past and the locality; and as such it constitutes what John Dorst has called an 'auto-ethnography' (1987: 4) – a text that culture has produced about itself (1987: 2). It is a formalised and self-conscious cultural account, though one which inevitably bears the imprint of more than its creators' conscious intentions. While Dorst limits his analysis to the finished representation, here I look, too, at its makers, their relationship to the locality, and their claims. The makers are, after all, themselves thoroughly and professionally engaged in questions of identity, locality and authenticity (cf. Bruner 1994: 398); and their authorial intentions are worth examining in their own right. Moreover, attention to the producers highlights the specific position from which they speak and signals that they may be well aware that the history and identity which their representations attempt to articulate are by no means uncontroversial or uncontested.

Heritage representations, like performances of culture and history for tourists more generally, are regarded in a good deal of tourism research as inherently 'artificial' or 'inauthentic'. MacCannell's (1989) notion of 'staged authenticity', for example, highlights the ersatz nature of that which the tourist is offered; and Hewison's characterisation of heritage as 'bogus history' (Hewison 1987: 144) likewise emphasises fraudulence. Not only is it tourists who are duped, according to these analyses, but also those who perform for them. According to Davydd Greenwood, for example, local people risk losing the 'authentic meanings' of their culture and debasing it to mere 'local color' by performing for outsiders (Greenwood 1989). In similar vein, MacCannell argues that highlighting ethnic difference ('a kind of going native for tourism'; MacCannell 1992: 159) puts its performers in danger of 'a distinctive modern form of alienation, a kind of loss of soul' (MacCannell 1992: 168). For Greenwood, the debasement is a result of making explicit meanings which were previously implicit; and of 'the commodification of culture' – turning culture into something which can be bought and sold. The alienation which MacCannell describes also stems from commodification, a process in which phenomena such as ethnicity or authenticity cease simply to 'be' – to have *use-value* – but come to have *exchange value* in a cultural system which peddles numerous formulae for translating between, or exchanging, things and categories which would be thought incommensurable in other 'modalities'. The market, and market-values, subsume everything, according to MacCannell, 'to the exclusion of all other values' (1992: 169). Nothing is valued in itself but only as currency.

A heritage representation like *Aros* certainly involves some of the processes which Greenwood and MacCannell implicate in the 'inauthenticating' of culture. First, it clearly involves a kind of 'making explicit'. Indeed, a heritage representation is, intentionally, a cultural explicating device. Moreover, the heritage format as used at *Aros*, with its staged sets and mannequins, and its claims to be '*The Skye Story*' (cf. *The Oxford Story*, *The Queenstown Story* (Cobh, Ireland), *The Story of Hull*, *The People's Story* (Edinburgh) etc.), has become rather a standardised model for proclaiming and establishing 'place myths' (Shields 1991: 6). It is in itself a generalised sign of 'being' or 'having' a culture (cf. Handler 1985, 1988). In MacCannell's terms this standardisation (a touristic technology for going native?) is itself evidence of inauthenticity and alienation. *Aros* is also in the business of making a profit, and it does so through the sale of its depiction of local culture and history. Clearly, it could be argued that it treats culture and history as commodities. Moreover, as we shall see, *Aros*'s representation of culture and history involves a good deal of translating of the local into categories with more global *semantic reach*. Again, this is part of a process – here, the translation of categories with local use-value into wider systems of exchange

– which MacCannell regards as an alienating reconstruction of the local. It is a process in which, he suggests, the local is 'subsumed' to the global.

My argument here, however, is that the matter is not so equivocal. Although *Aros* uses what has become a standardised and indeed transnational format ('the heritage model') – and one which relies mainly upon display technologies which have been associated with inauthenticity (reconstructions) – its creators are very concerned with authenticity and with presenting a sense of local distinctiveness. However, both their understandings of authenticity and their notions of local identity and culture, in relation to the wider system which impinges upon it, are a good deal more sophisticated than many of the models for interpreting heritage and touristic performance would allow.

This chapter proceeds as follows. I first provide some background to the creation of *Aros* and to its creators. I then discuss their notions of 'history' and 'story', before going on to describe and locate the kind of identity which the exhibition constructs and the authenticating devices which it uses. This is followed by a discussion of some of the particular features of heritage representations – their suitability and unsuitability for certain kinds of stories and identities; and possible variations in ways in which they may be read. In conclusion, I return to the question of the models which we use to analyse heritage and tourism, and from the basis of my attempt to understand some of the local conceptions of these matters suggest some alternative analytical possibilities.

MAKING HERITAGE

The island of Skye has been a highly romanticised tourist location since the mid-nineteenth century, when its wild landscape and exotic history and culture began to appeal to wealthy, cultured tourists from the South (Cooper 1979). Over the past century, Skye's tourist appeal has become much broader and many new tourist facilities have developed to try to tap what is one of the major sources of income and employment on the island. *Aros* – which is advertised in the tourist brochures and which provides its commentary in French, German, Italian, Spanish and Japanese, as well as Gaelic and English – is clearly intended to attract tourists. And the heritage format which it uses to do so – professionally produced period sets, Walkmans with commentary and sound-effects, a gift shop and restaurant   has become a familiar genre in tourist development projects. Indeed, what sparked off the idea of creating a heritage centre on Skye was a visit to the Jorvik Viking Centre by one of the centre's founders. Later on, in formulating their proposals, the makers of *Aros* visited other heritage sites and museums too. In this 'pirating' of the 'heritage model', *Aros*'s makers were also able to draw on an established 'technical means' for putting the model into operation (cf. Anderson 1983: 30, 66). This technical means included the Edinburgh-based heritage companies which provided the mannequins, period dress, graphic panels and audio-visual technologies, and which gave advice on matters such as how to write an engaging story, how best to display artefacts, and how to entice visitors into the exhibition and gift shop. National, and indeed transnational, notions and technologies of heritage, then, thoroughly played their part in the creation of the Skye heritage centre.

Aros is a purpose-built heritage centre containing an exhibition (*The Skye Story*), and a restaurant and gift shop which together cover a much larger area than does the exhibition itself. It is situated on the main road into Portree (Skye's capital) from the mainland. Its large car-park contains a notice welcoming coach parties, though in late 1994, when I carried out my research, *Aros* had not yet succeeded in establishing itself on the agenda of any of the numerous Highland coach tours which drive past. The centre cost around £800,000 to set up; and this was financed by a combination of private share capital (about 25 per cent), state funding in the form of grants from the Highlands and Islands Development Board (now Highlands and Islands Enterprise) and the Local Enterprise Council, and bank loans. It was intended to be both a money spinner (to repay the loans and generate dividends for share-holders) and a significant local employer in what is an area of high unemployment. In 1993–94 it employed seventeen full-time staff during the summer and twelve in winter, which is relatively high by comparison with many similar operations and is by no means trivial in the local jobs market. So far, the exhibition has received rather fewer visitors than was hoped; though the financial consequences of this have been compensated by the fact that the centre has made considerably more from its gift shop and restaurant than was anticipated. Although detailed figures have not been kept, it seems that this pattern is largely accounted for by local people, who visit the shop and restaurant far more than they do the exhibition (among my contacts, local people seemed to be more forthcoming on its restaurant, praising its 'good plain fare', than on the exhibition itself). Nevertheless, in economic terms, the centre seems so far to be more successful than many such ventures; though, ironically, its success may be founded less on its attempt to present a 'quality' vision of local heritage than on a semi-internationalised style of fast food.

THE HERITAGE MAKERS

The idea of setting up a heritage centre on Skye was devised and put in motion by two local Gaelic speakers, Donald and Calein, both of whom, then in their thirties, had been involved in a number of Gaelic revival projects on the island. The 'Gaelic revival' or 'Gaelic renaissance' is a movement to maintain and increase the amount of Gaelic spoken in Scotland which, particularly since the mid-1980s, has spawned numerous Gaelic developments, including Gaelic play groups, Gaelic medium primary schooling, community history projects, community cooperatives, Gaelic festivals, and enormous increases in the number of hours of Gaelic television broadcasting throughout Scotland. In the late 1980s Donald and Calein were both 'looking around for something new', a future source of employment and income, when Calein's visit to the Jorvik Viking Centre inspired them to investigate the possibility of a similar kind of heritage representation on Skye. They were later joined by two of their Gaelic-speaking peers who had complementary skills; and invited the historian, James Hunter, to help them formulate the ideas for the exhibition.

Donald and Calein are representative of a younger generation of Gaelic speakers who, were it not for the Gaelic revival and the jobs (mostly in the cultural industries) which it has created, would almost certainly have had to leave the island to find work elsewhere. In using their 'Gaelicness' to stay on the island and also 'attain a certain standard [of living]', as Donald puts it, this 'revival generation' has to ally Gaelic with ideas of commercial enterprise. When Donald talks of *Aros*, and his own experiences in the revival more generally, he repeatedly assimilates Gaelic to enterprise. He refers to 'the revival or business or whatever you call it', taking them as apparently synonymous; he accounts for his own participation in the revival in terms of the life experience that turned him into an enterprising person; and he tells me that the name of the centre, 'Aros', was chosen both because it means 'dwelling' or 'home' in Gaelic and the exhibition was to be 'the home of the Skye story' and because 'from the marketing point of view it starts with an A, so it's important to be top of the list and that sort of thing.'

This linkage of Gaelic and commercial enterprise is antithetical to the romanticism which has long been a principal lens for viewing the Scottish Highlands. Within romantic discourse, Gaelic culture seems to act as a repository for many of the qualities which the urban, industrialised and rational world to the south lacks (Chapman 1982: 129; see also Chapman 1978); so making the association of Gaelic culture with those 'Southern' qualities feel like category errors (or jokes). For many older Gaelic speakers too, though for different reasons, Gaelic and enterprise are often seen as opposed. In this case, it is a view of Gaelic as a 'waste of public money', and suspicions over the use of Gaelic for social mobility, that inform their distrust of the association. Revivalists are well aware of older Gaels' alternative view, but they contest it. As one involved in the island's heritage strategy said to me: 'Gaelic is not just about the old folks. If it is to have a future it has to be about us too. That's what we've got to change. We've got to say it's not about a dying way of life.' Accommodating Gaelic with commercialism, then, is seen by revivalists as a way of giving new strength to the language and culture. In the revivalists' vision, the market and tourism are appropriated and put to the service of Gaelic culture. In some ways we could argue that this is seen by them, not so much as the commodification of culture, as the Gaelicisation of commerce; though it is probably more accurate to argue that the two exist alongside one another and are not seen as mutually exclusive. In some ways, this articulation of enterprise with Gaelic is like that between enterprise and heritage more broadly. As Corner and Harvey have argued, although these might appear to be 'self-evidently in opposition', both involve a 'powerful articulation of past, present and future' and can act in a mutually supportive way (Corner and Harvey 1991b: 46). What is more, they suggest that, although enterprise and heritage have been particularly used to support one another in the discourse of 'the Right', they also 'connect with alternative visions of society' (Corner and Harvey 1991b: 75). In other words, they and their linkage contain the potential for articulating with other kinds of politics (cf. Urry 1990: 110; McCrone et al. 1995: 23f.). This certainly seems to be the case with Aros.

Donald, who is the manager of the centre, describes what he and his colleagues have been trying to do as 'cultural tourism'. He argues that this is distinct from much of Skye's tourism in that it is 'for the people', i.e. the people who live in Skye, rather than primarily 'for the tourist'. In making this argument he refers me to various documents that have been issued by Highlands and Islands Enterprise (a government-funded organisation which oversees development in the Scottish Highlands) and Commun na Gàidhlig (an organisation concerned mainly with the support of Gaelic) which explain and make a case for the promotion of 'cultural tourism' in the Highlands. They do so by casting 'Gaelic heritage' as 'an under-utilised resource' which can be used as a 'development tool' to attract tourists

(Pedersen and Shaw 1993: 1). Although on the one hand this might be seen as a model in which Gaelic culture becomes a commodity, it is important to note that this model of tourism does not presuppose that 'Gaelic culture' can, therefore, be 'bought' and exchanged by whoever should wish to do so. Gaelic culture is a 'resource' not so much in the sense of being something available to be transformed and used, though there is something of that involved, but in the sense of being Gaels' own repository of 'inner reserves' on which they can draw. This is a conception of 'resource' as potentially active, as a transformative tool, which can play a part in 'enhanc[ing] ... the development of Gaelic culture and society' (Pedersen and Shaw 1993: 1). Rather than as material to be acted upon, Gaelic culture is perceived as an agent which can shape the course of development. And 'development' here is not accepted as meaning conversion into an industrial, urban archetype but as strengthening and extending the local and traditional. This is a process which McKean, in his discussion of Balinese tourism, has described, after Geertz (1963), as 'cultural involution' (McKean 1989: 126). Instead of development being conceptualised as distinct from local culture, in a dualistic model which assumes that 'change' is imposed from the outside, it is fully incorporated within it, and, as such, carried out on local terms and potentially used to strengthen local pride and interest in traditional culture. In this way, cultural involution can lead to the conservation and elaboration of the traditional. Where conventional tourism might lead to cultural 'dilution', 'cultural tourism' aims to produce its intensification.

The makers of *Aros*, then, are local Gaelic speakers who have a vested interest in local heritage and Gaelic culture, and this is both for employment and as a source of their identities. As young, upwardly-mobile individuals whose self-definition is also formed partly in opposition to that of many older Gaels, their interest and engagement is also just as much with the future as with the past, and with change as with tradition. It is their specific vision, and in particular their attempt to forge a new Gaelic identity, which informs and indeed is part of the motive force for the story that the exhibition tells.

MYTHS, HISTORIES AND STORIES

The makers of *Aros* are emphatic that the centre is not just intended for tourists. On the practical front they point to the jobs it provides and say that, as the majority of these are held by young Gaelic speakers, the centre helps to curb some of the out-migration that Highland areas typically suffer. Just as significantly, however, *Aros is also seen as a resource for local people in 'understanding their history'. The exhibition is aimed primarily, Donald argues:*

> [at] the people. It's for the people. It's for the ordinary person who lives on a croft, really. That's who it's done for. It's aimed at a lot of people, you know, whoever's interested in their history and in their culture who wants to get a wee bit extra from what they would get in most of the story books.

Telling local people of their history, and going beyond 'the story books', is particularly important, according to Donald, because:

> we find that a lot of them are not well versed in their history in this part of the

world. There's an awful lot of myths told about their history. So we feel
that...somebody had to deal with them.

The tourist industry is a particularly powerful player in the perpetration of these
myths; so what *Aros* does is to use the technical means of this industry, the heritage
display, to tell what is intended to be 'quite a radical story'. This telling is not,
however, openly confrontational. Rather than refer outright to the accounts told by
Skye's other main tellers of Skye heritage, namely the clan centres (the Clan Donald
centre at Armadale Castle, ancestral home of the MacDonalds, and Dunvegan
Castle, ancestral home of the MacLeods), *Aros* provides an alternative account:

> The story we tell is very different from what is told elsewhere in Skye, especially
> Dunvegan Castle and Clan Donald. I'm not criticising what they are doing at
> all but it is a very different story, told from a different point of view. But we were
> also very careful not to step on their toes.

The clan centres deal mainly with history surrounding the clan system, which is
generally said to have ended with the Battle of Culloden in 1746. *Aros* deals mainly
with more recent history. The clan centres focus on the history of the lairds, whereas
Aros deals primarily with 'the people', that is, the crofters. However, there are areas of
overlap, especially in dealing with Bonnie Prince Charlie. What is more, *Aros*
incorporates a good deal of implicit intertextual reference to more romantic historical
accounts and it also very pointedly depicts some aspects of the activities of clan chiefs
which are certainly not mentioned in the clan centres (e.g. the 'slavery' episode,
discussed later in the chapter).

By Donald's own account, many visitors seem readily to perceive *Aros*'s difference
from the histories that they have previously encountered:

> One of the things we find...if a bus comes in here and they go through the
> exhibition, so many of them come out and say 'That's totally different from
> what the courier told me.' The courier loves to tell the romantic side of things,
> Bonnie Prince Charlie as being, you know, this wonderful character who, you
> know, ran up the hills and sort of slept in caves and...invented Drambuie and
> all this sort of nonsense. And that's not how it was. So we do open a few
> people's eyes.

Using heritage to counter alternative heritage accounts is, then, one feature of *Aros*.
This is no simple matter, however, for why should visitors believe the account at *Aros*
rather than that at the other sites? Donald himself repeatedly refers to *Aros* as a 'story'
– 'we tried to tell a story which...', 'we tell the story and let them make up their own
minds', and indeed the exhibition's title is *The Skye Story*. In using the term 'story',
Donald signals awareness of the fact that the exhibition, as with historical accounts in
books, is a particular *version* of history, told from a particular 'point of view'. It is also
only a very small part of what might potentially be told ('we could only go into so
much'); and is significantly different from many other accounts of Skye history ('it's a
very different story from that told elsewhere'). Donald clearly leaves space then for
alternative accounts of history. This vision of history as having alternatives, and as
only ever being partially represented and from particular perspectives, is very
different from the crude opposition of 'true history' versus 'bogus history' which is

used by Hewison in his critique of the heritage industry (1987). Perhaps, as Angela Morris (1991) has suggested, this vision of history as having alternative versions is more easily accepted in Scotland, where there has long been an awareness that Scottish history is not the same as English history or even that which passes as British.

Yet, despite the careful characterisation of history as story, Donald and the other creators of *Aros* are certainly not licensing a view that all accounts are equally correct or that veracity is unimportant:

> It was very important to us that we were factually correct. We did a lot of research. And we were very careful. If we were in doubt about anything we didn't use it.

A central aim of the exhibition, Donald says, is 'to uncover the myths' that are told about Skye history. Myths in this context are not simply accounts told from different vantage points (as are stories) but are factually incorrect and get in the way of a version of history both more authentic and more meaningful to local people. Myths are based on lies which should be revealed.

Moreover, although the exhibition uses technologies of display which have been associated by various cultural theorists with the decline of authenticity, and in particular with what Benjamin calls 'the withering of aura' (1973: 215), it by no means abandons authenticating devices and ploys. As we shall see below, although the exhibition consists almost entirely of reproductions rather than 'real' old artefacts, it finds plenty of non-auratic means to attempt to enlist visitors to its account. So, although *Aros* admits to being a story, we should observe that it also claims to be *the* Skye story, the story *of* Skye, and the story *from* the Skye point of view.

Aros is not, however, only an account of the past. Nor can its version of the past be described as 'nostalgic', as has been the accusation levelled at many heritage centres. Far from attempting to 'draw...a screen between ourselves and our true past', as Hewison (1987: 10) argues is characteristic of the heritage industry, *Aros* is very directly concerned with making links between past and present. Rather than being a 'denial of the future' (Hewison 1987: 46), it is an assertion of it.

THE SKYE STORY

While the clan centres concentrate particularly upon an aristocratic history of clan chiefs, *Aros* focuses upon the history of 'the people', a term used in the Highlands to refer to 'crofters' as opposed to 'lairds', and which also has wider socialist connotations (Macdonald 1997; Bennett 1988). *Aros* is also much more consciously politicised than Skye's various folklife museums, which nostalgically depict a way of life that has largely passed. *Aros*'s story is very different from that at the clan centres, principally in that it depicts the clan chiefs as largely responsible for the historical hardships which Skye people have suffered. It tells a story of atrocities endured and of the way in which the people resisted and are now enjoying a renaissance of their culture and language. As such, *Aros* attempts to point out the political causes for the depopulation of the Highlands and the decline of Gaelic culture and language; and to attribute agency for overcoming these problems to the people themselves. The exhibition seeks, in various ways, to tie the idea of the people and resistance together with the Gaelic language and culture, so making contemporary efforts to revitalise

Gaelic (the 'Gaelic Revival') the outcome of a long-standing popular battle against oppression. In so doing, it selects a particular set of events and figures to create its story, a process inevitably involving inclusion and exclusion.

The opening vignette at *Aros*, a woman sitting at a fire with a kettle, is the beginning point of establishing this linkage (see Figure 8.1). Although she looks like the stereotypical old woman from the past that can be seen at so many heritage centres and folklife museums (and was no doubt from the same cast and intended perhaps to remind us of the folklife model), she is intended here to be a specific person, Mary MacPherson or Màiri Mhór nan Oran (Big Mary of the Songs). She was a nineteenth-century Skye poetess who is a heroine of the Crofters' Wars (or Land Wars) when local people demonstrated against their removal from the land to make way for sheep. Although the exhibition does not mention it, Màiri also made flattering references in her poems to MacDonald of Sleat, one of Skye's worst landlords (Mac Gill-eain 1985).

The linkage of the Gaelic language and popular resistance is also made in a reconstruction of a Napier Commission hearing. The Napier Commission, established in the 1880s by the Government as a way of trying to assess the crofters' grievances that had been demonstrated in the Land Wars, toured the Highlands

Figure 8.1 Màiri Mhr nan Oran: Gaelic poet and clearances heroine

taking evidence from crofter representatives; and the Commission's report led to considerably improved legislation for crofters, giving them security of tenure and distributing land that had been taken from crofters back to them. At the hearing shown at *Aros* the crofter representative, Angus Stewart from Braes, stated that he preferred to give testimony in Gaelic rather than English. Quite why he did so is not clear. Perhaps he was more confident of his fluency in Gaelic, perhaps he thought his account would be less likely to get back to his landlord, or perhaps it was indeed a political statement as it is interpreted at *Aros*, where Stewart is commended for standing up for his people and his language.

The Gaelic language is more specifically commented on in various other sections of the exhibition. Its status as 'high culture' is established through reproductions from the Book of the Deer and the Book of Kells which are intended to illustrate that Gaeldom was 'a beacon of civilisation when the surrounding countries were heathen and illiterate' (as the exhibition states). Although the books are reproductions, they are placed under glass casing, using a museum representational technique to confirm their auratic and international value. This is one of a number of ways in which Gaelic's significance is extended out from the local. Through referring to Gaelic as 'The Lion's Tongue', the exhibition defines Gaelic as the language of Scotland, not merely of the Highlands (see MacKinnon 1974).

Yet in fact Gaelic has never been spoken by all the population within what is now Scotland; and the idea that the Gaelic language should be seen as 'Scotland's language' today is controversial (Withers 1984). The exhibition tells no direct lies here, it simply heads the section on Gaelic with what is a well-known slogan, but it makes implications which are questionable. Gaelic is also defined as a Celtic, a European and a minority language. A map of Europe shows 'minority languages', visually establishing their minority ethnic kinship (McDonald 1986), and notes that they have been driven from their previous strongholds. No explanation of the processes involved or of their variations is given, but an agency is implied that the rest of the exhibition can fill in for the Gaelic case. Again, the condensed means of exhibition presentation creates a less equivocal picture than a more discursive account might convey (see Figure 8.2).

Gaelic language and culture today are also specifically commented upon in a section near the end of the exhibition, entitled 'Contemporary Skye'. This includes a collage depicting various indicators of Gaelic revivalism: Gaelic road signs; Gaelic cartoon figures (*Angus Og*, apparently modelled on a man from North Skye; and Postman Pat in his Gaelic incarnation as *Padraig Post*); and bagpipes and posters for *Runrig* (a successful rock group from Skye who sing in both Gaelic and English and blend mainstream rock with Gaelic traditional song). Here we are shown a thriving and modern Gaelic culture, and one which merges seamlessly with the past.

Aros also deals with the favourite Skye romantic subject: Bonnie Prince Charlie. However, it does not present the heroic tale that is favoured in many popular histories. The Jacobite rebellion which the Prince led in 1745, and the Battle of Culloden (1746) at which the cause was lost, are not related as a near triumph of Scotland over England but as something of a disaster for Highland people (see Pittock 1991). The romantic construction of the episode seems to be commented upon through the display styles, where Culloden is portrayed in a (specially commissioned) painting which seems to parody depictions of heroic battle scenes rather than attempt

Figure 8.2 Contemporary Skye: collage with Padraig Post (Postman Pat) and Angus Og

to be realistic (see Figure 8.3). Aesthetic intertextualism continues with gilt-framed reproductions of famous paintings of the Prince and Flora MacDonald (see Figure 8.4). These are hung above the words of two carefully juxtaposed songs: the Skye Boat Song ('Fly bonnie boat like a bird on the wing...'), which is described as being one of the sources of romantic versions of the episode; and a Gaelic song of the period which laments loved ones lost in battle.

A walk-in reconstruction depicts what Donald tells me is one of the few well-evidenced aspects of the Young Pretender's stay on Skye. It is a scene from MacNab's Inn in Portree, where the Prince stayed briefly. However, rather than showing him as a Highland hero, the reconstruction illustrates that he was an aristocratic outsider who did not know or understand the codes of the place. He is shown, and described on the taped commentary, as not wanting to share a drinking cup (as was Highland practice), and tipping the inn keeper lavishly, so leading MacNab to suspect his true identity (see Figure 8.5).

The account of the Prince also addresses the lack of support he received from Skye's main clan chiefs, MacDonald of Sleat and MacLeod of Dunvegan. Many histories account for this in terms of the chiefs' reluctance to participate in an ill-

Figure 8.3 Culloden: representing the battle

Figure 8.4 Bonnie Prince Charlie and Flora MacDonald: representing representations

Figure 8.5 A suspicious MacNab: breaking the myth

planned and under-resourced campaign by the headstrong Young Pretender. *The Skye Story*, however, argues that the chiefs were in effect bribed into inaction because their roles in a 'slave trade' from Skye had been rumbled. Skye people were being rounded up and sent out to America to work as slaves. In the most dramatic set of the exhibition, there is a large reconstruction of part of the slave ship – referred to as 'The Ship of the People' (*Soitheach nan Daoine*; see Figure 8.6). In most histories of the Highlands this fairly brief episode is given much less weight than the Clearances, which were a considerably more extensive and drawn-out process of people being either induced or forced to emigrate or otherwise moved off their land. By focusing on an event referred to as 'slavery', however, the exhibition deploys a more widely recognised, and indeed transnational, category. By doing so, the local is translated into terms which have greater semantic reach. This also sidesteps continuing and rancorous debate among historians over the extent to which the clan chief landlords were to blame for the Clearances, or whether they were themselves victims of wider economic forces (Hunter 1976; Richards 1982). Slavery, however, being universally regarded as morally disgraceful, provides an unequivocal symbolic statement countering the image of the clan chief as paternalistic benefactor.

Again, this is not simply a matter of the past, of 'dead heritage'. The role of landlords, many of whom are still clan chiefs, is also a contemporary issue, a long-standing source of dispute being over landlords' responsibility for the well-being of their tenants versus their aim to make profit from their estates. The historian James Hunter, who wrote the storyline of the exhibition in collaboration with Donald and Calein, has taken public issue with historians who he feels absolve the landlords of blame, and has made clear that he sees this as a contemporary as well as a historical matter. He has also been actively involved in contemporary crofting politics, particularly through having played a key role in the establishment of the Crofters Union, which works for crofters' rights today (Hunter 1991). His vision, and that of

Figure 8.6 The Ship of the People: Highland slavery

the others involved in creating *The Skye Story*, is one in which history is a matter of highly politicised contemporary significance. This is not to say that the exhibition is a polemic. On the contrary, the past–present linkages are mostly implicit, constructed through the linkage of sets, and the recurrence of the theme of the oppression of Gaels and their resistance to oppression. The creators of *The Skye Story* are well aware that to present too ostensibly political an account risks alienating visitors and thereby reducing the exhibition's power to compel its audience. Although Donald tells me that the aim of the exhibition is to 'let visitors make up their own minds', we have already seen that it contains a carefully orchestrated narrative and that the exhibition-makers have certainly not relinquished either the notion of 'fact' or a sense of the importance of the past. If visitors are being allowed to 'make up their own minds', they are not being allowed to make them up in conditions of their own choosing. The display technologies of *Aros*, to which we now turn, are directed towards leading visitors in particular, chosen, directions.

AUTHENTICITY AT AROS

Aros's attempt to be *the* Skye story inevitably, if indirectly, brings it into competition with Skye's other heritage sites and other versions of history. Lacking most of the features which stamp these sites as authentic, *Aros* nevertheless is concerned to present itself as an important and true account.

The island's clan history is the basis for its most commercially successful heritage sites, Dunvegan Castle and the Clan Donald Centre. Both make their claims to authenticity through place or *siting* and through genealogy, a putative connection through blood over time. In both cases, though, we might note that the present castles were largely created in the nineteenth century (the fashion for towers and castellation being inspired partly by Sir Walter Scott), although as they partly incorporated former buildings they can claim to be older and are widely assumed to be so. In addition to their own fairly aristocratic histories, both sites also lay claims upon what is perhaps the most famous aspect of Skye's myth-history, Bonnie Prince Charlie's attempt for the throne in the mid-eighteenth century, and in particular the assistance he received from 'Skye lass' Flora MacDonald. This is partly established through artefacts: Dunvegan has a lock of the Prince's hair and Flora's stays, and Clan Donald has some shoe buckles of the Prince and a wine glass out of which he is said to have drunk. Any such object is 'auratic' in Benjamin's terms; it has an authenticity which 'is the essence of all that is transmissible from its beginning, ranging from its substantive duration to its testimony to the history which it has experienced' (Benjamin 1973: 215). Its unique existence is based in its 'historical testimony' (1973: 214). It is imbued with the magic of having 'been there'.

It is through the auratic modalities of age, site and artefact that Skye's many other castles, ruins, historic houses and folklife museums are authenticated. This is the case for the history of crofters as well as of the clan chiefs. The Skye Museum of Island Life at Kilmuir, for example, consists of 'black houses', nineteenth-century thatched cottages which have been either restored or moved to the site and are mostly filled with artefacts of the period (and some Flora MacDonald items). When talking with the creator and manager of this museum, he repeatedly uses the phrase 'old things...I would not have anything artificial, no'. The idea of the museum as an amassing of old things is what predominates. Although these aged artefacts are arranged into different houses (such as the Smithy, the Weaver's house, the Ceilidh house), and although there is an attempt in some of them to reconstruct room settings, this is secondary to the collection principle. What is more, the reconstructions do not aim for the historical accuracy of a kind of photo-snapshot of a particular time and place in the past ('token-isomorphism' as Handler and Saxton term it; 1988: 423). For example, the dresser of the main room of the Croft house is crammed with diverse objects, egg-cups, books, butter-shapers, a photograph of the museum's opening, all probably dating from between the mid-nineteenth century right up to the 1960s and 1970s. In the Smithy there are numerous rusting iron tools, many more surely than in a Smithy at that time; and whose dilapidated surfaces spell long-standing disuse. Rather than being true to their moment of use, these objects have a patina of age that 'serves as a kind of visual proof of status' (McCracken 1988: 32). It is age *per se* and the aura conveyed by having been part of a now-past way of life that legitimates these sites and their contents.

Aros, by contrast, does not for the most part contain original historical artefacts. Certainly, the reconstructions contain various apparently old objects, an iron kettle, creels, a butter churn, but we are not told whether they are reproductions or originals. When I ask about where they have come from, Donald tells me that he found most of them himself at home. Their material status, their *provenance*, does not particularly matter: what matters is that they convey the right kind of picture, for at *Aros* authenticity lies not in the aura of artefacts, but in the 'story' which gets told.

So how is this story, which competes with alternative, more established stories, made compelling and authoritative? There are a number of strategies at work here. One is the presentation of 'facts'. In much of the written text and in the audio narrative 'the story' is related in terms of 'such and such happened'. It is told as given. This, of course, is the *modus operandi* of heritage presentations: they do not normally discuss sources or alternatives; and their physical, material form itself connotes 'fact'. The exhibition is also a relatively closed or coercive one. A narrator, a male Highland voice, ties it all together into a seamless account; and unless visitors forgo the commentary altogether, they must traverse this exhibition at a fixed speed and in a particular direction. The use of headsets also makes it very difficult to talk with other visitors, so making the visitor experience very much an individual, and rather concentrated, one; and, again, shutting out some of the possible sources of unplanned and alternative readings.

An exhibition such as *The Skye Story* contains only a small amount of carefully selected material: as Donald says: 'We were very careful not to overload it'. This means, however, that details which do not neatly fit the story have been eliminated. There is none of the messiness which can generate alternative accounts, which is not to say that people may not come out with alternative interpretations but *Aros* does its best to prevent this. Its makers may recognise that *Aros* is only one story, only one interpretation, but they are nevertheless keen to make it as compelling as possible for those who visit.

However, the exhibition does not wholly abandon sourcing. In one section, about famine and hardship, the visitor is presented (in large, stark white print on a black background) with eye-witness evidence in the form of dated quotations from observers of the Highlands, Dr Johnson, Lady MacAskill and Sir Archibald Geikie. That even well-to-do English and Lowland outsiders should have been in no doubt about the dreadfulness of the situation is undoubtedly rhetorically persuasive, if ironic, in establishing such a picture as objectively the case.

The exhibition also makes selective use of realism in the form of three-dimensional naturalistic sets built to scale and often accompanied by appropriate sound effects (such as the lapping of waves). Here, the visitor enters into a bounded world which conceals, albeit momentarily and incompletely, the limits which give lie to its constructedness. Such realist representations are used for the most part to depict events which the exhibition-makers wish to foreground as central to understanding the people's experience: especially, the slave ship and the Napier Commission hearing, powerful symbols respectively of the oppression of the people and their resistance. The Bonnie Prince Charlie myth is also countered with a rather mundane realist scene, the Prince in MacNab's Inn. Its ordinariness serves as a metaphorical deflation of the romance which more usually characterises representations of the Prince.

As Haraway has argued, realism is both an epistemological and an aesthetic stance – the two are mutually supportive – whose:

> power... [lies] in its magical effects: what is so painfully constructed appears

effortlessly, spontaneously, found, discovered, simply there if one will only look. Realism does not appear to be a point of view.

(Haraway 1991: 38)

Realism is a powerful strategy for presenting an event in as incontrovertible a manner as possible. It makes it *look* real, 'and therefore it is real; in any case the fact that it seems real is real even if, like Alice in Wonderland, it never existed' (Eco 1986: 16). Such an emphasis on the visual, increasingly supplemented by other sensory modes, has been argued to be supplanting auratic, or what Eco calls 'historical', modes of authenticating (Eco 1986: 16). While this is surely not the case to the extent implied by both Benjamin and Eco (see Lumley 1988: 15), *Aros* clearly makes much use of an established, and perhaps increasingly widespread, means of authenticating its account.

The exhibition is not realist throughout, however, and indeed in some places, especially the depiction of Culloden, non-realist styles are used ironically to signal the constructed nature of the representations which have come down to us. The exhibition plays with different styles and juxtapositions; and sometimes it uses these to authorise its own selections (as when a piece of Skye rock, or reproductions of famous Celtic books, are put in glass casing), and at others to hint at the contrivance of accepted images (the gilt-framed portraits of the Prince and Flora). If the audience is assumed to be 'not well-versed in their history', their intertextual interpretative skills, by contrast, are expected, it seems, to be rather sophisticated. Although it has been suggested that visitors are increasingly well-capable of recognising and enjoying irony, and indeed this is a characteristic of 'post-tourists' (Feifer 1985; Urry 1990: 100), there is always a danger in such representations that this sophistication is overestimated (Riegel 1996). Perhaps partly in recognition of this, the taped commentary in *The Skye Story* is more direct and less ironic than are the visual exhibits. Throughout the exhibition, however, irony and intertextualism are only used to make particular points: there is no play with styles for their own sake. The story the exhibition tells, a story of Gaelic identity, past, present and future, is too important to the exhibition's makers for that.

If *The Skye Story* uses many technologies of display that have been associated with the proliferation of, and even revelling in, inauthenticity, and more generally with a post-modern emphasis on style and surface rather than depth and processes of production (see, for example, Harvey 1989; Jameson 1991), it does not do so in order to dispense with questions of authenticity, authority, narrative and origins. Nevertheless, display strategies are not all equally compelling, nor all equally suited to telling certain kinds of stories. While the emphasis on reproductions and 'mechanically produced' visual realism, rather than on original artefacts with their 'unique historical testimony' (Benjamin 1973: 215), has sometimes been associated with a politics of the Right, in *The Skye Story* the very malleability of reproductions (including reproductions without originals), the fact that 'the story' can predominate, seems to afford a popular or radical potential. Such reproductions can be used to tell stories where artefacts are typically mute: stories of hardship, of linguistic oppression, of power relations. Moreover, they seem particularly well-suited to creating the kind of past–present linkages and the vision of a dynamic and changing culture and identity that is attempted at *Aros*.

Appropriate though the representational technologies of *Aros* may be for articulating a changing rather than a static identity, they have by no means ousted either alternative modes of authenticating or alternative visions of 'Skye' or 'Gaelic' identity. Sites such as the castles and the folklife museums, not to mention Skye's dramatic physical landscape, have a hold on what are undoubtedly very powerful auratic forms of authenticity. These show no signs of 'withering', and, if visitor numbers are anything to go by, clearly exceed those of *Aros*. Perhaps *Aros*'s techniques, the techniques of the heritage model, will not be able effectively to compete. Why go to look at a set of reconstructions when the island abounds with what appears to be 'the real thing'?

Just as *Aros*'s modes of authenticating must compete with those of other heritage sites, so too must its (and its makers') constructions of culture and identity. One of the key questions here is how far the account presented in *The Skye Story* will be perceived as 'the people's history' by local people – will it be seen as theirs, and as an account to visit and revisit?

I have not conducted systematic research upon this topic but, on the basis of comments made to me by local people, the following might be noted. The 'de-mythifying' intention of *Aros* does seem to strike a chord with some. As one woman said of other accounts: 'they've kept so much from us', implying that *Aros* uncovers a conspiracy of silence. For others, however, the exhibition was regarded as having been intended for tourists. In only one case was this related to the content of the exhibition. In this case, an elderly man told me that it was clearly not directed at local people as, in his view, the history it presents would already be well known to them. 'It's very thin,' he said, comparing it unfavourably with a local folk museum where you could find pictures and names of people or relatives that you knew and where 'you could spend a month reading and not be done'. The relatively coercive directed technologies of *Aros* and the heritage model do not offer themselves up for the alternative readings and openness to independent historical research that this particular visitor preferred. For those others who viewed the exhibition as being directed more at tourists than themselves, it was the classification of *Aros* within a broader range of enterprises which were all assumed to be intended for outsiders. Its commercial dimensions almost always figured in this, with the exhibition's admission cost (£3 per adult) often given as a reason not to visit more than once. One man made the generality very clear: 'It's a commercial venture – they're all commercial ventures. They're for tourists, not for the likes of us'. He went on to disparage the general attempt to link Gaelic with business and to argue that the Gaelic revival was based upon a set of 'gimmicks' – to be inauthentic in his terms. An older Gaelic speaker, his view was part of an alternative cultural view that the younger revivalists hope to conquer.

INALIENABLE HERITAGE

Heritage has been seen by various commentators, especially Hewison (1987) and Wright (1985), as particularly bound up with a conservative politics. What we see at *Aros*, however, is heritage put to more radical use; a potential which Samuel (1994) argues has long been thoroughly part of the heritage movement (see also Urry 1990: 110, 1996; McCrone *et al.* 1995; and see Chapter 1 above).

The Skye Story has been constructed by a particular group of local people, young, fairly successful Gaelic speakers who are making a living from their 'Gaelicness'. It is a story they tell themselves about themselves (Geertz 1985: 448). This is a story of a distinctive local historical experience; a story of continued Gaelic resilience in the face of outside threat. It is a story which, I have suggested, the heritage format (which does not rely upon originals) may be well-suited to telling, though it is certainly neither uncontested nor without its problems (in particular, the danger that it may be misread or dismissed). But what of the charge that this kind of representation entails a commodification of culture and history?

How do the makers of *Aros* see the matter? As we have discussed, while they intend the centre to make money, they reject the opposition between Gaelic culture and commercial enterprise. Such an opposition would be to condemn their way of life to marginality and spell the end of their language; and it is an opposition which itself is imposed, at least in part, from outside. However, this is not to say that they see themselves as in any sense selling their heritage, for heritage is not conceptualised as a commodity.

In Gaelic, *Aros* is subtitled *Dualchas an Eilein*, which might be translated as 'the heritage of the Island' (an Eilein, the Island, being colloquially used to refer to Skye). However, *dualchas* means heritage in rather a specific sense. Rather than referring to the property, or material, that is inherited from generation to generation, for which the term *oighreachd* would be used (and which most dictionaries give as the standard translation of heritage), *dualchas* refers to more intangible matters of nature, character and duty. The following glosses are given in Gaelic's most comprehensive dictionary (which also notes the difficulty of translating the term literally):

> 1. Hereditary disposition or right. 2. Imitation of the ways of one's ancestors. 3. Bias of character. 4. Nature, temper. 5. Native place. 6. Hire, wages, dues. 6. [sic.] Duty.
>
> (Dwelly 1977: 367)

Dualchas is a kind of imperative, something to which one is obviously and undeniably connected. It might manifest itself in various ways (a child is not identical to its parents), and might be put to various uses, but at root it is inalienable, it is kept even while it is passed on (such as from one generation to the next).

This idea of the inalienable, and its embodiment in material form, as Weiner has argued, is a very different kind of relationship to objects than that of commodity-relations (Weiner 1992: 6). In commodity-exchange, ownership is transmitted from seller to buyer. 'Inalienable possessions', by contrast, involve what Weiner calls 'the paradox of keeping-while-giving': even while they enter into systems of exchange and social relations, they are 'kept' and 'imbued with the intrinsic and ineffable identities of their owners' (Weiner 1992: 6). This paradoxical quality of inalienable possessions means that they are also well-suited to mediating the paradox of continuity (or identity) through change. Weiner says:

> In one sense, an inalienable possession acts as a stabilizing force against change because its presence authenticates cosmological origins, kinship, and political histories.
>
> (1992: 9)

And yet precisely because of its role in cosmological authentication, an inalienable possession is likely to be a focus of struggles for change. Heritage is just such an inalienable possession (McCrone *et al.* 1995: 197). Outsiders may come to look, to learn and to admire, and they may take away souvenirs, knowledge and images, but this does not lead to a diminishment in what is 'kept' by the people. *Dualchas* is thus not a commodity; and nor does it have 'commodity candidacy' (Appadurai 1986a: 13), that is, the likelihood of becoming a commodity.

However, in using what has become a standardised model for proclaiming their heritage as distinctive, do *Aros*'s makers reduce the local to a familiar, and ultimately undistinctive, transnational archetype? Is it the case, as MacCannell (1992: 170) argues for the Amish, Black, Chicano, Dervish, Eskimo and Guyanan, that Gaels will find themselves subsumed in a wider system in which 'They can never *be* the body, they can only be incorporated, contained, "assimilated", taken into the body, eaten up'? Again, it is important to consider how they see the matter.

The story that *Aros* tells is not of a pristine, untouched culture. On the contrary, much of the story concerns contact and relations with outsiders. However, as 'heritage' is not conceptualised as a bounded body of material, these interactions often highlight the manifestation of *dualchas* (particularly resilience) rather than its corruption; and in the story which is told, it is Gaelic culture which incorporates and appropriates material and practices from outside. *The Skye Story* has no problem with showing Gaels making use of outside agencies (such as the Napier Commission) or of defining that which has been appropriated as Gaelic (Postman Pat). The primary origins of things and practices are not what matters. What matters, and this meshes with the view of history being told from alternative vantage points, is the perspective from which they are now seen. Heritage is, in part, a strategy of appropriation.

To some extent, what is also involved here is a strong sense of the inalienability of *dualchas*. As Weiner has argued for inalienable possessions, this alters the character of exchange:

> Because each inalienable possession is subjectively unique ... exchange does not produce a homogeneous totality, but rather is an arena where heterogeneity is determined.... The possession not only authenticates the authority of its owner, but affects all other transactions even if it is not being exchanged.
>
> (Weiner 1992: 10)

Not only does this imply that heritage can be an arena for determining identity; it also suggests that the commodity relations which also surround heritage might be seen as distinct from ordinary commodity relations. Not so much a commodification of history and culture, what might be involved here (as Miller has argued for Christmas) is a 'sacralisation' of consumption (Miller 1994: 106).

CONCLUSION

These local understandings can be used to alert us to some of our own analytical presuppositions. On culture and the tourist encounter, they show that we need not conceptualise culture as 'an original pure state ... like the ethnographic present, before contact ... as if history begins with tourism, which then pollutes the world' (Bruner 1994: 408; see Chapter 1 above). Alternative, more dynamic, notions of culture are available – notions which allow for local, as well as global, appropriation (Gewertz and Errington 1991). Moreover, they highlight some of the dangers of a proprietorial discourse of 'origins'. Categories such as cultural identity and heritage are part of 'an international political model that people all over the globe use to construct images of others and themselves' (Handler and Linnekin 1984: 287). They act as a transnational symbolic resource for self-definition, though they may also be given their own local inflections (Appadurai and Breckenridge 1992). While there undoubtedly are differentials in the global flow of images and meanings (see Lash and Urry 1994; Hannerz 1992), the reflexive layerings and multiple borrowings have, by now, surely become so complex that we cannot easily assign ownership. Wherever we live, we do so to some extent in categories which have been defined elsewhere. As Eco wrote of the 'global village': 'all are in it, and all are outside it: Power is elusive, and there is no telling where the "plan" comes from' (Eco 1986: 149).

To see local people as merely the passive recipients of an external world which impinges upon them is rather like the conceit of tourists who assign local people only the role of object of the tourist gaze. As we have seen here, not only may they be well aware of external images of them, they may also attempt actively to counter those images and to construct alternative visions of their history and culture. Using a transnational and commodified format to do this does not necessarily mean abandoning local notions of heritage and identity, and may, moreover, help establish the significance of local experience. The heritage centre, and cultural tourism more generally, *can* be a way of telling the people's story, and of helping to make sure that it will be heard.

ACKNOWLEDGEMENTS

I offer grateful thanks to all those in Skye who helped me with this research, especially Donald MacDonald, Jonathan Macdonald and Sìne Gillespie. The following made many helpful comments on earlier versions of this chapter: Mike Beaney, Kevin Hetherington, John Urry, and participants at Sussex University and St Andrews Social Anthropology seminars.

9

TOURISM AND THE PHOTOGRAPHIC EYE

Carol Crawshaw and John Urry

INTRODUCTION

It has become relatively commonplace to discuss the different ways in which travel and tourism are bound up with photographic practices. In going beyond existing literature, it is our aim in this chapter to explore these interconnections in more depth. First, we shall establish general links between photography and the debates surrounding the role and significance of 'the visual'. The photographic practices and discourses which serve to represent tourism and travel are shown to be variants of more far-reaching and influential themes within Western social thought. Second, we examine some of the sources of photographic discourse and especially how the desire to photograph came to be historically established. Third, while there has been much speculation about the relationships between tourism and photography, there has been little empirical investigation into their connections. In setting the photography/tourism relationship within a wider debate, we draw upon our recent qualitative research into the practices of professional photographers and the influence of photographic images on tourists' perceptions of place.

THE NATURE OF THE VISUAL[1]

In *The Tourist Gaze*, the fundamentally visual nature of the tourism experience was analysed (Urry 1990). This book described how changes in tourism practices could be related to the way in which people perceive – 'gaze at' – objects and places and condition what they expect to gaze upon. The emphasis on the visual did not imply that 'gazing' was a purely individual activity (see Chapter 4 above). On the contrary, it was argued that the nature of tourists' perceptions is often collective and depends on a variety of social discourses organised by professionals, including photographers, travel writers, travel agents, tour operators, TV presenters and tourism policy-makers.

Different gazes are 'authorised' by different discourses. Examples include the discourse of *education* which conditioned the experience of the European Grand Tour, that of *health* which defines a type of tourism whose aim is to restore the individual to a state of physical well-being, and the discourse of *play* which surrounds what can be called 'liminal' tourism. Different discourses imply different socialities. In *The Tourist Gaze*, a distinction was drawn between 'romantic' and 'collective' tourist gazes. In the former, the emphasis is upon solitude, privacy and a personal, semi-spiritual relationship with the object of the gaze. The presence of other people detracts from the quality of the experience. The 'collective' gaze by contrast involves conviviality. Other people are necessary to give atmosphere to the experience of place which then becomes a shared process of visual consumption.

In order to understand the complex connections between seeing and perception, it is important to reconsider the very notion of the visual and more generally the privileging of the eye over other senses. In the history of Western societies, sight has long been regarded as the noblest of the senses. It has been viewed as the most discriminating and reliable of the sensual mediators between people and their physical environment (Jay 1986: 178). Epistemologically, Rorty (1980) asserts that in post-Cartesian thought, mental representations of the external world have been based primarily on internalised visual images, 'in the mind's eye'. As he puts it:

> It is pictures rather than propositions, metaphors rather than statements, which determine most of our philosophical convictions ... the story of the domination of the mind of the West by ocular metaphors.
>
> (Rorty 1980: 12–13; and see Chapter 1 above)

However, as certain French social philosophers, notably Foucault, have argued, the primacy of the visual does not necessarily have positive social implications. Ocularcentrism also has a dark side. In *Madness and Civilisation* (1967), Foucault describes how, in seventeenth- and eighteenth-century France, madness was treated as an object of pure spectacle, detached from the worlds of human understanding and compassion. He shows how, with the development of the asylum in the nineteenth century, this essentially visual representation of insanity became institutionalised, a process further explored in *The Birth of the Clinic* (1976). This study is concerned with the complicity of visual domination in the control exercised by scientific knowledge. Foucault describes the heightened faith in medical evidence as being vested in the 'sovereign power of the empirical gaze', which is said to have 'marvellous density of perception, offering the grain of things as the first face of truth' (Foucault 1976: xiii). Within science generally, and medicine specifically, the eye develops as the 'depository and source of clarity' (Foucault 1976: xii, 88). This process became institutionalised with the development of the medical clinic, 'probably the first attempt to order a science on the exercise and decisions of the gaze' (Foucault 1976: 89). Within the context of the clinic, the gaze of the healer is not merely that of an observer, but of a medical 'expert', a 'doctor' endowed with the authority of an institution. Thus the visual becomes central to the power of medical discourse.

In *The Archaeology of Knowledge* (1972) Foucault criticises the notion of a single synthetic subject as the source of a sovereign gaze. Here, Foucault presents the complexities of discourse as being 'not the majestically unfolding manifestation of a thinking, knowing subject, but, on the contrary, a totality ... a space of exteriority in which a network of sites is deployed' (Foucault 1972: 55). This complexity of discourse is demonstrated in *Discipline and Punish* (1979). He shows, through the famous example of Bentham's model prison, how ocular discipline is fundamentally spatial, being rooted in the architectural geography of the building which is represented as a panopticon. In an environment such as this, where control is exercised through the 'benevolently sadistic gaze of a diffuse and anonymous power' (Jay 1986: 191), the individual is both surveyor and surveyed. Each inmate interiorises the gaze 'to the point that he is his own overseer, each individual thus exercising this surveillance over, and against, himself' (Foucault 1980: 155). Almost anyone could operate the panopticon. By extension, Foucault asserts that contemporary society as a whole is: 'not one of spectacle, but of surveillance. . . . We are neither in the amphitheatre nor on the stage, but in the panoptic machine' (1979: 217). Thus for Foucault the all-seeing eye has exacted a terrible revenge; and except in his concept of heterotopia, he ignores the possibilities of alternative seeings and viewings (Foucault 1970; Jay 1986: 194).

How can these expositions of the visual help to illuminate travel and tourism practices? What are the leisure equivalencies of these effects of the gaze? Since tourism involves observation and spectacle, does tourism imply systems of panopticon-like surveillance? By the end of the eighteenth century the focus of travel in Europe shifted from scholastic pursuits to visual pleasure, from the traveller's ear to the traveller's eye (Adler 1989: 7). From then on, sight becomes highly significant in the ordering of tourist and travel discourses. In most such discourses there is a particular emphasis upon the seeing and collecting of sights. Everyday expressions such as 'seeing the sights', 'capturing the view', 'eye-catching scenery', 'picturesque villages', 'pretty as a postcard', illustrate the significance of the eye to both the traveller and the travel promoter. Sometimes tourism seems to be understood as little more than the collection of disparate and unconnected sights which are given an objectified form in travel brochures, postcards and photographs. Furthermore, the promotion and practice of collecting sights can dominate the very pattern of travel, which is often organised to facilitate fleeting views of spectacular scapes (see Urry 1990: 138–40).

Despite the apparent popularity of sightseeing among the travelling public, this type of tourism is commonly denigrated. The experience is generally taken to be irreducibly superficial, both because it only involves the sense of sight and because the tourist follows well-trodden routes leading to very familiar viewing points. To be seen as mere sightseers will embarrass even the most seasoned tourists. For some, the very term 'tourist' itself is pejorative and many people will seek to describe themselves instead as 'visitor' or 'traveller'. By analogy with Foucault's analysis of the dark side of sight, there is a tendency to denigrate the visual within the academic literature concerned with tourism. Sight is not seen as the noblest of the senses in travel, but as one which may get in the way of what are deemed to be real experiences, which ideally should involve a variety of senses (see Boorstin 1964). Criticism is levelled both at the sight-seeing tourists, and at the agencies which promote places primarily for visual consumption (see Buzard 1993).

Tourism practices can involve an equivalent process to the surveillance of people behind bars. The 'bars' here can be the camera, or the ethnic costumes, or the picturesque honey-pot. In each case visitors are thought to possess all-seeing eyes which are able to identify real, authentic local people and local customs.

MacCannell (1989) has analysed the 'staged authenticity' of many tourist sites. In popular places the gaze of tourists, and especially the all-seeing lens, can intrude upon the everyday lives of local people. Apparently authentic back-stages may be artificially created by local people and entrepreneurs to redirect the gaze and hence reduce the degree of intrusion. Staged authenticity thus arises from the socio-spatial relations built around the attempts by visitors to consume places and people visually, and by the activities of locals to manage and limit the effects of the all-seeing eye (and see Chapter 7 on employment relations and staged authenticity).

Moreover, we can see something analogous to the processes of interiorisation as produced by the panopticon. Those living in tourist 'honey-pots' may believe that they are always being gazed upon, even if they are not in fact visible. So locals may not venture out, or they may do so only in ways appropriate to the gaze. Thus, the gaze may be interiorised, creating a universal visibility which serves a meticulous, rigorous, powerful eye. Locals may seek to restrict the length of the tourist season, to preserve part of the year 'out of season – out of sight' of the eye and the lens (Crawshaw 1994a).

Finally, there are ways of being a tourist that can challenge and disturb dominant constructions of the spaces of a town or city, heterotopias. This notion takes up the idea of a flâneur, the strolling pedestrian who is able to travel, arrive, gaze, move on, be anonymous in a kind of liminal zone. The flâneur is attracted to the city's dark corners, to chance encounters to confront the unexpected, to engage in a kind of counter-tourism that involves a poetic confrontation with the 'dark corners' occupied by the dispossessed and marginal of a town or city, and to experience supposedly 'real' 'authentic' life uncluttered by the dominant visual/tourist images of that place (see Tester 1994a).

We have so far presumed that tourism does predominantly involve the visual appropriation of place. However, one issue centrally important in tourism is that of memory. Much tourism involves memory. In a kind of way tourism is the appropriation of the memories of others. And yet it might be argued that the sense of sight is not so significant in relationship to memory as are various other senses. It could be claimed that it is the body that knows and remembers, through a whole variety of senses and actions. This is not just a question of the visual but of what Bachelard terms 'reverberations'. This is a metaphor of sound waves, rather than of sight (Bachelard 1969). Part at least of what is remembered consists of certain bodily configurations, especially as they relate to touch, hearing, and smell as well as sight. In Proust's inimitable phrase, 'our arms and legs are full of torpid memories' (cited Lowenthal 1985: 203; and see Lash and Urry 1994: 240–1).

Nevertheless, the visual is centrally important in the construction of touristic memories. When we are away from our usual surroundings, travelling for pleasure or necessity, all of our senses are heightened by the experience of different food and drink, temperatures, sounds and so on (see Rodaway 1994, on the geography of the senses). But it is the visual images of places that give shape and meaning to the anticipation, experience and memories of travelling. First, people's memories of tourist sites are often invoked because of particular visual images which they have seen in advance or seen while they are visiting. Second, visitors themselves help to construct their memories through the photographs they take and the postcards they purchase. Tourism involves going away from the normal environment and coming back again, with suntans, souvenirs, snapshots. Photographs provide evidence – that you have been away, that the mountains were that high, that the weather was so good. At home, afterwards, visual images are interwoven with verbal commentary to remember the experience and to tell others about it (Crawshaw 1994a: 14). This process of memory-production is significantly social and involves working at the realisation of memory (see Middleton and Edwards 1990). Third, many of the images that we visually consume when we are travelling are, in effect, the memories of others which are then visually consumed by us. But finally, there is an enormous array of photographic images within tourism which we are exposed to and which can bombard and overload our memories, images that may provide little in the way of meaning and which make it hard to put together and hang on to our personal memories of a particular place.

In the next section we turn more directly to the relationships of tourism and photography, which we have already noted particularly represents the omnipotent eye for both tourists and those who are visited and subject to its power of surveillance.

THE DESIRE TO TRAVEL AND TO PHOTOGRAPH

The development of photography and the growth of tourism have been closely bound together. The invention of the camera, the manufacture of the ubiquitous box camera, the development of daylight loading film and the mass-production of picture postcards, have all coincided with landmarks in the democratisation of travel and the expansion of tourism.

It is customary to date the invention of photography to 1839. In France in that year Louis Daguerre announced the production of the daguerreotype, and in England Fox Talbot publicised the discovery of the photographic process involving the negative and a paper-based image (Crary 1990; Batchen 1991: 14). These more or less simultaneous inventions coincided with other events and developments which established tourism as an industry and as a novel sociological-geographical phenomenon. Thus, just two years later in 1841, Thomas Cook organised the first-ever large-scale tour, taking four to five hundred temperance excursionists from Leicester to Loughborough and back again. In that year, too, the first national railway timetable was published, the first railway terminus hotel was built in York, the first Atlantic steamship service was launched (Cunard), and the first major travel company (Wells Fargo) appeared in the USA (see Lash and Urry 1994: 261). And by the turn of the century, travel for pleasure had become well-established, and picture taking was becoming a popular pastime, particularly on holiday.

Why did all these developments in photography and the tourism industry appear more or less coincidentally? What was it in the 1830s that seemed to initiate modern travel and some of the particular tropes of the modern world? As Crary asks, what was it during that period that produced 'an observing subject who was both a product and at the same time constitutive of modernity in the nineteenth century?' (1990: 9)

Considering just the issue of photography, we encounter an interesting paradox. In his seminal *The Origins of Photography*, Gernsheim argues that 'the circumstances that photography was not invented earlier remains the greatest mystery in its history' (Gernsheim 1982: 6). Much of the scientific basis of photography was known in the second quarter of the eighteenth century, and yet none of the artists who employed the 'camera obscura' in its various forms sought to fix images permanently. Why was this? Why was there so little desire to produce permanent photographs until well into the nineteenth century?

Foucault again provides some insights. For him the method of 'archaeology' is not a search for inventions, nor a concern for the average, but seeks to 'uncover the regularity of a discursive practice' (Foucault 1972: 144–5). Thus, in relationship to the emergence of 'photography', Batchen argues that we should shift our emphasis away from the inventions of Daguerre and Fox Talbot and focus instead on the appearance of a regular discursive practice which has, as its desired object, what we now know as photography (Batchen 1991: 15). When and why did there develop a widespread social imperative for fixed rather than fleeting images? When, in other words, 'did evidence of a desire to photograph begin to appear with sufficient regularity and internal consistency to be described . . . as a discursive practice?' (Batchen 1991: 15). There were three tributaries of such a desire.

First, there were what Batchen calls the 'photo-photographers', authors and experimenters who in the late eighteenth and early nineteenth centuries expressed a desire to 'photograph'. This list of notable inventors included Morse, Wedgwood, Davy and the younger Daguerre, who all in various ways expressed frustration at not being able permanently to fix their impressions and experiences of the environment (Batchen 1991: 16).

Second, there was the striking shift in the nature of landscape appreciation. Adler shows that, before the eighteenth century, travel had been based upon discourse and scholarship (through the ear), but over the course of the eighteenth century travellers could no longer expect that their scholastic observations would become part of the scientific understanding of the world (Adler 1989). Travel came to be justified, not scientifically, but through connoisseurship, first of buildings and works of art and later of landscapes. Adler summarises:

> Experiences of beauty and sublimity, sought through the sense of sight, were valued for their spiritual significance to the individuals who cultivated them. . . . In its aesthetic transformation, sightseeing became simultaneously a more effusive passionate activity and a more private one.
>
> (Adler 1989: 22)

Such connoisseurship unambiguously came to involve new ways of seeing, new kinds of observations. Bryson describes such a gaze as involving a 'prolonged, contemplative [look] regarding the field of vision with a certain aloofness and disengagement, across a tranquil interval' (1983: 94; see Taylor 1994: 13).

Third, from the end of the eighteenth century onwards, influential writers and artists began to articulate a desire for fixing their sensations of landscape. In 1782, for example, the famous proponent of the picturesque, the Reverend William Gilpin, expressed certain annoyance at not being able to contain and capture the fleeting visual sensations that he experienced on a journey down the river Wye. On a later excursion, he wrote of the frustration at not being able to 'fix and appropriate the scene' viewed through his Claude Glass (Batchen 1991: 17). William Cowper expressed similar sentiments in 1785, a desire:

> To arrest the fleeting images that fill
> The mirror of the mind, and hold them fast
> (cited Batchen 1991: 17)

William Taylor Coleridge, Thomas Gray, John Clare and John Constable all expressed similar frustrations at not being able to capture and to fix their fleeting images, especially the transient images of nature.

These three tributaries coalesced from the 1790s onwards. Prior to then there is relatively little talk which expresses the photographic desire. But from then on such talk becomes a torrent. The discourse of photographic desire was established from the 1790s; and by the 1830s this discourse was well-represented among an intelligentsia in Europe and parts of North America.

Paralleling these developments around 1800 was the discovery of the other great ocularcentric system of the modern world, namely Bentham's panopticon (see Foucault 1970; Batchen 1991). This, too, was an apparatus with a prescribed set of relations between a light source, a focusing cell and a directed way of looking. The reverberating economy of gazes that is established is taken by Foucault as a mechanism of surveillance which can then be widely applied. And it is a mechanism which has parallels with photography, as the modern traveller both subjects others, and is subject to, an increasingly interiorised gaze. Both the panopticon and photography involve the material production of bodies, of the bodies that are gazed upon and the bodies that undertake the gazing (Batchen 1991: 25). Crary interestingly argues that Foucault's opposition of surveillance and spectacle seems to overlook how the effects of the two regimes of power can in effect coincide (1990: 18). This is because of the ways in which people become objects of observation, and in particular how vision itself becomes a modality of surveillance and discipline. And this in turn stems from the more general nineteenth-century process by which there is a 'separation of the senses', especially of the visual sense from that of touch. The autonomisation of sight enabled the quantification and homogenization of visual experience, as radically new objects of the visual began to circulate (including commodities, mirrors, places, photographs, phantasmagoria, and various 'tourist-objects'; see Chapter 4).

Thus photography is not to be viewed as part of the gradually unfolding and continuous history of visual representation. Rather, it is a crucial element in a 'new and homogenous terrain of consumption and circulation in which an observer becomes lodged' (Crary 1990: 13). Photography is one of a number of new nineteenth-century techniques which involved the 'industrialization of image making' (Crary 1990: 13). It is the most significant component of a new cultural economy of value and exchange in which visual images are given extraordinary mobility and exchangeability. Such visual experiences are bound up with 'non-veridical' theories of vision – by contrast with the veridical theories which authorised the camera obscura. Photography is ineluctably bound up with the modern world and with the subjectivity of the observer and the extraordinary proliferation of signs and images that that world ushered in during the first half of the nineteenth century, a process which began well before the 'modernist' Impressionism of the 1870s and 1880s (as Crary points out; 1990: 149).

Two claims have thus been advanced so far in this section. First, around 1800 a productive desire emerges which some decades later culminates in modern regimes of surveillance and in the extraordinary promiscuity of the photographic eye. And second, photography is part of a general process of the autonomisation of vision and of the rapidly circulating signs and images that serves to create the modern observing-and-observed subject.

What, then, are the social consequences of this new autonomous sense of the visual and especially of its icon, the camera? First, photographic images provide a kind of 'mirror' on the society within which they are located. Rudisill, for example, explains how the early daguerrotypists 'taught Americans to be American more completely; they confronted Americans with themselves and sought to help them recognize their own significance' (Rudisill 1971: 238). The relentless, revealing photographic images which we are exposed to today, of war, poverty, famine, crime, have similar effects within different cultural contexts. Within the last decade the increased reflexivity about the environment has partly come about because of still and live photographic images of the visual and other effects upon nature of unrestrained economic development.

Second, photography is a socially organised set of rituals. It involves a set of rules and roles which people take up in new or special environments. A sense of being out of place can be offset by following a set of photographic rituals. It involves a repertoire of actions when confronted by the 'other' – an other which may be awesome, threatening, mysterious. Taking a picture is, as Sontag notes, reassuring, so enabling people:

> to take possession of space in which they are insecure.... The very activity of taking pictures is soothing, and assuages general feelings of disorientation. Unsure of other responses, they take a picture.
>
> (Sontag 1979: 9–10)

This is a specific variant of the more general feature of tourist developments, that is, to ensure that pleasures will outweigh anxieties, that familiarity will overcome uncertainty, and that risks are regulated and contextualised (Taylor 1994: 70, 243).

Third, photography provides some of the language by which we learn to describe and appreciate the environment. Photography has significantly given us the terms in which we recollect, explain, justify how and why we have visited various places. Discourses of travel are saturated with ocular metaphors, especially those that play upon the analogies between the eye and the lens (Jay 1993; Urry 1995).

Finally, and most importantly, there has been a tendency to understand the practices of everyday and holiday photography through the prism of public photography. On this account photography is viewed as a particularly powerful signifying practice which reproduces a dominant set of visual images, at the very same time that it conceals its constructed character. Photography can thus be seen as part of the dominant ideology of a society, reproducing and enhancing its preferred images while appearing to present entirely accurate representations (see Berger 1972; Sontag 1979; Albers and James 1988; Urry 1990). Taylor (1994) provides many examples of how in the last hundred years or so new modes of photographic representation have developed which have apparently functioned in this manner. He particularly brings out how our conception of landscape has typically involved the notion of 'mastery'. The photographer, and then the viewer, are seen to be above and dominant over a static and subordinate landscape, which lies out beyond us inert and inviting our inspection (Taylor 1994: 38–9). Such photographic practices thus demonstrate how nature was to be viewed, as dominated by humans and subject to their mastery; the mode of viewing being taken as emblematic of the relationship of domination of humans over nature, and also of men over women. Nature/landscape is often presumed to be female and similarly waiting to be 'mastered' (see Plumwood 1993).

But this visual dominant ideology thesis has been perceptively criticised:

> The 'empire of the Gaze' then owes its theoretical dominance to a belief that technology stands over and against us, that the gaze that fixes us in its glare is

non-reflexive, denying the possibility of dialogue. It is this blindness to the existence of multiple gazes, the existence of other 'scopic regimes' that traps us in the 'empire'.

(Guy 1993: 4)

The critique of this dominant ideology thesis with regard to photography involves a number of points. First, we should avoid a technological determinism where new photographic technologies are seen as necessarily generating new ways of seeing. As we noted above, we should understand how and where the desire for photographic images comes from and historically mutates (see Guy 1993). Technologies do not determine such discursively constructed desires. Further, there are a number of visual systems operating within modernity, as Taylor convincingly shows (1994). Crary says of the camera obscura:

> By the early 1800's, however, the rigidity of the camera obscura, its linear optical system, its fixed positions, its categorical distinction between inside and outside, its identification of perception and object, were all too inflexible and unwieldy for the needs of the next century.
>
> (1990: 42)

Also we should note the ways in which photographic images become a kind of currency, becoming part of the 'economies of signs' in the late twentieth century. Photographs are material objects, not simply a reflection or mirror of an already existent world.

Finally, photographs help not just to panopticalise, to ontologise the visual realm, but also to subvert and oppose. Taylor interestingly brings out the role of resistance in contemporary photography, particularly in the ways that it can disrupt normal tourist imagery (Taylor 1994: ch. 8). Such photographers especially use parody and irony but do not simply distance themselves from the tourist experience. In Britain, Martin Parr and Ingrid Pollard are perhaps the best-known subverters of the tourist photograph, concentrating much more on the ambiguities of the tourist than on the supposed tourist site/sight itself (see Parr 1995). More generally Batchen talks of the 'materiality of photography in the constitution of our subjectivity' (1988: 9; see also Guy 1993).

This set of issues, photography as mirror, as ritual, as language, as dominant ideology, and as resistance, will now be examined in relationship to research we conducted in the English Lake District.

CONTEMPORARY PHOTOGRAPHY AND TOURISM

One of the most popular tourist destinations in Britain, the English Lake District is associated with powerful and enduring images. In sonnets and surveys, postcards, prose, policies and tourists' photographs, the region is portrayed in terms of romantic imagery, of nature as a source of inspiration, tranquillity, solitude and harmony. Today, a favourite image of the Lake District is a photograph of Ullswater taken from the lake shore with daffodils slightly offset in the foreground. According to literary historians, this is the scene that inspired William Wordsworth to write his poem 'The Daffodils'. Various views of the spring flowers at Ullswater are photographed and reproduced each year in calendars, books, travel guides, and as postcards. The apparently realistic images are metonymic of the District. Without descriptive text or explanation, these photographs promise the experience of 'wandering lonely as a cloud' over the hills, in the traces of one of England's most celebrated poets.

The Romantic imagery of the Lake District which is widely accepted as natural was in fact culturally constructed from the middle of the eighteenth century onwards. Before 1750 or thereabouts the region was described in the journals of notable travellers as wild, barren, frightful (see Urry 1995: ch. 13). Defoe considered the landscape as 'all barren and wild'; it was a wilderness far removed from civilisation (see Raban 1987: 35). The transformation of this bleak, empty wilderness into an arcadia was not essentially a material transformation, but involved a new way of viewing nature. It was influenced by a small group of people, mainly writers and artists, and translated into a public taste for scenery. The cult of the picturesque, and the Romantic movement that followed, played a decisive role in the discovery of the region by tourists and in the development of a particular style of scenic tourism which involved visualising the travel experience. Following the 'invention' of the camera in 1839, photography played a dominant part in the emergence of a tourism industry in the Lakes and in the visualisation and democratisation of the 'Lakeland experience'. Raban (1987: 36) talks of how the 'Lake District was turned into Britain's first theme park' as the mighty mountains were dotted with hikers. Through the work of professional photographers, tourism promoters and tourists themselves, the Lake District has become the exemplar of a certain type of tourism, certain tourist practices (especially walking and climbing), and of particular kinds of landscape photography (see Crawshaw 1994a).

The Lake District thus appears to demonstrate the power of a visual discourse organised around a romantic conception of the visual and which is undertaken by professional photographers. It is also a place much visited, revisited and photographed, where taking photographs is essential in people's appropriation of the place. It would seem to exemplify the effect of a dominant visual ideology.

We explored such notions first through the work of various prominent professional photographers, and second through visitors' responses to popular tourist photographs of the Lakes. We were interested to understand how photographic images provide a kind of 'mirror on society'. We examined the rules, roles and rituals which professional photographers engage in, the images and language which they use to describe the Lake District and the ways in which their photographs are understood and appreciated by tourists. We were interested in the relationship between the professionals who promote particular images of the Lakes and the people who receive them. We were also concerned to discuss whether the images are imposed or whether there is a kind of 'dialogue'.

First, we interviewed ten professional photographers who live and work in the Lake District. Their photographs appear annually in the holiday guide of the regional tourist board which is distributed to 250,000 potential visitors to the area, and in much other tourism material circulated nationally and internationally. While their work and working practices varied, they all had an interest and involvement in landscape photography. Working in a field which they described as being placed somewhere between art and advertising, the photographers were conscious of and articulate about the rules of photography they followed and about their creative and commercial roles. 'To be any good', said one, 'you have to have the eye to select a picture which is beautiful and a picture which is commercial. You have to combine the two'. Another said that 'the most important thing was to capture and create artistically a pleasing subject, because if you did that then you knew that you had a good selling subject'. Describing his role as artist, technician and businessman, one said that he aimed to produce 'instantly recognisable, technically perfect, beautiful images for tourists'. The relationship between rules and roles, between the creation of beautiful images and saleable images, was a recurrent theme throughout the interviews:

> I enjoy making pictures on the camera. I enjoy composition. . . . It may be an art form. . . . Once it's taken, you've produced it, it's finished. And it becomes a saleable, or not, commodity.

For most of the photographers that we interviewed their rules of photography were rooted in a kind of combination of picturesque principles and romantic imagery, in which the viewing point was a paramount consideration. The Lake District photographers emphasised the importance of knowing 'where the good views were' and of 'knowing a good view when you see it'. With a library of thousands of transparencies after forty years working in the Lake District, one photographer advised:

> I always used to think, yes, there is only one perfect position or perfect angle. So you have to juggle about until you are satisfied that you have composed something. . . . Up the Langdale valley there is a very good view looking up the river showing the Pikes and so on. In the river if you get Coniston just right, there's quite a large pool and you can get the Pikes reflected in the pool.

Another suggested:

> If it was a calm, totally calm day, I probably would head towards the western lakes. If there was good movement of clouds in the sky, I would probably head somewhere upland. I do have favourite places and favourite views.

Indeed, as with the proponents of the picturesque in the eighteenth century, most of the photographers interviewed had lists of views which they wanted to capture. 'I used to have a list of subjects I would like to capture in that one year. You never really get everything.' Many mentioned views that they were missing in their photographic libraries, such as 'Haweswater in autumn, Bassenthwaite at sunset, Wastwater in the mist'. Reminiscent of Wordsworth's 'chace from hill to hill, from rock to rock still craving combinations of new forms' (quoted in Bezencenet 1983: 14), one photographer confided:

> even on the most perfect day I'm going to be thinking, ah, wait a moment. Isn't it going to be better from the fellside? Oh God, I've made the wrong choice again. I should have gone into that valley. The mist is drifting more beautifully. There is a kind of constant feeling of, oh, it's better on the other side of the mountain range . . . .

As well as the skill of identifying viewing points, the art of composition, 'the disposition of lines, lights, shades, masses', and an instinct for local weather conditions were seen by the photographers as prerequisite qualities for successful landscape photography. While they acknowledged the changeability of Lakeland weather conditions, most preferred high contrast images taken in the sunshine. 'It is just a question of waiting, finding some good viewpoints and waiting until the light is right.' Clearly the weather is often not appropriate and so those days are not appropriate for such photography. Different photographers claimed:

> For me there has got to be some sunshine, even if it is intermittent sunshine. The clearer the better. I do not take landscape photographs in murky weather... you have got to have that clarity of light to take the right sort of photographs of the Lake District.

> If you are taking something that is going to sell you want the blue sky and the white cloud and the clarity of image.... The image is the light.

So part of what is involved here is following a set of rules about what the photographers deem people expect. There is, of course, something reassuring here – to confirm that at least sometimes the weather is that nice and the scenery is that splendid, at least for some visitors some of the time.

These photographers went on to argue that the elements of a beautiful and commercial photograph of the Lake District were predominantly natural features which are combined together to convey a 'romantic scene', or rather a picturesque reworking of Romanticism. Two further photographers argued:

> The majority of requests that I get in the library of Lake District shots are a lake and a mountain. They don't want any of the houses or the country life or anything like that. It's straightforward. A lake and a mountain. Nature.

> They (the tourists) are looking for some of the images that they have had presented to them in the many writings about the Lake District... the tranquillity, nice clear images of the fells and sunny days and the natural environment... open fells with sheep.

There was agreement between the photographers on this. No prominent buildings and especially no local people were deemed appropriate to the scenery. This then is a conception of the countryside as landscape, as bereft of most signs of human habitation (except sheep, dry stone walls, deforestation, distant white-painted farmhouses and so on). They maintained that promotional images should exclude:

> vehicles, cars, anything that would date a picture.... Anything that is obtrusive and jars. People with bright clothes on, people carrying plastic bags... dead trees, barbed wire... derelict buildings, scaffolding. Road signs, litter, car parks, crowds, traffic jams, low-flying planes, Bermuda shorts.

The question of whether people should be excluded was seen as more complicated. Some said that they included people if they were 'attractive and appropriately dressed', and this meant that they were 'middle class, youngish, wearing walking gear that's not too dirty or frayed'. In other words, only some categories of visitor are viewed as appropriate; and local people are almost always seen as inappropriate even if it is they who mainly produce the look of the landscape. Others said that including people 'involves a bit of personal interface which actually makes it harder work'. Several said that tourism clients 'asked for people in pictures, but they didn't sell'. We will return to this issue below.

Also, in composing the beautiful and saleable photograph, some photographers admitted to using the occasional prop so as to reproduce the dominant visual ideology. The art of composition, of arranging natural elements, was occasionally assisted by the judiciously placed rock, foxglove, fishing rod, or even daffodils:

> You obviously know the daffodils by Ullswater. Many years ago, there wasn't a mass of daffodils. I remember, probably forty years ago, we took a few bucketfuls of daffodils and put them in.

> There used to be a photographer who...had one of those fake lawn fields...plastered with flowers. They used to have them on greengrocer's stalls...he would whip it out and roll it off into a shot somewhere in the corner to add a bit of colour.

More generally, it was claimed that:

> you do a bit of gardening, you move things. I don't destroy anything, apart from the odd twig that might be obtrusive in the foreground, framing something that might be a bit too close, or a reed that is blowing in the wind that you want to remove.

The judgement about what would sell to tourists and tourism clients was based, for most, on a combination of experience, instinct and market research:

> We work from our instincts. We do market research in sales. That tells us what we need to make things sell.

One photographer said, 'I am taking the photograph for the tourist.' He went on to suggest:

> I like the people to be able to drive around in their cars, and perhaps go over the brow of a hill and see the shot that I have done and say 'I recognise that'...I like people to have an instant recognition of what they see and think 'I've seen that place'.

One photographer said that he was 'selling dreams'. Others said they were reinforcing long-established images of the Lake District. 'Tourists are looking for some of the images that they have had presented to them in the many writings of the Lake District.' 'People have a tendency to think that they know what they want to see.' 'Give the people what they want. That is what I always try to do.'

While opinions varied about whether tourism photography created images or reinforced them, the photographers generally agreed that their work involved selecting, shaping and structuring elements of the physical environment to reflect mental images: their own images, their clients' images or the tourists' dreams. 'Photography is about endeavouring to make something....It's the challenge of creating something.'

In tourism, the nature of photography as a socially constructed way of seeing has several dimensions. The work of the Lakeland photographers demonstrated a conscious interweaving of the art of the picturesque, the imagery of the Romantics and the principles of photographic pictorialism. Viewpoints, pleasing subjects, the right conditions, good lighting, were the essential considerations. Their work reflected their cultural values and attitudes and their mixed roles as artistic photographers and business people.

However, it also reflected their perceptions about what visitors to the Lake District actually wanted to see or imagined that they would see. The photographs reflected the photographers' perceptions of the nature of tourism and of the tourist gaze. The romanticised photographs of the Lake District, stripped of signs of modernity, 'bad weather' and items that were 'out of place' reinforced the tourists' images of the area as tranquil, timeless, natural. Many of the Lakeland photographers saw themselves, not as image-makers, but as illustrators, reinforcing deeply held mental images with visual ones. One suggested that: 'My photographs are illustrative, beautiful, romantic. That is how we try to present places. That is what people want. That is how they imagine it will be'.

It is not difficult to interpret these photographers as reinforcing dominant visual conceptions of the area, conceptions that are in fact more picturesque than sublime, and present the Lakes as an immensely 'civilised' reworking of 'nature'. Indeed, in focus group interviews with visitors, many remarked on the way that the Lakes are remarkably 'neat and tidy', more so than nature could 'on its own' ever be (see Urry 1995: ch. 13, on the civilising of nature; see also Crawshaw 1994b).

We then turned to the tourists themselves to see whether these dominant images were in fact how they imagined the Lake District. Do the photographs in promotional publications shape new conceptions of place or do they reflect and reinforce deeply held cultural values and feelings? Are travel photographers image-makers, imposing their views on travellers, or are they illustrators, translating the experiences, memories and mental images of travellers into visual, material ones which can be stored away and brought out again at any time? Are there ways in which visitors disrupt and alter these dominant conceptions?

Two questions were included in a market research questionnaire, circulated with a sample of Cumbria Tourist Board's 1993 annual holiday guide to the region which is widely distributed around the United Kingdom. People were asked which photograph in the guide most closely represents the type of experience which they would hope to enjoy during a visit to Cumbria and why this was so. There were 120 colour photographs to choose from in various sizes and covering a wide range of subjects: images with people and without; people cycling, swimming, fishing, climbing, eating, shopping, resting; historic houses, gardens, museums, monuments, castles; steam trains and steam boats; hotels, restaurants, caravan sites; villages, towns, city centres; images of lakes, hills and mountains.

About 350 people responded to the questions on photography. What was particularly surprising was that an extraordinary 60 per cent of those who answered the first question chose one of only four photographs from the wide selection of high quality, evocative photographs that could have been chosen. So most of the photographs were rejected. The four chosen in such numbers can be seen in Figures 9.1, 9.2, 9.3 and 9.4. Eighty per cent chose one of only ten photographs.

One explanation for this selection is that certain photographers are particularly skilful semioticians and influential image-makers; reproducers of a dominant ideology. They know the signs and symbols that make up saleable pictures. In one

Figure 9.1 Brotherswater

Figure 9.2 Ullswater

The time is always right to come to Cumbria. Daffodils and lambs greet visitors in spring, summer guarantees plenty to enjoy - and room to enjoy it. In Autumn the countryside is a blaze of colour whilst in winter, the warmth is in the welcome!

Figure 9.3 Derwentwater

Figure 9.4 Windermere

sense, reading the popular photographs rests with the romanticised picturesque images deeply embedded in the discourses surrounding the Lake District. The imagery and discourse pre-date photography and organised tourism. But in another way the four photographic images say as much about the nature of tourism in the Lake District as they do about the romantic images of Nature. They suggest a more complex analysis of popular photography and of the relationship between the tourism photographer and the tourist.

Most importantly, and partially contradicting the views of the professionals, each of the photographs chosen includes people; young couples at Ullswater and Waterhead Bay, a woman and child at Derwentwater, and a family at Brotherswater. They are all appropriately dressed as visitors, in ways which, outside the Lake District, might be thought of as 'fancy dress' (see Urry 1995: 207). They are unmistakably not local people. And they are all almost certainly white (see Taylor 1994, on Ingrid Pollard's 'I wandered lonely as a BLACK face in a sea of white'). Those photographed are looking, enjoying the view, all are engaged in a tourist gaze. There are no other people about and hence those photographed might be said to be experiencing what we have termed the 'romantic tourist gaze'. They are taking in the landscape visually and, in the case of Ullswater and Brotherswater, are clearly exerting 'mastery' of the scene.

So what people prefer in a quite striking fashion is not the quintessential view bereft of people. It is not a scene (of which there were many) which is literally empty of people. The pictures chosen all involve scenes in which the observer appears to identify with the people in the photograph gazing at, on and in cases over, the scene in question. So the scenes chosen as 'typical' provide not a representation of an auratic romantic landscape but in fact one that has been tamed by humans and especially by visitors much like themselves.

Second, the choice of the photographs is explained in diverse ways. Some people said that they selected photographs which depicted activities that they enjoyed:

It is what I most enjoy about the Lake District – fell-walking.

I am a keen fell-walker who has walked over most of the District.

Others replied that certain images evoked emotions which they felt or would like to feel:

It depicts remoteness, peace and tranquillity.

Solitude – no people.

Some respondents explained their choice of photograph in terms of physical features:

Water and hills – landscape.

Water, boats, birds and beautiful trees.

A fourth group described the chosen photographs in terms of mental images and memories:

It's what the Lakes mean to us.

A true picture of my idea of a Cumbrian holiday.

Thus the choice of particular photographs was justified in contradictory terms. A photograph of Brotherswater (Figure 9.1), for example, was selected because it shows 'fell-walking; it looks peaceful, relaxing; it includes mountains, lakes, clean air; because it typifies everything I love about the Lake District and because it reminds me of past holidays and those to come'. Explaining why he selected the photograph of Brotherswater, one respondent wrote 'obvious'. But this selection process is in fact not so obvious, since different respondents gave quite divergent justifications of the similar choices made.

In particular, some respondents were very keen to emphasise, in describing the photographs chosen, not only the well-known symbols, but also their hopes, memories, feelings, families, activities, other tourists, and so on. The landscape aesthetic shared by modern-day Lakers appears to connect a certain type of scenery with various kinds of everyday activity, experiences, events, people, even clothing. Thus the Lake District photographs are associated not only with landscape, outdoor pursuits, healthy living, but also with enjoyable social relationships with friends, families, partners. In choosing a favourite photograph, these respondents identify with the people in the pictures, hoping for the experience which they themselves seem to be enjoying.

It shows children walking happily.

Represents ideal family holiday – outdoors, sun shining, smiling faces.

[H]oping my husband will appreciate views like this.

If travel photographs shape, reflect and reinforce peoples' holiday hopes, they also organise their memories of past visits. Significantly, 80 per cent of the respondents had previously visited Cumbria. Over a third selected photographs because they 'reminded them of previous visits' or 'showed the Lakes as they knew it'. A particular photograph was chosen:

Because of the many memories it invokes.

It has fond memories for us.

[A]s I knew Cumberland as a child – evacuee!

My earliest memory of this spot – some 60-odd years ago.

It is THE LAKES. It has memories of holidays with our kids.

Although not of their own making, the professionally produced images of the Lake District are apparently ones which many visitors would like to remember and look forward to. 'It reminds me of past holidays', said one respondent, 'and my hopes for future ones'.

How can highly stylised photographs composed by professional photographers represent the 'real' Lake District for so many visitors and remind them of their personal, past experiences there? In an interesting study conducted in Durham, tourists were asked about the photographs which they had taken at a popular beauty spot (Pocock 1982). It showed that people were rather disappointed by their own pictures because their memories of the view were in fact much richer and fuller.

Similarly, one of the professional photographers argued that: 'Photographic images, however created, can never match the spectacle of the Lake District'.

So on the one hand, the photographs of the area idealise the scenes and experiences by only being shot in certain weather conditions and by excluding all sorts of items that would be out of place. And yet on the other hand, people's memories are more complex and diverse than can be captured in a photographic image. Such photographs are then triggers for processes of reminiscence; where people's feelings about the place are much more bound up with particular family and personal experiences. In this case the photographs are two-dimensional and, as in Durham, do not capture the complex sense of place as people have experienced and remember it (see Chapter 1 on the significance for tourist sites of the social practices of reminiscence).

CONCLUSION

The interconnections between modern tourism and photography serve to emphasise that visual consumption has become one of the dominant ways in which societies intersect with their respective environments. The historical development of scenic tourism in England's Lake District is a clear example. Under the influence of cultured travellers, artists and writers, emptiness and barren nature were transformed into landscape and scenery to be appreciated and appropriated in particular ways, by particular people for personal reasons. Discourses surrounding seeing the Lake District which were culturally constructed in the eighteenth century have been reproduced, passed down and altered over time through the processes of tourism and photography. Photography in the Lake District is thus partly a matter of dominant conceptions. We have shown how professional photographers follow the dictates of a dominant conception and construct images in accordance with it.

Indeed the travel photographer and the tourist seem to engage in a mutually reinforcing social process of constructing and altering images of places and experiences. In the case of the Lake District, they almost collude in the transformation of the physical environment into a resource for recreation, personal enjoyment, good health and happiness.

But everyone knows that places are not as perfect as they are represented. And we have also shown that people choose, use, relate to and talk about photographs in different ways, something similar to the different modes in which Benjamin argued people experience the city. He talked of the 'distracted' way that people see the city, something which can disrupt the received cultural traditions through the practice of flânerie (Benjamin 1969; and see Chapter 2 above on the gendering of the flâneur). The urban flâneur samples aspects of urban life in an unpremeditated and voyeuristic fashion, so allowing involuntary memory to operate. This may enable the present to be incorporated into the past. Benjamin talked of how, in a state of distraction, memories from the past could be ignited by a current event, so combining the two (Savage and Warde 1993: 136–8). Sontag also notes that photography is the contemporary form taken by flânerie so that this also suggests that photographic practices do not simply reinforce a dominant visual aesthetic (Sontag 1979: 55). Odd memories and feelings can be so ignited; and this may in no way coincide with dominant visual images.

Photography is thus part of the process by which subjectivities are formed; it interconnects in many ways with people's hopes, fears, memories, activities, likes, loves, and so on; it is the contemporary form taken by flânerie so that disconnected memories can be brought together in unpredictable ways; and the complex relationships between photography and travel require further theoretical reflection and empirical interrogation, to look further into how the photographic eye is both continuously intrusive and actively employed.

ACKOWLEDGEMENTS

The research reported here was conducted by Carol Crawshaw and generously funded by the ESRC.

NOTE

1 See Urry 1992b for more detail.

BIBLIOGRAPHY

Adams, P. G. (1962) *Travelers and Travel Liars 1660–1800*, New York: Dover.

Adkins, L. (1992) 'Sexual work and the employment of women in service industries', in M. Savage and A. Witz (eds), *Gender and Bureaucracy*, Oxford: Blackwell.

Adler, J. (1989) 'Origins of sightseeing', *Annals of Tourism Research*, 16: 7–29.

Adler, J. (1992) 'Mobility and the Creation of the Subject: Theorizing movement and the self in early Christian monasticism', *International Tourism Between Tradition and Modernity Colloquium*, Nice, France, November.

Adler, J. (1994) 'Virile Travellers and Cloistered Virgins: Mobility, space and gender in early Christian ascetism', *XIIIth World Congress of Sociology*, Bielefeld, Germany, July.

Adorno, T. and Horkheimer, M. (1944) *Dialectic of Enlightenment*, London: Verso.

Albers, P. and James, W. (1988) 'Travel photography. A methodological approach', *Annals of Tourism Research*, 15: 134–58.

Anderson, B. (1983) *Imagined Communities*, London: Verso

Anderson, P. (1996) 'Copyright and wrongs', *Bulletin*, 20 February, p. 81.

Anger, K. (1975) *Hollywood Babylon 1*, New York: Dell.

Anger, K. (1984) *Hollywood Babylon 2*, London: Arrow.

Anon. (1994) 'Shopping vacations; millions make pilgrimages to mega-mall meccas', *Seattle Times*, 13 November.

Anon. (1995) 'A different woman every night: men on a sex hunt on holiday in Greece', *Marie Claire*, 81: 10–15.

Anon. (1995) 'One big happy family', *Travel Weekly*, 16 March.

Appadurai, A. (1986a) 'Introduction: commodities and the politics of value', in A. Appadurai (ed.), *The Social Life of Things: Commodities in cultural perspective*, New York: Cambridge University Press.

Appadurai, A. (ed.) (1986b) *The Social Life of Things: Commodities in cultural perspective*, New York: Cambridge University Press.

Appadurai, A. (1990) 'Disjuncture and difference in the global cultural economy', *Theory, Culture and Society*, 7: 295–310.

Appadurai, A. (1993) 'Disjuncture and difference in the global community', in B. Robbins (ed.), *The Phantom Public Sphere*, Minneapolis and London: University of Minnesota Press.

Appadurai, A. and Breckenbridge, C. (1992) 'Museums are good to think: heritage on view in India', in I. Karp, C. Kreamer and S. Lavine (eds), *Museums and Communities*, Washington and London: Smithsonian Institute.

Arendt, H. (1978) *The Life of the Mind*, London: Secker and Warburg.

Arendt, H. (1979) 'Introduction. Walter Benjamin: 1892–1940', in W. Benjamin, *Illuminations*, Glasgow: Fontana.

Armstrong, P. (1989) 'Limits and possibilities for HRM in an age of management accountancy', in J. Storey (ed.), *New Perspectives in Human Resource Management*, London: Routledge.

Arts Queensland (1995) *Hidden Heritage. A Development Plan for Museums in Queensland 1995–2001*, prepared by Jane Lennon, Brisbane: Queensland Office of Arts and Cultural Development.

Ashworth, G. J. and Tunbridge, J. E. (1990) *The Tourist-Historic City*, London and New York: Belhaven Press.

Australia Council (1991) *Art Galleries: Who Goes? A Study of Visitors to Three Australian Art Galleries, with International Comparisons*, prepared by Tony Bennett and John Frow, Sydney: Australia Council.

Bachelard, G. (1969) *The Poetics of Space*, Boston: Beacon Press.

Bagguley, P. (1991) 'Gender and labour flexibility in Hotel and Catering', *The Service Industries Journal*, 10: 737–47.

Bakhtin, M. (1968) *Rabelais and his World*, Cambridge: MIT Press.

Barber, B. (1995) *Jihad vs the World*, New York: Times Books.

Barrell, J. (1972) *The Idea of Landscape and the Sense of Place 1730–1840*, Cambridge: Cambridge University Press.

Barthes, R. (1957) *Mythologies*, St Albans: Paladin.

Barthes, R. (1981) *Camera Lucida*, New York: Hill and Wang.

Batchen, G. (1988) 'Photography, power and representation', *Afterimage*, 16: 7–9.

Batchen, G. (1991) 'Desiring production itself: Notes on the invention of photography', in R. Diprose and R. Ferrell (eds), *Cartographies*, London: Allen and Unwin.

Baudrillard, J. (1981) *For a Critique of the Economy of the Sign*, St Louis: Telos.

Baudrillard, J. (1983) *Simulations*, New York: Semiotext(e).

Baudrillard, J. (1988) 'Consumer society', in M. Poster (ed.), *Jean Baudrillard. Selected Writings*, Stanford: Stanford University Press.

Baudrillard, J. (1990) *Fatal Strategies*, New York: Semiotext(e).

Baudrillard, J. (1993) *Symbolic Exchange and Death*, London: Sage.

Bauman, Z. (1989) *Modernity and the Holocaust*, Ithaca: Cornell University Press.

Bauman, Z. (1991) *Modernity and Ambivalence*, Ithaca: Cornell University Press.

Bauman, Z. (1992) *Intimations of Postmodernity*, London: Routledge.

Bauman, Z. (1993) *Postmodern Ethics*, Oxford: Blackwell.

Bauman, Z. (1994) 'Från pilgrim till turist (From Pilgrim to Tourist)', *Moderna Tider*, September: 20–34.

Beck, U. (1992) *Risk Society*, London: Sage.

Bell, D. (1973) *The Coming of Post-Industrial Society. A Venture in Social Forecasting*, New York: Basic Books.

Belleville, B. (1995) 'Eco-tourism offers cure for evils visited on land', *The Orlando Sentinel*, February 26.

Benjamin, W. (1969) *Charles Baudelaire or the Lyric Priest of High Capitalism*, London: New Left Books.

Benjamin, W. (1973) *Illuminations*, Glasgow: Fontana.

Benjamin, W. (1979) *One Way Street*, London: New Left Books.

Benjamin, W. (1985) 'Central Park', *New German Critique*, Winter 34: 32–58.

Bennett, T. (1988) 'Museums and "the people" ', in R. Lumley (ed.), *The Museum Time-Machine*, London: Routledge.

Berger, J. (1972) *Ways of Seeing*, Harmondsworth: Penguin.

Berman, M. (1983) *All That Is Solid Melts Into Air*, London: Verso.

Berry, L. L., Zeithaml, V. A. and Parasuraman, A. (1988) 'Quality counts in services, too', in C. H. Lovelock (ed.), *Managing Services: Marketing, Operations and Human Resources*, Englewood Cliffs: Prentice Hall International.

Bezencenet, S. (1983) 'Landscape Image Property', *Ten 8*, 12: 14–15.

Bhabha, R. (ed.) (1990) *Nation and Narration*, London: Routledge.

Blomstedt, J. (1986) 'Benjamin ja Baudelaire, melankoliset muukalaiset (Benjamin and Baudelaire, the melancholic strangers)', *Helsingin Sanomat*, 11 May.

Blundell, V. (1993) 'Aboriginal empowerment and the souvenir trade in Canada', *Annals of Tourism Research*, 20: 64–87.

Blundell, V. (1996) 'Riding the Polar Bear Express: and other encounters between tourists and first peoples in Canada', *Journal of Canadian Studies*, 30(4): 1–23.

Boissevain, J. (1989) 'Tourism as anti-structure', *Kultur Anthropologisch*, 30: 145–59.

Bolger, J. (1994) 'Site of Schindler Story Repackaged as City of the Film', *Guardian*, 17 May.

Boniface, P. and Fowler, P. (1993) *Heritage and Tourism in 'the Global Village'*, London and New York: Routledge.

Boorstin, D. (1964) *The Image: A Guide to Pseudo-Events in America*, New York: Harper.

Bouquet, M. (1987) 'Bed, breakfast and an evening meal: commensality in the nineteenth and twentieth century farm household in Hartland', in M. Bouquet and M. Winter (eds), *Who From Their Labours Rest? Conflict and Practice in Rural Tourism*, Aldershot: Avebury.

Bourdieu, P. (1984) *Distinction: A Social Critique of the Judgement of Taste*, Cambridge, Mass.: Harvard University Press.

Bowen, D. E. and Schneider, B. (1985) 'Boundary-spanning-role employees and the service encounter: some guidelines for management and research', in J. A. Czepiel, M. R. Solomon and C. F. Surprenant (eds), *The Service Encounter*, Lexington: Lexington Books.

Bowlby, R. (1992) *Still Crazy After All These Years. Women, Writing and Psychoanalysis*, London: Routledge.

Braidotti, R. (1994) *Nomadic Subjects. Embodiment and Sexual Difference in Contemporary Feminist Theory*, New York: Columbia University Press.

Braverman, H. (1974) *Labour and Monopoly Capital. The Degradation of Work in the Twentieth Century*, New York: Monthly Review Press.

Britton, S. (1991) 'Tourism, capital, and place: towards a critical geography of tourism', *Environment and Planning D: Society and Space*, 9: 451–78.

Bruner, E. (1994) 'Abraham Lincoln as authentic reproduction: a critique of postmodernism', *American Anthropologist*, 96: 397–415.

Bryman, A. (1995) *Disney and his Worlds*, London: Routledge.

Bryson, N. (1983) *Vision and Painting. The Logic of the Gaze*, London: Macmillan.

Buci-Glucksmann, C. (1994) *Baroque Reason. The Aesthetics of Modernity*, London: Sage.

Buck-Morss, S. (1989) *Ways of Seeing*, Cambridge, Mass.: MIT Press.

Burke, P. (1978) *Popular Culture in Early Modern Europe*, London: Temple Smith.

Burr, S. (1994) 'What research says about sustainable tourism development', *Parks and Recreation*, September.

Buzard, J. (1993) *The Beaten Track*, Oxford: Oxford University Press.

Bywater, M. (1993) 'The market for cultural tourism in Europe', *EIU Travel and Tourism Analyst*, 6: 30–46.

Carlzon, J. (1987) *Moments of Truth*, Cambridge: Ballinger.

Carpenter, R. (1994) 'Memories come abroad on an SS Norway cruise to Caribbean Islands', *The Boston Globe*, 6 February.

Casey, C. (1995) *Work, Self and Society: After Industrialism*, London: Routledge.

Chaney, D. (1993) *Fictions of Collective Life*, London: Routledge.

Chapman, M. (1978) *The Gaelic Vision in Scottish Culture*, London: Croom Helm.

Chapman, M. (1982) ' "Semantics" and the "Celt" ', in D. Parkin (ed.), *Semantic Anthropology*, London: Academic Press.

Chase, R. B. (1981) 'The customer approach to services: theoretical bases and practical extensions', *Operations Research*, 29: 698–706.

Chesney-Lind, M. and Lind, I. (1986) 'Visitors as victims. Crimes against tourists in Hawaii', *Annals of Tourism Research*, 13: 167–91.

Chivers, T. (1973) 'The proletarianisation of a service worker', *Sociological Review*, 21: 633–56.

Christiansen, R. (1994) *Tales of the New Babylon: Paris 1869–1875*, London: Sinclair Stevenson.

Clarke, J. and Critcher, C. (1985) *The Devil Makes Work*, London: Macmillan.

Classen, C., Howes, D. and Synnott, A. (1994) *Aroma*, London: Routledge.

Clayton, P. and Price, M. (eds) (1988) *The Seven Wonders of the World*, London: Routledge.

Clifford, J. (1988) *The Predicament of Culture*, Cambridge, Mass.: Harvard University Press.

Clifford, J. (1989) 'Notes on travel and theory', *Inscriptions*, 5.

Clifford, J. (1992) 'Travelling cultures', in L. Grossberg, C. Nelson and P. A. Treichler (eds), *Cultural Studies*, New York and London: Routledge.

Clift, S. (1994) *Romance and Sex on Holidays Abroad: A Study of Magazine Representations*, Travel, Lifestyles and Health Working Paper no. 4, Canterbury: Christ Church College.

Cohen, E. (1971) 'Arab boys and tourist girls in a mixed Jewish–Arab community', *International Journal of Comparative Sociology*, 12: 217–33.

Cohen, E. (1972) 'Towards a sociology of international tourism', *Social Research*, 39: 164–89.

Cohen, E. (1982) 'Thai girls and farang men', *Annals of Tourism Research*, 9: 403–28.

Cohen, E. (1987) 'Authenticity and commoditisation in tourism', *Annals of Tourism Research*, 15: 371–86.

Cohen, E. (1988) 'Tourism and AIDS in Thailand', *Annals of Tourism Research*, 15: 467–86.

Cohen, E. (1989) ' "Primitive and remote": hill tribe trekking in Thailand', *Annals of Tourism Research*, 16: 30–61.

Cohen, E. (1992) 'Tourist arts', in C. Cooper and A. Lockwood (eds), *Progress in Tourism, Recreation and Hospitality Management*, vol. 4, London: Belhaven Press, 3–31.

Cohen, E. (1993) 'Introduction. Investigating tourist arts', *Annals of Tourism Research*, 20: 1–8.

Cohen, E. (1995) 'Contemporary tourism – trends and challenges: sustainable authenticity or contrived post-modernity?', in R. Butler and D. Pearce (eds), *Change in Tourism. People, Places, Processes*, London and New York: Routledge.

Connell, J. (1993) 'Bali revisited: death, rejuvenation, and the tourist cycle', *Environment and Planning D: Society and Space*, 11: 641–62.

Cooper, D. (1979) *Road to the Isles: Travellers in the Hebrides, 1770–1914*, London: Routledge.

Corbin, A. (1986) *The foul and the fragrant: odor and the French social imagination*, Leamington Spa: Berg.

Corbin, A. (1992) *The lure of the sea: the discovery of the seaside in the western world, 1750–1840*, Cambridge: Polity Press.

Corner, J. and Harvey, S. (eds) (1991a) *Enterprise and Heritage: crosscurrents of national culture*, London: Routledge.

Corner, J. and Harvey, S. (1991b) 'Mediating tradition and modernity: the heritage/enterprise couplet', in *Enterprise and Heritage: crosscurrents of national culture*, London: Routledge.

Cosgrove, D. (1985) 'Prospect, perspective and the evolution of the landscape idea', *Transaction of the Institute of British Geographers*, 10: 45–62.

Craig-Smith, S. and French, C. (1994) *Learning to Live with Tourism*, Melbourne: Pitman Publishing.

Craik, J. (1991) *Resorting to Tourism. Cultural Policies for Tourist Development in Australia*, Sydney: Allen and Unwin.

Craik, J. (1992) 'Australian tourism: the emergence of a state-coordinated consultative policy framework', in S. Bell and J. Wanna (eds), *Business–Government Relations in Australia*, Sydney: Harcourt Brace Jovanovich.

Craik, J. (1995a) 'Are there cultural limits to tourism?', *Journal of Sustainable Tourism*, 3: 87–98.

Craik, J. (1995b) 'Is cultural tourism viable?', *Smarts*, 2: 6–7.

Crang, M. (1994) 'On the heritage trail: maps of and journeys to olde Englande', *Environment and Planning D: Society and Space*, 12: 341–55.

Crang, P. (1994) 'It's showtime: on the workplace geographies of display in a restaurant in Southeast England', *Environment and Planning D: Society and Space*, 12: 675–704.

Crang, P. (1996) 'Displacement, consumption and identity', *Environment and Planning A*, 28: 47–67.

Crang, P. (forthcoming) *Spaces of Service*, London: Routledge.

Crary, J. (1990) *Techniques of the Observer*, Cambridge, Mass.: MIT Press.

Crawshaw, C. (1994a) *Altered Images: Tourism and Photography in the Lake District*, Tourism and the Environment Project Working Paper No. 1, Lancaster: Lancaster University.

Crawshaw, C. (1994b) *Romancing the Lake District: Tourist Expectations and Experiences*, Tourism and the Environment Project Working Paper No. 3, Lancaster: Lancaster University

Crick, M. (1989) 'Representations of international tourism in the social sciences: sun, sex, sights, savings and servility', *Annual Review of Anthropology*, 18: 307–44.

Crompton, R. and Jones, G. (1984) *White-Collar Proletariat*, London: Macmillan.

Crush, J. and Wellings, P. (1987) 'Forbidden fruit and the export of vice', in S. Britton and W. Clarke (eds), *Ambiguous Alternative. Tourism in Small Developing Countries*, Suva, Fiji: University of the South Pacific Press.

Cukier-Snow, J. and Wall, G. (1993) 'Tourism employment. Perspectives from Bali', *Annals of Tourism Research*, 14: 195–201.

Culbertson, J. and Randall, T. (1986) *Permanent Parisians: An Illustrated Guide to the Cemeteries of Paris*, London: Robson Books.

Culbertson, J. and Randall, T. (1991) *Permanent Londoners: An Illustrated Guide to the Cemeteries of London*, London: Robson Books.

Culler, J. (1981) 'Semiotics of tourism', *American Journal of Semiotics*, 1: 127–40.

Culler, J. (1988) *Framing the Sign: criticism and its institutions*, Oxford: Blackwell.

Curtis, B. and Pajaczkowska, C. (1994) ' "Getting there": travel, time and narrative', in G. Robertson *et al.* (eds), *Travellers' Tales. Narratives of Home and Displacement*, London: Routledge.

Czepiel, J. A., Solomon, M. R. and Surprenant, C. F. (eds) (1985) *The Service Encounter*, Lexington, Mass.: Lexington Books.

Dandeker, C. (1990) *Surveillance, Power and Modernity: Bureaucracy and Discipline from 1700 to the Present Day*, Cambridge: Polity Press.

Davidson, J. (1995) 'Fair game when the chips are down', *Glasgow Herald*, 24 February.

Davis, B. (1994) 'The digital museum', *Aperture*, Summer 136: 68–70.

de Certeau, M. (1984) *The Practice of Everyday Life*, Berkeley: University of California Press.

Dearden, P. and Harron, S. (1992) 'Tourism and the hilltribes of Thailand', in B. Weiler and M. Hall (eds), *Special Interest Tourism*, London: Belhaven Press.

Dearden, P. and Harron, S. (1994) 'Alternative tourism and adaptive change', *Annals of Tourism Research*, 21(1): 81–102.

Debord, G. (1983) *Society of the Spectacle*, Detroit: Black & Red.

di Maggio, P. (1983a) 'Can culture survive the marketplace?', *Journal of Arts Management and the Law*, 13: 61–87.

di Maggio, P. (1983b) 'Cultural policy studies: what they are and why we need them', *Journal of Arts Management and the Law*, 13: 241–8.

Dorst, J. (1987) *The Written Suburb: An American Site. An Ethnographic Dilemma*, Philadelphia: University of Pennsylvania Press.

Douglas, M. (1991) 'The Idea of Space', *Social Research*, 58: 287–307.

Drew, P. and Heritage, J. (eds) (1992) *Talk at Work: Interaction in Institutional Settings*, Cambridge: Cambridge University Press.

Drew, P. and Wootton, A. (eds) (1988) *Erving Goffman: Exploring the Interaction Order*, Cambridge: Polity.

Du Gay, P. (1993) ' "Numbers and souls": retailing and the de-differentiation of economy and culture', *British Journal of Sociology*, 44: 563–87.

Dwelly, E. (1977) *Faclair Gaidhlig gu Beurla le Dealbhan (Dwelly's Illustrated Gaelic to English Dictionary)*, Glasgow: Gairm.

Eco, U. (1986) *Travels in Hyper-Reality*, London: Picador.

Edensor, T. (1996) *Touring the Taj*, PhD Dept of Sociology, Lancaster: Lancaster University

Edensor, T. and Kothari, U. (1994) 'The masculinisation of Stirling's heritage', in V. Kinnaird and D. Hall (eds), *Tourism: A Gender Analysis*, Chichester: John Wiley and Sons.

Eichberg, H. (1984) 'Hverdagslivets parceller', *Den Jyske Historika*, 29–30: 53–73.

Elam, D. (1992) *Romancing the Postmodern*, London: Routledge.

Enloe, C. (1989) *Bananas, Beaches and Bases: Making Feminist Sense of International Politics*, London: Pandora.

Faiola, A. (1996) 'Net worth: it's never been easier to click and go – but does travel really compute?', *Washington Post – Travel*, 11 February.

Fairbairn-Dunlop, P. (1994) 'Gender, culture and tourism development in Western Samoa', in V. Kinnaird and D. Hall (eds), *Tourism: A Gender Analysis*, Chichester: John Wiley and Sons.

Falk, P. (1994) *The Consuming Body*, London: Sage.

Featherstone, M. (1983) 'Consumer culture: an introduction', *Theory, Culture and Society*, 1: 18–33.

Featherstone, M. (1991) *Consumer Culture and Postmodernism*, London: Sage.

Feifer, M. (1985) *Going Places*, London: Macmillan.

Feifer, M. (1986) *Tourism in History*, New York: Stein and Day.

Filby, M. (1992) ' "The figures, the personality, and the bums": service work and sexuality', *Work, Employment and Society*, 6: 23–42.

Fine, B. and Leopold, E. (1993) *The World of Consumption*, London: Routledge.

Finn, A. and Erdem, T. (1995) 'The economic impact of a mega-multi-mall', *Tourism Management*, 16: 367–73.

Fodness, D. and Milner, L. (1992) 'A perceptual mapping approach to theme park visitor segmentation', *Tourism Management*, 13: 95–101.

Foucault, M. (1967) *Madness and Civilization*, London: Tavistock.

Foucault, M. (1970) *The Order of Things*, New York: Random House.

Foucault, M. (1972) *The Archaeology of Knowledge*, London: Tavistock.

Foucault, M. (1976) *The Birth of the Clinic*, London: Tavistock.

Foucault, M. (1979) *Discipline and Punish: The birth of the prison*, New York: Vintage.

Foucault, M. (1980) 'The eye of power', in C. Gordon (ed.), *Power/knowledge: Selected Writings, 1972–77*, New York: Pantheon.

Foucault, M. (1981) *The History of Sexuality*, Harmondsworth: Penguin.

Freud, S. (1984) 'A disturbance of memory on the Acropolis', in *On Metapsychology*, Harmondsworth: Penguin.

Friedman, J. (1994a) *Cultural Identity and Global Process*, London: Sage.

Friedman, J. (ed.) (1994b) *Consumption and Identity*, Switzerland: Harwood Academic Publishers.

Frisby, D. (1992) *Simmel and Since. Essays on Georg Simmel's Social Theory*, London: Routledge.

Frow, J. (1991) 'Tourism and the semiotics of tourism', *October*, 57.

Gabriel, Y. (1988) *Working Lives in Catering*, London: Routledge.

Game, A. (1991) *Undoing the Social*, Milton Keynes: Open University Press.

Gauntlett, M. (1993) 'Theatre-going, theatre programmes, tourism', *Australasian Drama Studies*, 22: 113–27.

Geertz, C. (1963) *Agricultural Involution*, Berkeley: University of California Press.

Geertz, C. (1985) 'Deep play: notes on the Balinese cockfight', in C. Geertz, *The Interpretation of Cultures*, New York: Basic Books.

Gernsheim, H. (1982) *The Origins of Photography*, London: Thames and Hudson.

Gershuny, J. (1978) *After Industrial Society? The Emerging Self-Service Economy*, London: Macmillan.

Getz, D., Joncas, D. and Kelly, M. (1994) 'Tourist shopping villages in the Calgary region', *Journal of Tourism Studies*, 5: 2–15.

Gewertz, D. and Errington, F. (1991) *Twisted Histories, Altered Contexts: Representing the Chambri in a World System*, Cambridge: Cambridge University Press.

Giddens, A. (1990) *The Consequences of Modernity*, Stanford: Stanford University Press.

Giddens, A. (1991) *Modernity and Self-Identity*, Stanford: Stanford University Press.

Giddens, A. (1992) *The Transformation of Intimacy: sexuality, love and eroticism in the late modern age*, Stanford: Stanford University Press.

Gilroy, P. (1993) *The black Atlantic: modernity and double consciousness*, London: Verso.

Goethe, J. (1962) *Italian Journey*, Harmondsworth: Penguin.

Goffman, E. (1956) *The Presentation of Self in Everyday Life*, Edinburgh: University of Edinburgh.

Goffman, E. (1961) *Asylums*, Garden City, New York: Anchor Books.

Goffman, E. (1967) *Interaction Ritual: Essays on Face-to-Face Behavior*, New York: Doubleday.

Goffman, E. (1983) 'The interaction order', *American Sociological Review*, 48: 1–17.

Goss, J. (1993) 'Placing the market and marketing place: tourist advertising of the Hawaiian islands, 1972–92', *Environment and Planning D: Society and Space*, 11: 663–88.

Graburn, N. (1995) 'The past in the present in Japan: nostalgia and neo-traditionalism in contemporary Japanese domestic tourism', in R. Butler and D. Pearce (eds), *Change in Tourism. People, Places, Processes*, London and New York: Routledge.

Green, N. (1990) *The Spectacle of Nature*, Manchester: Manchester University Press.

Greenwood, D. (1989) 'Culture by the pound: an anthropological perspective on tourism as cultural commoditization', in V. Smith (ed.), *Hosts and Guests*, Philadelphia: University of Pennsylvania Press.

Gregory, D. (1994) *Geographical Imaginations*, Oxford: Blackwell.

Grochowski, J. (1995) 'Vegas' virtual reality: the city of illusion keeps gambling on reinvention', *Chicago Sun-Times*, 8 October.

Guest, D. E. (1992) 'Right enough to be dangerously wrong: an analysis of the In Search of Excellence phenomenon', in G. Salaman *et al.* (eds), *Human Resource Strategies*, London: Sage.

Guy, S. (1993) *Popular Photography: Within the Empire of the Gaze*, unpublished paper, Sunderland: University of Sunderland.

Hall, M. (1994) 'Gender and economic interests in tourism prostitution: the nature, development and implications of sex tourism in South-east Asia', in V. Kinnaird and D. Hall (eds), *Tourism: A Gender Analysis*, Chichester: John Wiley and Sons.

Hall, M. (1995) *Tourism in the Pacific Rim*, Melbourne: Longman Australia.

Hall, M. and McArthur, S. (eds) (1993) *Heritage Management in New Zealand and Australia*, Auckland: Oxford University Press.

Hall, M. and Zeppel, H. (1990) 'Cultural and heritage tourism: the new Grand Tour?', *Historic Environment*, 7: 86–98.

Hall, S., Hobson, D., Lowe, A. and Willis, P. (1980) *Culture, Media and Language*, London: Heinemann.

Hall, S. and Jacques, M. (eds) (1989) *New Times*, London: Lawrence and Wishart.

Hall, S. and Jefferson, T. (eds) (1975) *Resistance Through Rituals*, London: Hutchinson.

Handler, R. (1985) 'On having a culture: nationalism and the preservation of Quebec's Patrimony', in G. Stocking (ed.), *Objects and Others. Essays on Museums and Material Culture*, Wisconsin: Wisconsin University Press.

Handler, R. (1988) *Nationalism and the Politics of Culture in Quebec*, Wisconsin: Wisconsin University Press.

Handler, R. and Linnekin, J. (1984) 'Tradition, genuine or spurious', *Journal of American Folklore*, 97: 273–90.

Handler, R. and Saxton, W. (1988) 'Living history: dissimulation, reflexivity and narrative', *Cultural Anthropology*, 3: 242–60.

Hannerz, U. (1990) 'Cosmopolitans and locals in world culture', in M. Featherstone (ed.), *Global Culture*, London: Sage.

Hannerz, U. (1992) *Cultural Complexity: Studies in the Social Organization of Meaning*, New York: University of Columbia Press.

Hannerz, U. (1993) 'The withering away of the nation?', *Ethnos*, 3–4: 377–91.

Haraway, D. (1991) *Simians, Cyborgs, and Women. The Reinvention of Nature*, New York: Routledge.

Harkin, M. (1995) 'Modernist anthropology and tourism of the authentic', *Annals of Tourism Research*, 22: 650–70.

Harvey, D. (1989) *The Condition of Postmodernity*, Oxford: Blackwell.

Harvey, P. (1996) *Hybrids of Modernity. Anthropology, the Nation State and the Universal Exhibition*, London: Routledge.

Hayner, N. (1936) *Hotel Life*, Chapel Hill: University of North Carolina Press.

Hebdige, D. (1995) 'Fabulous confusion! Pop before Pop?', in C. Jenks (ed.), *Visual Culture*, London: Routledge.

Heidegger, M. (1977) *The Question Concerning Technology and Other Essays*, New York: Harper Torchbooks.

Henshall Momsen, J. (1994) 'Tourism, gender and development in the Caribbean', in V. Kinnaird and D. Hall (eds), *Tourism: A Gender Analysis*, Chichester: John Wiley and Sons.

Herman, G. (1982) *Rock 'n' Roll Babylon*, London: Plexus.

Hewison, R. (1987) *The Heritage Industry*, London: Methuen.

Heywood, I. (1994) 'Urgent dreams: climbing, rationalization and ambivalence', *Leisure Studies*, 13: 179–94.

Hibbert, C. (1969) *The Grand Tour*, London: Weidenfeld and Nicolson.

Hill, B. (1995) 'A guide to adventure travel', *Parks and Recreation*, September.

Hochschild, A. (1983) *The Managed Heart: Commercialization of Human Feeling*, Berkeley: University of California Press.

Hoggett, P. and Bishop, J. (1986) *Organizing around Enthusiasms: patterns of mutual aid in leisure*, London: Comedia.

Houser, D. (1994) 'In expeditions at sea, passengers get excitement without loss of comfort', *The Baltimore Sun*, 20 Febuary.

Hovinen, G. (1995) 'Heritage issues in urban tourism', *Tourism Management*, 16: 381–8.

Hughes, H. (1987) 'Culture as a tourist resource: a theoretical consideration', *Tourism Management*, 8: 205–16.

Hughes, H. (1989) 'Tourism and the arts. A potentially destructive relationship?', *Tourism Management*, 10: 97–9.

Humphreys, R. (1985) 'The survival of scientific management', *International Journal of Hospitality Management*, 4: 124–7.

Hunter, J. (1976) *The Making of the Crofting Community*, Edinburgh: James Donald.

Hunter, J. (1991) *The Claim of Crofting: The Scottish Highlands and Islands 1930–1990*, Edinburgh: Mainstream.

Huyssen, A. (1995) *Twilight Memories*, London: Routledge.

Ireland, M. (1993) 'Gender and class relations in tourism employment', *Annals of Tourism Research*, 20: 666–84.

Irigaray, L. (1985a) *Speculum of the Other Woman*, Ithaca, N.Y.: Cornell University Press.

Irigaray, L. (1985b) *The Sex Which Is Not One*, Ithaca, N.Y.: Cornell University Press.

Irigaray, L. (1993) *Sexes and Genealogies*, trans. Gillian G. Gill, New York: Columbia University Press.

Jacobs, J. (1995) ' "That dangerous fantasy of authenticity": a review of the J. C. Slaughter Falls community arts project, Brisbane', *Ecumene*, 2: 211–14.

Jameson, F. (1991) *Postmodernism, or the Cultural Logic of Late Capitalism*, London: Verso.

Jay, M. (1986) 'In the Empire of the gaze: Foucault and the denigration of the visual in twentieth-century French thought', in D. Hoy (ed.), *Foucault: A Critical Reader*, Oxford: Blackwell.

Jay, M. (1993) *Downcast Eyes: the denigration of vision in twentieth-century French thought*, Berkeley: University of California Press.

Jenks, C. (1995a) 'Introduction' to *Visual Culture*, London: Routledge.

Jenks, C. (1995b) *Visual Culture*, London: Routledge.

Jokinen, E. and Veijola, S. (1994) 'The Death of the Tourist. Seven Improvisations', *XIIIth World Congress of Sociology*, Bielefeld, Germany, July.

Jones, C. and Decotiis, T. A. (1988) 'A better way to select service employees: video-assisted testing', in C. H. Lovelock (ed.), *Managing Services: Marketing, Operations and Human Resources*, Englewood Cliffs: Prentice Hall International..

Jones, P. (1988) 'Quality, capacity and productivity in service industries', *International Journal of Hospitality Management*, 7: 104–12.

Jusserand, J. (1888) *English Wayfaring Life in the Middle Ages*, London: Fisher-Unwin.

Kaplan, C. (1990) 'Deterritorializations: The Rewriting of Home and Exile in Western Feminist Discourse', in A. R. JanMohamed and D. Lloyd (eds), *The Nature and Context of Minority Discourse*, Oxford: Oxford University Press.

Kelliher, C. (1989) 'Flexibility in employment: developments in the hospitality industry', *International Journal of Hospitality Management*, 82: 157–66.

Kendon, A. (1988) 'Goffman's approach to face-to-face interaction', in P. Drew and A. Wootton (eds), *Erving Goffman: Exploring the Interaction Order*, Cambridge: Polity.

Kershaw, B. (1993) 'Reminiscing history: memory, performance, empowerment', *De-traditionalisation Conference*, Lancaster University, July.

Kinnaird, V. and Hall, D. (eds) (1994) *Tourism: A Gender Analysis*, Chichester: John Wiley and Sons.

Klaus, P. G. (1985) 'Quality epiphenomenon: the conceptual understanding of quality in face-to-face service encounters', in J. A. Czepiel, M. R. Solomon and C. E. Surprenant (eds), *The Service Encounter*, Lexington, Mass.: Lexington Books.

Klemm, M. (1989) 'Tourism and the arts – a response', *Tourism Management*, December: 347.

Knights, D. and Willmott, H. (eds) (1990) *Labour Process Theory*, London: Macmillan.

Kracauer, S. (1995) *The Mass Ornament*, Cambridge, Mass.: Harvard University Press.

Kraus, K. (1920) *No Compromise*, New York: Ungar Press.

Krippendorf, J. (1984) *The Holidaymakers*, London: Heinemann.

Kristeva, J. (1986) *The Kristeva Reader*, T. Moi (ed.), Oxford: Basil Blackwell.

Kristeva, J. (1993) 'L'abjet d'amour (Freud ja rakkaus. Ahdistava hoito)', in *Puhuva subjekti – tekstej 1967–1993 (A Speaking Subject – texts 1967–1993)*, Tampere: Gaudeamus.

Kroc, R. and Anderson, R. (1977) *Grinding It Out: The Making of McDonald's*, Chicago: Contemporary Books.

Kumar, K. (1978) *Prophecy and Progress*, Harmondsworth: Pelican.

Lasch, C. (1984) *The Minimal Self*, London: Picador.

Lash, S. (1990) *Sociology of Postmodernism*, London: Routledge.

Lash, S. and Urry, J. (1994) *Economies of Signs and Spaces*, London: Sage.

Lee, W. (1991) 'Prostitution and tourism in South-East Asia', in N. Redclift and M. T. Sinclair (eds), *Working Women: International Perspectives on Labour and Gender Ideology*, London: Routledge.

Leed, E. (1992) *The Mind of the Traveller*, New York: Basic Books.

Lefebvre, H. (1991) *The Production of Space*, Oxford: Blackwell.

Legge, K. (1989) 'Human Resource Management: a critical analysis', in J. Storey (ed.), *New Perspectives on Human Resource Management*, London: Routledge.

Lehtinen, U. and Lehtinen, J. R. (1991) 'Two approaches to service quality dimensions', *The Services Industry Journal*, 11: 287–303.

Leidner, R. (1993) *Fast Food, Fast Talk. Service Work and the Routinization of Everyday Life*, Berkeley: University of California Press.

Lennon, J. J. and Wood, R. C. (1989) 'The sociological analysis of hospitality labour and the neglect of accommodation workers', *International Journal of Hospitality Management*, 8: 227–35.

Leontidou, L. (1994) 'Gender dimensions of tourism in Greece: employment, sub-cultures and restructuring', in V. Kinnaird and D. Hall (eds), *Tourism: A Gender Analysis*, Chichester: John Wiley and Sons.

Levin, D. (1993) *Modernity and the Hegemony of Vision*, Berkeley: University of California Press.

Littrell, M., Anderson, L. and Brown, P. (1993) 'What makes a craft souvenir authentic?', *Annals of Tourism Research*, 20: 197–215.

Lodge, D. (1984) *Small World. An Academic Romance*, Harmondsworth: Penguin.

Lovelock, C. H. (1988) 'Classifying services to gain strategic marketing insights', in C. H. Lovelock (ed.), *Managing Services: Marketing, Operations and Human Resources*, Englewood Cliffs: Prentice Hall International.

Loving, B. (1996) 'Tripping on the Internet: virtual journeys', *Star Tribune*, 7 January.

Lowenthal, D. (1985) *The Past is a Foreign Country*, Cambridge: Cambridge University Press.

Luhmann, N. (1989) *Ecological Communication*, Cambridge: Polity.

Lumley, R. (1988) 'Introduction', in *The Museum Time-Machine*, London: Routledge.

Lury, C. (1993) *Cultural Rights*, London: Routledge.

Lury, C. (1996) *Consumer Culture*, Cambridge: Polity.

Lynch, K. (1972) *What Time is this Place?*, Cambridge, Mass.: MIT Press.

Lyotard, J.-F. (1984) *The Postmodern Condition*, Minneapolis: University of Minneapolis Press.

Mac Gill-eain, S. (1985) 'Màiri Mhr nan Oran', in S. Mac Gill-eain, *Ris a' Bhruthaich*, Stornoway: Acair.

MacCannell, D. (1973) 'Staged authenticity: on arrangements of social space in tourist settings', *American Journal of Sociology*, 79: 589–603.

MacCannell, D. (1984) 'Reconstructed ethnicity: tourism and cultural identity in third world communities', *Annals of Tourism Research*, 11: 361–77.

MacCannell, D. (1989) *The Tourist*, 2nd edn, London: Macmillan.

MacCannell, D. (1992) *Empty Meeting Grounds: The Tourist Papers*, London: Routledge.

Macdonald, S. (1997) *Reimagining Culture: Community, Identity and the Gaelic Renaissance*, Oxford and Providence: Berg.

MacKinnon, K. (1974) *The Lion's Tongue*, Inverness: Club Leabhar.

Maffesoli, M. (1995) *The Time of the Tribes*, London: Sage.

Marcuse, H. (1964) *One Dimensional Man*, London: Abacus.

Mars, G. (1973) 'Hotel pilferage: a case study in occupational theft', in M. Warner (ed.), *Sociology of the Workplace*, London: Allen and Unwin.

Mars, G. and Nicod, M. (1984) *The World of Waiters*, London: Allen and Unwin.

Mars, G., Bryant, D. and Mitchell, P. (1979) *Manpower Problems in the Hotel and Catering Industry*, Farnborough: Saxon House.

Marshall, G. (1986) 'The workplace culture of a licensed restaurant', *Theory, Culture and Society*, 3: 33–47.

Marx, K. (1973) *Grundrisse*, Harmondsworth: Penguin.

May, T. (1995) 'Millions journey among the junk-food mountains to give their sensations a whirl', *The Guardian*, 19 August.

McCarthy, J. (1994) *Are Sweet Dreams Made of This? Tourism in Bali and Eastern Indonesia*, Northcote, Vic.: Indonesia Resources and Information Program.

McCole, J. (1993) *Walter Benjamin and the Antinomies of Tradition*, New York: Cornell University Press.

McCracken, G. (1988) *Culture and Consumption*, Bloomington and Indianapolis: Indiana University Press.

McCrone, D., Morris, A. and Kiely, R. (1995) *Scotland – the Brand*, Edinburgh: Edinburgh University Press.

McDonald, M. (1986) 'Celtic ethnic kinship and the problem of being English', *Current Anthropology*, 1.

McEnery, M. (1995) 'Outlet shopping guide: bare-bones factory stores give way to a bargain hunter's nirvana', *The Bergen Record*, 5 October.

McKean, P. (1989) Towards a theoretical analysis of tourism: economic dualism and cultural involution in Bali', in V. Smith (ed.), *Hosts and Guests*, Philadelphia: University of Pennsylvania Press.

McLuhan, M. (1967) *The Gutenberg Galaxy*, London: Routledge and Kegan Paul.

McLuhan, M. (1973) *Understanding Media*, London: Routledge and Kegan Paul.

McLynn, F. (1990) *Burton: Snow upon the Desert*, London: John Murray.

Mellor, A. (1991) 'Enterprise and heritage in the dock', in J. Corner and S. Harvey (eds), *Enterprise and Heritage*, London: Routledge.

Meyerowitz, J. (1985) *No Sense of Place*, Oxford: Oxford University Press.

Middleton, D. and Edwards, D. (eds) (1990) *Collective Remembering*, London: Sage

Mill, R. C. (1989) 'The practice of Human Resource Management within the hospitality industry', in C. P. Cooper (ed.), *Progress in Tourism, Recreation and Hospitality Management*, vol. 1, London: Belhaven Press.

Millar, S. (1989) 'Heritage management for heritage tourism', *Tourism Management*, March: 9–14.

Miller, D. (1987) *Material Culture and Mass Consumption*, Oxford: Blackwell.

Miller, D. (1994) *Modernity: An Ethnographic Approach. Dualism and Mass Consumption in Trinidad*, Oxford and Providence: Berg.

Miller, S. (1996) 'Between a rock and a hard place', *RealTime*, February–March: 3.

Moi, T. (ed.) (1986) *The Kristeva Reader*, Oxford: Basil Blackwell.

Morris, A. (1991) 'Popping the cork: history, heritage and the stately home in the Scottish borders', in G. Day and G. Rees (eds), *Regions, Nations and European Integration: Remaking the Celtic Fringe*, Cardiff: University of Wales.

Morris, M. (1988) 'At Henry Parkes motel', *Cultural Studies*, 2: 1–47.

Morris, M. (1995) 'Life as a tourist object in Australia', in M.-F. Lanfant, J. Allcock and E. Bruner (eds), *International Tourism*, London: Sage.

Moulin, C. (1990) 'Packaging and marketing cultural heritage resources', *Historic Environment*, 7: 82–5.

Mulvey, L. (1981) 'Visual pleasure and narrative cinema', in T. Bennett *et al.* (eds), *Popular Film and Television*, London: Open University Press.

Munt, I. (1994) 'The other postmodern tourist: culture, travel and the new middle classes', *Theory, Culture and Society*, 11: 101–24.

Newbern, K. and Fletcher, J. (1995) 'Leisurely cruise the Caribbean', *The Washington Times*, 27 August.

Noro, A. (1995) 'Uudemman kulutussosiologian mallit ja figuurit (Models and figures in present-day sociology of consumption)', *Sosiologia*, 32: 1–11.

Orwell, G. (1933) *Down and Out in Paris and London*, Harmondsworth: Penguin.

Papadopoulus, N. and Heslop, L. A. (1993) *Product-Country Images: Impact and Role in International Marketing*, New York: Haworth Press.

Parkhurst Ferguson, P. (1994) 'The flâneur on and off the streets of Paris', in K. Tester (ed.), *The Flâneur*, London: Routledge.

Parr, M. (1995) *Small World*, Stockport: Dewi Lewis.

Parrinello, G. (1993) 'Motivation and anticipation in post-industrial tourism', *Annals of Tourism Research*, 20: 233–49.

Pearce, P. (1988) *The Ulysses Factor*, New York: Springer-Verlag.

Pedersen, R. and Shaw, J. (1993) *Gaelic Tourism Concepts*, Inverness: Highlands and Islands Enterprise.

Peters, T. (1994) 'Theatre on the retail stage', *The Independent on Sunday*, 6 March.

Pittock, M. (1991) *The Invention of Scotland: the Stuart Myth and the Scottish Identity, 1638 to the Present*, London: Routledge.

Plant, S. (1992) *Most Radical Gesture*, London: Routledge.

Plumwood, V. (1993) *Feminism and the mastery of nature*, London: Routledge.

Pocock, D. (1982) 'Valued landscape in memory: the view from Prebends' Bridge', *Transactions of the Institute of British Geographers*, 71: 354–64.

Porteous, J. (1985) 'Smellscape', *Progress in Human Geography*, 9: 356–78.

Porter, R. (1994) *London: A Social History*, London: Hamish Hamilton.

Prentice, R. (1993) 'Community-driven tourism planning and residents' preferences', *Tourism Management*, 14: 218–26.

Prus, R. and Vasilokopoulos, S. (1979) 'Desk clerks and hookers – hustling in a "shady" hotel', *Urban Life*, 8: 52–71.

Queensland Art Gallery (1994) *Annual Report 1993–94*, Brisbane: Queensland Art Gallery.

Raban, J. (1987) *Coasting*, London: Picador.

Rabinow, P. (1992) 'Artificiality and Enlightenment: from sociobiology to biosociality', in J. Crary and S. Kwinter (eds), *Incorporations*, New York: Zone.

Rajanti, T. (1993) ' "Tässä on minun katuni" – kaupunkilainen elämäntapa Mary Marckin koululaisromaaneissa (This is my street – urban life style in the juvenile novels of Mary Marck)', *Tiede & Edistys*, 2: 115–26.

Rajotte, F. (1987) 'Safari and beach-resort tourism', in S. Britton and W. Clarke (eds), *Ambiguous Alternative. Tourism in Small Developing Countries*, Suva, Fiji: University of the South Pacific Press.

Reimer, G. D. (1990) 'Packaging dreams: Canadian tour operators at work', *Annals of Tourism Research*, 17: 501–12.

Relph, R. (1981) *The Modern Urban Landscape*, London: Croom Helm.

Richards, E. (1982) *A History of Highland Clearances*, London: Croom Helm.

Richter, L. (1995) 'Gender and race: neglected variables in tourism research', in R. Butler and D. Pearce (eds), *Change in Tourism: People, Places, Processes*, London and New York: Routledge.

Riegel, H. (1996) 'Into the heart of irony', in S. Macdonald and G. Fyfe (eds), *Theorising Museums*, Oxford: Blackwell.

Ritzer, G. (1995) *Expressing America: A critique of the global credit card society*, Thousand Oaks, CA: Pine Forge Press.

Ritzer, G. (1996) *The McDonaldization of Society*, rev. ed., Thousand Oaks, CA: Pine Forge Press.

Ritzer, G. (forthcoming a) *Postmodern Social Theory*, New York: McGraw Hill.

Ritzer, G. (forthcoming b) *Consuming Society*, Thousand Oaks, CA: Pine Forge Press.

Robertson, G., Tickner, L., Bird, J., Curtis, B. and Putnam, T. (1994) *Travellers' Tales*, London: Routledge.

Rodaway, P. (1994) *Sensuous Geographies*, London: Routledge.

Rojek, C. (1993) *Ways of Escape: Modern Transformations in Leisure and Travel*, London: Macmillan.

Rojek, C. (1994) 'Leisure and the dreamworld of Modernity', in I. Henry (ed.), *Leisure, Modernity, Postmodernity and Lifestyles*, Brighton: LSA.

Rojek, C. (1995) *Decentring Leisure. Rethinking Leisure Theory*, London: Sage.

Rojek, C. and Turner, B. (eds) (1993) *Forget Baudrillard?*, London: Routledge.

Rorty, R. (1980) *Philosophy and the Mirror of Nature*, Oxford: Blackwell.

Rosaldo, R. (1993) *Culture and Truth*, London: Routledge.

Rose, N. (1989) *Governing the Soul: the Shaping of the Private Self*, London: Routledge.

Rowling, M. (1971) *Everyday Life of Medieval Travellers*, New York: Dorset.

Rudisill, R. (1971) *Mirror Image*, Mexico: University of Mexico Press.

Ryan, C. (1991) *Recreational Tourism*, London and New York: Routledge.

Sack, R. (1993) *Place, Modernity and the Consumer's World. A Relational Framework for Geographical Analysis*, Baltimore: The Johns Hopkins University Press.

Said, E. (1978) *Orientalism*, London: Routledge.

Said, E. (1983) *The World, the Text and the Critic*, Cambridge, Mass.: Harvard University Press.

Saleh, F. and Ryan, C. (1991) 'Analysing service quality in the hospitality industry using the SERVQUAL model', *The Service Industries Journal*, 11: 324–43.

Samuel, R. (1994) *Theatres of Memory*, London: Verso.

Savage, M. and Warde, A. (1993) *Urban Sociology, Capitalism and Modernity*, London: Macmillan.

Schlentrich, U. (1992) 'The world of hospitality', *Hospitality*, 135: 14–16.

Schneider, B. (1988) 'Notes on climate and culture', in C. H. Lovelock (ed.), *Managing Services: Marketing, Operations and Human Resources*, Englewood Cliffs: Prentice Hall International.

Schudson, M. (1979) 'Review essay: tourism and modern culture', *American Journal of Sociology*, 85: 1249–58.

Schwartz, B. (1973) 'Waiting, exchange and power: the distribution of time in social systems', *American Journal of Sociology*, 79: 841–70.

Sennett, R. (1991) *Conscience of the Eye*, London: Faber.

Shaw, G. and Williams, A. (1994) *Critical Issues in Tourism. A Geographical Perspective*, Oxford: Blackwell.

Shaw, G. and Williams, A. (eds) (1996) *Riding the Big Dipper*, London: Mansell.

Sheldon, P. (1989) 'Professionalism in Tourism and Hospitality', *Annals of Tourism Research*, 16: 492–503.

Shields, R. (1991) *Places on the Margin: Alternative Geographies of Modernity*, London: Routledge.

Shields, R. (ed.) (1995) *Cultures of the Internet*, London: Sage.

Shurmer-Smith, P. and Hannam, K. (1994) *Worlds of Desire, Realms of Power*, London: Edward Arnold.

Silberberg, T. (1995) 'Cultural tourism and business opportunities for museums and heritage sites', *Tourism Management*, 16: 361–5.

Silver, I. (1993) 'Marketing authenticity in third world countries', *Annals of Tourism Research*, 20: 302–18.

Simmel, G. (1907) *Philosophy of Money*, London: Routledge.

Simmel, G. (1950) 'The Stranger', in K. H. Wolff (ed.), *The Sociology of Georg Simmel*, New York: Free Press.

Simmel, G. (1959) 'The Adventurer', in K. H. Wolff (ed.), *Georg Simmel. A collection of essays, with translations and bibliography*, Columbus: State University Press.

Simmel, G. (1983) 'Das Abenteuer', in *Philosophische Kultur*, Berlin: Verlag Klaus Wagerbach.

Slater, D. (1995) 'Photography and modern vision: the spectacle of "natural magic" ', in C. Jenks (ed.), *Visual Culture*, London: Routledge.

Smith, S. L. J. (1994) 'The tourism product', *Annals of Tourism Research*, 21: 582–95.

Smith, V. (1979) 'Women. The taste-makers in tourism', *Annals of Tourism Research*, 1: 49–60.

Smith, V. (ed.) (1989) *Hosts and Guests*, Oxford: Blackwell.

Solomon, M. R. (1985) 'Packaging the service provider', *The Service Industries Journal*, 5: 64–72.

Sontag, S. (1979) *On Photography*, Harmondsworth: Penguin.

Sparks, B. and Callan, V. J. (1992) 'Communication and the service encounter: the value of convergence', *International Journal of Hospitality Management*, 11: 213–24.

Squire, S. (1994) 'The cultural values of literary tourism', *Annals of Tourism Research*, 21: 103–20.

Stallybrass, P. and White, A. (1986) *The Politics and Poetics of Transgression*, London: Methuen.

Steadman Jones, G. (1981) *Outcast London*, Harmondsworth: Penguin.

Stille, A. (1995) 'Virtual antiquities could help real icons stand the test of time', *The Washington Post*, 25 December.

Strathern, M. (1991) *Partial Connections*, Maryland: Rowman and Littlefield.

Swain, M. (1993) 'Women producers of ethnic arts', *Annals of Tourism Research*, 20: 32–51.

Swain, M. (1995) 'Gender in tourism', *Annals of Tourism Research*, 22: 247–66.

Taylor, J. (1994) *A Dream of England*, Manchester: Manchester University Press.

Taylor, W. (1993) 'Message and muscle: an interview with Swatch titan Nicolas Hayek', *Harvard Business Review*, March–April, 98–110.

Tazzioli, T. (1995) 'Gay odyssey: learning to respect personal style within a "lifestyle" ', *The Seattle Times*, 7 May.

Tester, K. (ed.) (1994a) *The Flâneur*, London: Routledge.

Tester, K. (1994b) 'Introduction', in K. Tester (ed.), *The Flâneur*, London: Routledge.

Thanh-Dam, T. (1983) 'The dynamics of sex tourism: the case of Southeast Asia', *Development and Change*, 14: 533–53.

Thompson, E. P. (1994) *Witness against the Beast: William Blake and the Moral Law*, Cambridge: Cambridge University Press.

Timothy, D. and Butler, R. (1994) 'Cross-border shopping: a North American perspective', *Annals of Tourism Research*, 22: 16–34.

Towner, J. (1985) 'The grand tour: a key phase in the history of tourism', *Annals of Tourism Research*, 12: 293–333.

Townley, B. (1989) 'Selecting and appraisal: reconstituting "social relations"?', in J. Storey (ed.), *New Perspectives on Human Resource Management*, London: Routledge.

Transnationals Information Centre (1987) *Working for Big Mac*, London: Transnationals Information Centre.

Truong, T.-D. (1990) *Sex, Money and Morality: Prostitution and Tourism in Southeast Asia*, London and New Jersey: Zed Books.

Turner, B. S. (1994) 'Introduction', in C. Buci-Glucksmann, *Baroque Reason. The Aesthetics of Modernity*, London: Sage.

Turner, L. and Ash, J. (1976) *The Golden Horde: International Tourism and the Pleasure Periphery*, London: Constable.

Turner, R. H. (1962) 'Role-taking: process versus conformity', in A. M. Rose (ed.), *Human Behavior and Social Processes: An Interactionist Approach*, London: Routledge .

Upah, G. D. and Fulton, J. W. (1985) 'Situation creation in service marketing', in J. A. Czepiel, M. R. Solomon and C. F. Surprenant (eds), *The Service Encounter*, Lexington, Mass.: Lexington Books.

Urry, J. (1990) *The Tourist Gaze*, London: Sage.

Urry, J. (1992a) 'The Tourist Gaze and the Environment', *Theory, Culture and Society*, 9: 1–26.

Urry, J. (1992b) 'The Tourist Gaze "Revisited" ', *American Behavioral Scientist*, 36: 172–86.

Urry, J. (1994a) 'Cultural change and contemporary tourism', *Leisure Studies*, 13: 233–8.

Urry, J. (1994b) 'Time, leisure and social identity', *Time and Society*, 3: 131–49.

Urry, J. (1995) *Consuming Places*, London: Routledge.

Urry, J. (1996) 'How do societies remember the past?', in G. Fyfe and S. Macdonald (eds), *Theorising Museums: Representing Identity in a Changing World*, Sociological Review Monograph, Oxford: Blackwell.

Vähämäki, J. (no date) *Kalajuttu* (The fishing tale), unpublished manuscript.

Vattimo, G. (1992) *The Transparent Society*, Cambridge: Polity.

Veijola, S. and Jokinen, E. (1994) 'The body in tourism', *Theory, Culture and Society*, 11: 125–51.

Ventola, E. (1987) *The Structure of Social Interaction: A Systematic Approach to the Semiotics of Service Encounters*, London: Frances Pinter.

Venturi, R., Scott Brown, D. and Izenour, S. (1972) *Learning from Las Vegas*, Cambridge, Mass.: MIT Press.

Virilio, P. (1977) *Speed and Politics*, New York: Semiotext(e).

Virilio, P. (1991) *Lost Dimension*, New York: Semiotext(e).

Wagner, U. (1977) 'Out of time and place – mass tourism and charter trips', *Ethnos*, 42: 38–52.

Walker, R. (1985) 'Is there a service economy? The changing capitalist division of labour', *Science and Society*, 49: 42–83.

Weiner, A. (1992) *Inalienable Possessions. The Paradox of Keeping-while-Giving*, Berkeley: University of California Press.

Weitz, B. A. (1981) 'Effectiveness in sales interactions: a contingency framework', *Journal of Marketing*, 45: 85–103.

Whitford, M. (1991) *Luce Irigaray. Philosophy in the Feminine*, London: Routledge.

Whyte, W. F. (1948) *Human Relations in the Restaurant Industry*, New York: McGraw Hill.

Whyte, W. F. (1949) 'The social structure of the restaurant', *American Journal of Sociology*, LIV: 302–10.

Wilson, E. (1992) 'The Invisible Flâneur', *New Left Review*, 191: 90–110.

Withers, C. (1984) *Gaelic in Scotland, 1698–1981. The Geographical History of a Language*, Edinburgh: John Donald.

Wolff, J. (1985) 'The Invisible Flâneuse. Women and the Literature of Modernity', *Theory, Culture and Society,* 2: 37–46.

Wolff, J. (1993) 'On the Road Again: Metaphors of Travel in Cultural Criticism', *Cultural Studies,* 1 7: 224–39.

Wolff, J. (1995) *Feminist Sentences,* Oxford: Blackwell.

Wollheim, P. (1980) *Art and its Objects,* Cambridge: Cambridge University Press.

Wood, R. C. (1992a) 'Deviants and misfits: hotel and catering labour and the marginal worker thesis', *International Journal of Hospitality Management,* 11: 179–82.

Wood, R. C. (1992b) *Working in Hotels and Catering,* London: Routledge.

Wood, R. C. (1994) 'Hotel culture and social control', *Annals of Tourism Research,* 21: 65–80.

Wouters, C. (1986) 'Formalization and Informalization: Changing Tension Balances in the Civilizing process', *Theory, Culture and Society,* 3: 1–18.

Wouters, C. (1989) 'The Sociology of Emotions and Flight Attendants: Hochschild's Managed Heart', *Theory, Culture and Society,* 6, 95–124.

Wright, P. (1985) *On Living in an Old Country,* London: Verso.

Zeppel, H. and Hall, M. (1991) 'Selling art and history: cultural heritage and tourism', *Journal of Tourism Studies,* 2: 29–45.

Zeppel, H. and Hall, M. (1992) 'Arts and heritage tourism', in B. Weiler and M. Hall (eds), *Special Interest Tourism,* London: Belhaven Press.

Zukin, S. (1990) 'Socio-spatial prototypes of a new organisation of consumption: the role of real cultural capital', *Sociology,* 24: 37–55.

Zukin, S. (1991) *Landscapes of Power,* Berkeley: University of California Press.

NAME INDEX

SUBJECT INDEX